Seize the Trident

Seize the Trident

The Race for
Superliner Supremacy and
How It Altered the Great War

DOUGLAS R. BURGESS JR.

International Marine / McGraw-Hill

Camden, Maine • New York • Chicago • San Francisco • Lisbon • London • Madrid • Mexico City
Milan • New Delhi • San Juan • Seoul • Singapore • Sydney • Toronto

The **McGraw·Hill** Companies

1 2 3 4 5 6 7 8 9 10 DOC DOC 0 9 8 7 6 5

Library of Congress Cataloging-in-Publication Data
Burgess, Douglas R.
 Seize the trident : the race for superliner supremacy and how it altered the Great War /
Douglas R. Burgess Jr.— 1st US ed.
  p. cm.
 Includes bibliographical references and index.
 ISBN 0-07-143009-1
 1. Ocean liners—Great Britain—History—19th century. 2. Ocean liners—Germany—
History—19th century. 3. Ocean liners—Great Britain—History—20th century.
4. Ocean liners—Germany—History—20th century. 5. World War, 1914-1918—
Causes. I. Title.
 VM381.B87 2005
 387.5'42'094109041—dc22   2005002447

Dedication

For my dearest friend David Gritz, a true scholar, blind to hatred,
murdered by terrorists, Hebrew University of Jerusalem, July 31, 2002.

———

*"They are not dead who live in the lives they leave behind. In
those whom they have blessed they live a life again."*

—Eleanor Roosevelt

Contents

Photos follow page 86

Acknowledgments

THIS BOOK BEGAN WITH A VISIT TO MY FATHER'S OFFICE WHEN I WAS FIVE
years old. The ship brokerage firm of Simpson, Spence and Young
occupied an elderly Manhattan brownstone just north of Battery Park.
From the southern bank of its windows one could see the cemetery of
Trinity Church where Alexander Hamilton is buried; from the western side were the dockyards along West Side Drive. That was the view
from his office. It was there that I first saw the glistening white superstructures of the cruise ships, hovering like fairyland castles over the
gritty squalor of the piers. It was there too that I first heard the shattering blast of a ship's horn bellowing its cry of departure—a haunt-
ing, yet exhilarating sound.

From that day until this, I have shared my father's enduring love for
the sea and the ships that ply across it. Douglas R. Burgess Sr. began his
career selling motorboats at a local marina, then became a shipbroker,
and finally executive vice president of a cruise line. Even in later years,
when his financial interests turned from ships to real estate, our home
remained filled with the memorabilia of a hundred lost liners. It was his
library that provided the earliest sources for my own historical project.
It was he, moreover, who inspired me to take on this enterprise, and
his relentless drive which propelled it from concept to conclusion.
Nothing has been more valuable to the creation of this book than my
father's unflagging support and counsel. Throughout the long and often daunting process of research and writing, he has remained a cheerful and constant wellspring of ideas, suggestions, and good-natured critique. I cannot count the number of times the phone would ring and
his voice on the line would exuberantly say, "I just had a thought. . . ."

In the same breath I must also thank my mother, Shannon Burgess,
for her faith that all things are possible, and my grandparents, Don
and Elise Burgess and Irene Hagara, whose love and guidance have been
the most cherished constants of my life. Thanks as well to Omar Dia,

Curtis Fairclough, Jeff Lagendyk, Szeming Lau, Pete Matukas, and Laurent Tonet-Tyers for years of joyous friendship. Many, many thanks to my agent Elizabeth Frost-Knappman and to my editor Tris Coburn for all their advice and aid. Were it not for the unfailing support of all these friends and family, *Seize the Trident* would never have been begun, much less completed.

Introduction

AUGUST 15, 1889, WAS THE SORT OF DAY THAT COULD ONLY HAVE occurred at the very apogee of imperial rule, when the potency of the British royal house suddenly blazed forth in a momentary spectacle of color, light, and sound. The occasion was a Naval Review at the Spithead roadstead off the southern coast of England. Ranked at anchor were battleships, the striking force of the Royal Navy, resplendent in their sleek black hulls and buff-colored superstructures. Sailors in crisp white uniforms lined their decks at attention, while signal flags flew up and down halyards as a bewildering array of messages flashed back and forth between ships of the fleet. This was a time of transition for the British Navy, when the squat, gray, menacing figure of the dreadnought was still confined to the drawing boards of marine engineers, and the sweeping reforms of Admiral Sir John "Jackie" Fisher were almost two decades away. The fleet now assembled for royal inspection was thus little changed, in appearance or character, from the one Lord Nelson had led to victory against the French at Trafalgar more than eighty years before. The newer ships had iron hulls and screw propellers, but many more were built of oak, with great paddlewheels hanging incongruously over their flanks like hunchbacks. All had sails. In fact, the Admiralty had recently led a spirited resistance to abandoning the auxiliary sails on their vessels, however useless or ludicrous they might appear. Cadets were still taught to distinguish a topsail from a topgallant and gravely advised on the best way to stay in the lee of the Dover cliffs during a spot of dirty weather. It had been almost thirty years since the Royal Navy had seen regular combat, and its atrophy was marked by the increasing triumph of ceremony over practicality. Yet, even if obsolete and dowdy, Britain's peacetime fleet was still an impressive spectacle as launches bearing local dignitaries and eager sightseers darted in and out among the leviathans, blowing whistles and dipping their flags in salute.

On one of the larger battleships stood Albert Edward, Prince of Wales, and his nephew, Kaiser Wilhelm II of Germany. The Kaiser had made the brief trip across the English Channel in a cruiser of the German Navy, and was then piped aboard the British vessel with all the appropriate pomp and ceremony into the waiting embrace of his royal uncle. The two men made a strange contrast. The Prince of Wales, portly and middle aged, had almost twelve more years to wait before he would attain the throne so long held by his domineering mother, Queen Victoria. Something of an enfant terrible in mid-Victorian London, he indulged in excesses and eccentricities that were no longer novel enough to be notorious. He personified the era that would soon bear his name, Edwardian: doughty, dignified, perhaps a little inclined to fat, but radiant in self-confidence. Next to him stood Kaiser Wilhelm II, Emperor of Germany, nominal heir to the Holy Roman Empire and recent inheritor from Prince Otto von Bismarck of a virile new nation. Younger and leaner than his uncle, he wore his title with conscious arrogance. The prominent waxed moustache, polished boots, and dress sword—which would delight caricaturists of a later age— were very much in evidence. Etiquette demanded that each man appear in the regalia of their navies, a strange protocol that furthered the analogy between themselves and their fleets: the Prince of Wales was paunchy and somehow faintly old fashioned; the Kaiser was sharp and brash, with just a hint of boyish exuberance.

On this day, the pageantry of empire was at its zenith.

But it was also fiercely hot, and the Kaiser, the Prince, and their entourages, with no shade to provide relief, sweated profusely under layers of broadcloth and gold braid. The Naval Review, trumpeted as a congenial demonstration of Anglo-German entente, was in fact a masterpiece of British duplicity. The British Admiralty was only too well aware of Wilhelm's designs for a new German navy; he had made no secret of them. Hence, in effect, they arranged the circus to display the lion. The ships of the British battle fleet now clogging Spithead sent their own message perfectly clearly.

Yet the plan, brilliantly conceived, backfired. Among the many dignitaries gathered on the English battleship were executives from the White Star Line, Britain's passenger ship firm that was a friendly rival to the mighty and venerable Cunard Line. Leading the party was Thomas Ismay, White Star chairman and founder. They were there to escort the Kaiser aboard Britain's newest luxury liner, the aptly named *Teutonic*, which had been fully reconditioned as an armed merchant cruiser. It was this metamorphosis that they most wished to press upon him: for the first time, a peacetime passenger liner could be transformed almost instantly into an auxiliary warship. This was a gentle reminder, if one was needed, that Britain could and would turn every available hull into a defender of the Isles, if necessary. As soon as he crossed the gangway, Kaiser Wilhelm was whisked off at once to view *Teutonic*'s armor plating and artillery enclosures.

Wilhelm was impressed, but not in the way they had anticipated. Politely feigning interest, he examined the military trappings and made appropriate comments. But as soon as courtesy allowed, the Kaiser diverted the party to an unscheduled tour of the ship's First Class passenger spaces. Here the Kaiser was enthralled. The *Teutonic* was the last word in seagoing luxury, with a tapestry-lined smoking room, vaulted dining room with coffered ceiling, and full barber shop and beauty salon boasting electrical hairbrushes and fans to dry ladies' elaborate upswept coiffures. Her silhouette also contrasted sharply with the stodgy navy vessels around her. Long and sleek, the *Teutonic* was the first liner to replace traditional masts rigged for sail with truncated ones fit only for signaling. Her profile would come to characterize ships of the modern era: riveted steel hull, painted black; three decks of windowed superstructure, painted white; and two raked funnels bearing White Star's signature colors of black and beige. Her presence must have been an inadvertent embarrassment for the British, for she made their navy seem, in comparison, almost like a backdrop for a Gilbert and Sullivan operetta. The Kaiser spent two hours aboard the *Teutonic*, while the British admirals fidgeted and consulted their watches. When he finally returned to the waiting battleship, he turned to an aide and said, quite casually, "We really must have some of these."

So began the great race for the North Atlantic, a friendly contest between two nations that would ultimately change the course of history itself. When Kaiser Wilhelm returned to Germany he announced his intention to "seize the trident" from the British, matching them not only in navies but in merchant fleets as well. The next three decades would see the creation of vessels so grand and implausible that, even to our jaded eyes, they still defy belief. Between 1889 and 1919 the gross tonnage displaced by a flagship ocean liner would increase from

9,984 to 52,226 tons. Keel length would extend from 545 feet to 919. Average speed would jump from 17 to 24 knots, shortening the distance between the Old and New Worlds by a full day. In the relentless struggle for sybaritic supremacy on the Atlantic, ships whose forebears had been content with a single gathering area suddenly sprouted palm courts, verandas, Ritz-Carlton grills, Turkish baths, swimming pools, gymnasiums, libraries, nurseries, smoking rooms, writing rooms, three-deck-high dining rooms, entrance foyers, elevators, and dog kennels. Interior decoration evolved in less than a decade from a nautical functionalism not unlike that of the early clippers to a lavish indulgence in styles as varied as Jacobean, Rococo, Renaissance, Tudor, and Louis XIV, XV, and XVI. The German supership *Imperator* would boast a Pompeian Bath flawlessly reproduced from its smaller twin in the Royal Automobile Club; a passenger aboard the English *Aquitania* gushed that one might "sleep in a bed depicting one ruler's fancy, breakfast under a different dynasty altogether, lunch under a different flag and furniture scheme, play cards or smoke, or indulge in music, under three other monarchs. . . ." Locked in a game of furious one-upmanship, with nothing less than the symbolic might of the empire at stake, Edwardian craftsmen were given carte blanche for their wildest aspirations, in an age when the only standard of supremacy was excess.

But the race of the superliners was more than a battle of egos. Literally and figuratively, a passenger ship was a bridge between two continents and cultures. The French Line, for example, referred to their ships as "the longest gangplank in the world," an attitude shared by both the Germans and the British. Neither Cunard nor Hamburg-Amerika could have laid a single keel plate without the active sponsorship of their governments. British subsidies saved the Cunard Line from absorption by J. P. Morgan's combine in 1903, facilitated the construction of the *Lusitania* and *Mauretania*, and kept the proud designation of RMS (Royal Mail Steamer) on every British transatlantic liner. German sponsorship, personally awarded by the Kaiser himself, not only helped create the ships but vastly expanded the shipyards needed to build them. Thus, in every way, the Atlantic liners were the floating embodiments of their respective nations. The best local craftsmanship was incorporated into them, whether Parsons turbines in the *Mauretania* or hand-worked paneling in the First Class lounge of the

Vaterland. Like the *Teutonic*, every liner was built as both a passenger ship and a potential adjunct to the naval fleet. In peacetime, these liners were symbols of their nations' culture, might, and prowess. In war, they became a lifeline between allies.

Despite their pivotal importance to cultural, political, and military history, neither the liners nor their dual civilian and wartime roles have been given serious historical consideration. In contrast, the Anglo-German naval race is the subject of countless books, articles, even movies. The race between the passenger liners has been relegated to a footnote in that broader history. We remain fascinated by the great disasters, the *Titanic* of 1912 and the *Lusitania* of 1915, yet rarely are these events seen in their larger historical context. The history of the passenger-liner rivalry has received attention only in so-called social histories, books written on—as Frank Braynard titled his—the "lives of the liners." While many of these are excellent, their scope is, paradoxically, both too broad and too narrow to give the race of the superliners its due; too broad, because they usually cover a period much greater than 1889–1919; too narrow, because they confine themselves to the histories of individual ships with only perfunctory references to surrounding events.

This book places the prewar superliners in their proper context of intense national rivalry between Britain and Germany. This race, so long neglected by historians, had a crucial impact on early-twentieth-century history, rivaling that of the naval competition. Indeed, the Anglo-German passenger-ship race had repercussions in virtually every facet of contemporary history. It was an integral part of the naval race itself in that it spurred technological innovations such as the turbine, the Marconi wireless, and the double hull that became essential in every World War I warship. Even more importantly, the creation of the superliners facilitated a great wave of emigration to the United States in the first decade of the twentieth century. An average ship in the 1880s could carry 250 emigrants, all housed in open cargo areas in the bowels of the ship. The *Imperator* of 1912, however, carried 1,772 in what was called steerage class, not luxurious by any means but still in individual cabins with stewards and complimentary linen, though the washrooms were communal. Emigrants who had until recently huddled together in unheated spaces with creaking bulkheads now enjoyed a lounge, a dining room, a smoking room, and deck space. To fill all these cabins, passenger lines actively recruited emigrants with flashy advertising campaigns. Yet even without the ads, the holds would still have been filled. Mass migration to the United States at that time might be likened to an hourglass, with the Atlantic Ocean in the narrow middle. The superliners relieved that bottleneck, allowing millions of immigrants to cross and thus transform American society.

Finally, the race of the superliners may be credited with influencing and perhaps even altering the outcome of the First World War. When the fierce rivalry that produced these leviathans exploded into actual combat, they were abruptly left stranded all over the globe. After a brief, abortive career as armed merchant cruisers, English ships were enlisted to ferry troops from the mother country to the Dardanelles and from the dominions to the western front in France, and to bring vital matériel from the United States. The bulk of the German liner fleet was trapped in their docks in Hoboken, New Jersey, where they remained dormant until 1917. Then, with the entry of America into the war, these ships were swiftly commissioned by the U.S. Navy, renamed, and employed as troop carriers. With British and German superliners working in tandem, an almost unimaginable two million soldiers, the entire American Expeditionary Force, were ferried across in a matter of months. This mass influx is often credited with breaking the stalemate of trench warfare and bringing about the collapse of the German military one year later. Without those giant ships, this would not have been possible.

The symbolic significance of a prewar Atlantic liner also makes the Anglo-German passenger-ship race a perfect framework for examining the social conditions and interactions of the age. Each of these ships was a microcosm of its nation's social structure, perfectly reproduced in segregated hierarchical tiers. At the top, in First Class, were the aristocrats and the barons of industry. Beneath that was Second Class, the bourgeoisie. Beneath that was Steerage, the area for working-class emigrants. And beneath that, in the darkest, foulest recesses of the ship, were the stokers, trimmers, firemen, and engineers whose labors propelled and powered this floating city. To understand the social realities of the Edwardian era one could hardly do better than to examine the interactions among these classes on a transatlantic liner.

Finally, the race provides a tangible yardstick for observing the descent of Britain and Germany into war. Begun as a friendly competition, a sort of yachting cup writ large, the rivalry degenerated rapidly into an all-out clash of wills, which, while still ostensibly peaceful, was anything but friendly. The Kaiser's imperious demand for maritime supremacy eventually became a personal obsession; at the start of the war, one of his first directives was to choose the liner in which he would take his victory tour after Britain was defeated. Where the English and Germans initially felt pride in the accomplishments of their own ships, they would later rejoice at humbling and destroying the other's. The day the *Lusitania* was launched was declared a national holiday in England; the day she was torpedoed was reportedly declared a national holiday in Germany.

The breakneck pace set by Germany and England would also be the cause of other, more subtle tragedies. Aided by lightning advances in technology and driven by an unquenchable thirst for speed, size, and luxury, passenger liners grew exponentially in the first decade of the twentieth century. But the rest of society could not keep pace. The sinking of the *Titanic*, and the appalling loss of life, were directly attributable to the Anglo-German competition. Ships like the *Titanic* had become *too* big: too big for their captains, too big for their steering mechanisms, and too big for the antiquated lifeboat requirements of the Board of Trade. The race for maritime supremacy produced a breed of mammoths whose size exceeded the technological limitations of the age. Thus the loss of the *Titanic* represents not (as once supposed) the hand of God punishing the arrogance of man, but the arrogance of man collapsing inevitably upon itself with terrible results.

The average life span of an Atlantic liner, from dry dock to scrap yard, is thirty years. This book traces the history of the Atlantic race from its inception in 1889 through its zenith in the first decade of the twentieth century, the awesome maelstrom of war, and finally its ignominious, ironic conclusion in 1919. These thirty years, arguably the most important in modern history, saw the decline and fall of the Old World's smug complacency, the disastrous fruits of nationalism, the loss of innocence in the crucible of total war, the collapse of monarchies, and the birth, in 1919, of a new world order.

The history of the great Atlantic liners is, simultaneously, one of governments, societies, companies, and personalities. Rarely have so many disparate elements coalesced, interweaving separate threads of nationalism, technology, immigration, aristocracy, consumerism, tourism, empire, and big business. Like the liners themselves, the race brings together a cast of characters from every conceivable walk of life, from emperor to penniless migrant. It is also uniquely reflective of its time: a period of uncritical patriotism, faith in science and technology, absolute certainty about human progress, and optimism unbridled by defeat or tragedy. The Edwardian era was one of aspirations; everyone had an ambition. In Germany, Kaiser Wilhelm II wished to create floating monuments to Germany's magnificence, and his own. In England, Parliament subsidized the creation of the largest and fastest ships on earth to counter his challenge. In the offices of the Hamburg-Amerika Line, company chairman Albert Ballin envisioned a friendly competition among passenger liners that could replace the clash of navies and eliminate the need for war. In New York, financier and railroad entrepreneur J. P. Morgan sought to control the Atlantic as surely as he did the rails, forming a shipping trust that nearly drove both the Germans and the British off the seas. In Serbia, Ireland, Italy, Poland, and all across Europe, farmers, machinists, and tradesmen left their homelands and braved a reckless passage across unknown waters for the promise of work in the New World. The race for the Atlantic encompassed them all.

This is their story.

-1-

The Gauntlet

AS THE LAST HATFUL OF WIND FADED SLOWLY TO NOTHING, TWO magnificent racing yachts sat becalmed. Sails flapped listlessly, and the men scurrying about their decks had no more purpose or effect than ants on a log. Aboard the royal yacht *Britannia*, the Prince of Wales viewed the situation philosophically. Just over the horizon lay Cowes on the Isle of Wight where his mother, Queen Victoria, awaited him at her large residence, Osborne House. It had been a splendid August day, a chance to escape the ponderous responsibilities of royalty that Bertie, as he was known to his family and friends, detested. But it was nothing more than a temporary respite; just as a ship inevitably returns to shore, the Prince soon would have to relinquish his yachtsman's cap and again don the mantle of Heir Apparent to the British Empire.

Tonight's duty was particularly onerous: a full-dress dinner given in honor of his visiting nephew, Kaiser Wilhelm II, by the Queen. "Full-dress" meant considerably more in 1893 than it does today. The Prince of Wales would be decked with a breastplate of medals, the combined weight of which would drag his starched tunic perilously close to the tablecloth and endanger the soup. He would be seated not according to his own fancy, or even his mother's, but by the inflexible rules of protocol—which doubtless meant that he would be forced to spend the evening making polite conversation with Wilhelm, whom he disliked, or with whatever bull-necked Prussian baron Willie had brought along in his entourage. But the Prince understood his role, and accepted it. Lateness to table would not only be inexcusable, it would be unconscionable. "Signal the *Meteor*," he ordered, " 'Propose abandon race and return by train so as to reach Osborne in time for dinner.' "

Moments later the message came back: "I object. Race must be fought out. It doesn't matter when we reach Cowes."

There were few men in the world who could send such a message to the Prince of Wales, and only one with the appallingly bad manners to do so: Kaiser Wilhelm II. In Germany, His Imperial Majesty the Kaiser was the nominal inheritor of the Holy Roman Empire, a lineal descent that spanned history as far back (at least in theory) as Charlemagne. He was also granted the title "All Highest," and regularly penned under his signature "*Suprema lex, Regis voluntas*"—"the supreme law is the will of the king." More than any ruler except the Tsar (whose totalitarian power was already showing signs of strain), the German Kaiser was a monarch absolute, enjoying privileges of Divine Right that the English kings had not known since the execution of Charles I in 1649.

But in England he was "Willie," the obstreperous grandson of Queen Victoria, whose imperial affectations were regarded as little more than playground boastfulness. "To pretend that he is to be treated in *private* as well as public as 'His Imperial Majesty' is *perfect madness*," Victoria wrote scathingly to the Prime Minister, Lord Salisbury, "*If* he has *such* notions, he better *never* come here. The Queen will not swallow this affront." Nevertheless, she did. For despite their unconcealed disgust at Wilhelm's brash demeanor, the British royals felt a lingering pity toward their cousin not unlike that of popular boys at school toward a class twit who, in attempting to emulate them, becomes only a parody himself. Wilhelm had been a sickly child, underweight and not expected to live. His left arm, malformed at birth, was a withered stalk that he kept pinned to his side and always crooked, disguising its shape. Every photograph taken of the Kaiser is a three-quarters profile with the left arm concealed behind the trunk, often holding a pair of gloves. To compensate for this deformity, the child Wilhelm embarked on a Spartan regime of activity designed to strengthen the rest of him. He became a champion horseback rider and a deadly fencing opponent. In an age in which duels were still de rigueur for matters of honor (Chancellor Bismarck claimed to have fought scores of opponents in his early years), Wilhelm developed the reputation of a fierce duelist, though no one would dare challenge the Prince to anything more than a friendly match. Still, despite his athletic prowess, the Kaiser never overcame the shame of being—as his grandfather Wilhelm I cruelly dubbed him—a *"defective* prince." In relations with his English cousins, he was forever the boastful, arrogant, yet somehow pathetic parvenu.

Wilhelm thus occupied a strange dual role, Kaiser and cousin, depending on which side of the Channel he found himself. But what was most notable was not the difference between these roles, but their interrelatedness. Nineteenth-century diplomacy was very much a family affair, as it had been for many hundreds of years. The British royal family occupied the epicenter of a complicated web of alliances that encompassed the ruling and noble families of nearly every Continental power. These alliances were multiplied by a predilection among American plutocrats to marry their daughters into European nobility (Winston Churchill, for example, was born to a father who was a younger son of the Duke of Marlborough and a mother from New York). England's preeminence was largely the result of the fertility and longevity of Queen Victoria's reign. In her sixty years as monarch, she saw her nine children and many grandchildren become a new generation whose marriages and children would span all of Europe's royal houses. And of all the Continental powers wedded to the British Crown, none was closer than the German Kaiser. Victoria herself was of German ancestry: her father was the fourth son of King George III, who in turn was the grandson of George II, the Elector of Hanover. The first two Georges spoke hardly any English. George III married a German, as did Victoria herself—Prince Albert of Saxe-Coburg-Gotha. German was her first language, spoken exclusively until she was three years old.

When she spoke to her grandson, the Kaiser, she occasionally used the informal German *du*.

Just as the British royal family was predominantly German, Kaiser Wilhelm was as much an English gentleman as a Prussian monarch. His mother, Princess Victoria, disliked Germany almost as much as she loved her German husband, Crown Prince for years and only briefly Kaiser Friedrich III. Her son Wilhelm would later write of her: "She delivered judgment on everything and found everything wrong with us and better in England which she habitually called 'home.' " Perhaps it was in response to his mother's intense anglophilia that her headstrong son embraced German culture, or perhaps it was the lingering sense that his English blood "tainted" his title to the imperial throne. Nevertheless, from birth young Wilhelm was influenced by his English roots. He was taught to read English literature, and he enjoyed English poetry and conversed fluently with his mother and his brother, Prince Heinrich, in both languages. He also maintained a close and affectionate relationship with his grandmother, Queen Victoria, which endured despite politics and conflict until the British monarch's death in 1901.

Thus, it might have been familial feelings as much as good politics that led the Prince of Wales to recommend his nephew for membership in the Royal Yacht Squadron at Cowes. The honor was a singular one, for it meant that Wilhelm would be admitted into the inner sanctum of the Prince's social circle, the highest stratum of "high society." In the late nineteenth century, before movie stars and pop singers shifted the center of celebrity to the orange groves of California, the small English cove at Cowes formed one point of a social triangle that Newport and, later, Kiel would complete. In the summer, from June to August, each hosted races between the finest yachts in the world. It was the last sport of kings, as the English and German royals matched their razor-sharp hulls against those of industrial titans J. P. Morgan and William K. Vanderbilt. Like a flock of magnificently plumed migratory birds, the yachts sailed from one point of the triangle to the other, followed by a constellation of guests, minor aristocrats, lesser millionaires, *social aspirants*, servants, courtiers, and society columnists. At a time when J. P. Morgan could cynically remark of a yacht, "If you have to ask how much it costs, you can't afford it," the social register of Cowes was widely regarded as the apex of Western civilization.

Membership in the Royal Yacht Squadron was exclusive to the point of absurdity; Sir Thomas Lipton, possibly the most famous yachtsman of the nineteenth century, was not elected a member until the last year of his life. While all the world might forget that Sir Thomas was a self-made tea merchant, the club members at Cowes did not. Nevertheless when the Prince of Wales, as Commodore, proposed his young nephews Princes Wilhelm and Heinrich of Prussia, birthright won over nautical prowess and both were speedily elected. It was a poor choice, and Bertie would live to regret this gesture of magnanimity more than any other decision of his life.

For, whether as Willie or as His Imperial Majesty, the Kaiser's most defining characteristic was his fierce, almost pathological competitiveness. Historians have placed the blame on a deep-seated inferiority complex, arising from feelings of physical and social inadequacy due to his withered arm and lack of the easy charm of his Uncle Bertie and the English royal family. Personal doubts also mingled with political realities; in 1889, the year the Kaiser visited Cowes for the first time, England was at the pinnacle of her imperial glory, while Germany was less than twenty years past her unification and still depended for survival on her founding architect, Otto von Bismarck. Prussia's victory over France in 1871 seemed paltry compared with England's far greater triumph over Napoleon a half century earlier. In the interim, later known as the Pax Britannica, England adopted a policy of "splendid isolation" among her Continental neighbors and used the relative peace at home to forge a formidable empire abroad. By 1889, the combined efforts of empire-builders such as Disraeli and Rhodes had left England in possession of territories so vast that the proclamation "the sun never sets on the British Empire" was quite literally true. Queen Victoria became Empress of India, and a great white diamond was affixed to the center of her crown. Wilhelm, in contrast, held title over a loosely bound federation of squabbling principalities and an "empire" that existed more in ceremony than in fact. Hence, while Wilhelm as a man might feel belittled by the implacable serenity his British relatives enjoyed in their social position, Wilhelm the Emperor could not help but feel upstaged by the awesome might and historical primacy accorded the British Empire.

His frustrations came to be felt by his colleagues at the Royal Yacht

Squadron. Wilhelm was "the man nobody liked," a boorish pest whose persistent quibbling over rules and regulations was matched only by an impassioned, ungentlemanly desire to win. He was forever raising questions about handicaps and decisions, often implying or even stating outright that club members were slighting him in favor of his uncle. When he raced, he did so with dogged determination and a very loose regard for rules. Charlie Barr, the great American captain who piloted many millionaires' yachts to victory, once came perilously close to accusing the Kaiser of being a cheat. As a working captain in the pay of hired masters, Barr had considerable experience dealing with the arrogance and ignorance of the titled rich. Nevertheless, upon meeting the Kaiser at Kiel, he described him as "a bumptious, not altogether on-the-level yachtsman." During their first race Wilhelm blithely ignored the rules, refusing to give way whenever he held the advantage. As the distance closed between his *Meteor* (on port tack) and Barr's *Ingomar* (on starboard), and collision seemed imminent, Barr was forced to come about even though the rules accorded him right of way. The second time it occurred, Barr held fast. "But, sir," a German officer exclaimed, "it's the *Kaiser!*" "When he steps behind the helm of a racing yacht," Barr growled back, "he ceases to be the Kaiser." The two yachts drew closer together. An observer wrote that the German lieutenant, Baron von Kotwitz, sat on the *Ingomar*'s deck "with his mouth half open . . . wondering whether we had all gone stark raving mad . . . [and] were really going to send his All Highest Emperor to the bottom of the sea." At the very last moment, the *Meteor* retreated. Barr won the race, and the Kaiser stormed past him, refusing to acknowledge the victory. A contrite admiral later passed along the message that the Kaiser regretted the incident and accepted the blame. But the damage to the Kaiser's reputation was done. In a society where unflappable calm and "Jolly well played, sir" sportsmanship were the governing tenets, such behavior was as alien and bizarre as wearing a bathing suit to Ascot.

Between 1892 and 1895, Wilhelm's *Meteor* was matched against the Prince of Wales's *Britannia* for four consecutive summers. The *Britannia* proved the faster yacht, and the Prince won handily every time. After each race, the Kaiser retreated from the field angrily muttering accusations of favoritism, but it was nothing more than petty jealousy.

The *Britannia* was not only the better yacht, but her captain, the Prince of Wales, the better yachtsman. Count von Bülow, Wilhelm's acid-tongued adjutant, remarked that, "if the Kaiser steered himself, we regularly hit the buoy."

Even more galling than the Prince of Wales's repeated victories was his familiar presence on the Squadron club lawn. Magnificently self-assured, Bertie presided over club functions in a yachting outfit trimmed with gold braid—befitting a Commodore—and puffing complacently on a huge cigar. He was the very picture of the English sportsman. These functions were for him a form of relaxation and good fun: sunlight and sport by day, laughter and fellowship in the evenings. Try as he might, the Kaiser could never emulate his uncle's attitude. Races, for him, were about winning. Nothing else mattered—not rules, not sportsmanship, not even the strain on his relations with his English family. Hence his churlish response on that hot August afternoon. While the Prince of Wales might have been sorry to give up a lovely day to return to Osborne for a stuffy dinner with his mother, Wilhelm refused to relinquish the field to a detested opponent. The race was finished, and Bertie was again the victor. The two men arrived at Osborne long after dinner had ended, the Kaiser rushing in and hurriedly kissing his grandmother's proffered hand. As the belated guest of honor, he merited a mirthless smile. Poor Bertie, whose love of good sport Victoria doubtless blamed for the ruin of her dinner plans, got only a nod.

In 1895, the last year the Kaiser and the Prince of Wales would race, Wilhelm announced that he was withdrawing the *Meteor* from the Queen's Cup, faulting the handicapping set for the race. It was as close to an accusation of cheating as he would dare to make against his uncle, and it did not go unnoticed. Shortly thereafter he established his own Regatta Week at Kiel, which he deliberately scheduled two months ahead of the one at Cowes, hoping to steal some of its thunder. Yet despite marching bands, functionaries, gala balls, and innumerable state receptions, Kiel Week would never match the social importance Cowes enjoyed. It was too stiff, too contrived. The yachts looked as stunning as ever, but the social occasions (which were, after all, the heart and soul of yachting) never quite captured the aristocratic insouciance that Cowes and its benefactor, the Prince of Wales, achieved. Still, the Kaiser persisted. The *Meteor* would go on losing, though without

Wilhelm at the wheel. And Kiel Week would continue to attract the yachts, the millionaires, and their entourages every summer until that last, fateful season in 1914. But Wilhelm's heart was no longer in it. Even by 1895, his attention had turned. In Berlin, the ambitious Admiral Tirpitz set the Kaiser's mind toward matching England's navy. And in Bremen and Hamburg, Wilhelm's unforgotten promise to wrest the glory from Britain's merchant fleet was about to bear fruit. Even as the Kaiser lost interest in Cowes, his sights were set on a much larger race.

"An Enormous But Shapely Mass of Steel"

The Blue Riband, a prize given to the fastest steamship on the Atlantic, did not actually exist. There was no coveted blue silk banner, no trophy, no tangible sign that any honor had been awarded at all. It was not until the French liner *Normandie* released a 30-foot blue pennant from her mainmast—in 1935—that an actual "blue riband" even existed, and not until two years after that did a British enthusiast, Sir Jeffrey Hale, commission a large silver cup in honor of the transatlantic speed record, "Hale's Trophy." Yet since the mid-nineteenth century British and American liners had been locked in a feverish, often deadly competition for the honor, building larger and faster ships to court an early generation of wealthy tourists heading eastward and a burgeoning mass of emigrants flooding west into the New World.

Among the earliest of these entrepreneurs was a Canadian businessman living in England named Samuel Cunard. Founded in 1840 to carry mail from London to Halifax, the Cunard Line began inauspiciously with two 300-ton vessels and a government contract. At that time scores of such companies appeared and disappeared on the Atlantic so quickly that many left no trace except their newspaper advertisements. Cunard's line was unremarkable except that it emphasized safety over all other considerations, including speed and comfort. The early Cunard ships were smelly, and cramped. Charles Dickens, traveling aboard the Cunard liner *Britannia,* remarked of his cabin that nothing smaller had ever been made for sleeping, except coffins. The commodious stateroom advertised by sketch rendering ashore was in actuality a creaking, heaving box that could no more hold Dickens's trunks "than a giraffe could be persuaded into a flower pot." But the Cunard ships had one tremendous advantage over their competition: they did not sink. In an age when handbooks for lady passengers advised the wearing of good clothes on board "because a corpse washed ashore in good clothes is likely to be treated better than one dressed from the rag bag," this was indeed an accomplishment.

The wisdom of Cunard's emphasis on safety was quickly borne out by the grisly fate of his most dangerous rival, Edward Knight Collins. Collins, an American, envisioned a fleet of ocean liners that would sweep Cunard's spartan paddlewheelers off the Atlantic through a combination of unparalleled luxury, unmatched speed, and sheer élan. There was something of the carnival huckster about Collins: a big, burly, jovial man (in contrast to the spare, prim Cunard), his first commercial enterprise on the Atlantic had been the Dramatic Line, featuring ships named after the great figures of the American and English stages. When, in 1849 he approached Congress seeking a subsidy to build a newer, faster fleet, Collins was fortunate to arrive on the scene at a time when Cunard's unquestioned supremacy on the transatlantic run was beginning to wear thin. Armed with an annual subsidy of $385,000 and a mandate from Senator Bayard of Delaware to "proceed with the absolute conquest of this man Cunard," Collins began construction on no fewer than five ocean liners bearing names that seemed to lay claim to the oceans themselves: *Atlantic, Pacific, Arctic, Baltic,* and *Adriatic.* They were like nothing the world had ever seen.

The *Atlantic,* the first of Collins's ships, had an ice house, steam heating, bathrooms with hot and cold water, and a barber shop. Her dining room, compared with the "hearse with windows" Dickens had observed on the *Britannia,* was a sumptuous delight. Oriental rugs lined the floors, upon which rested heavily upholstered chairs and marble tables, all framed by panels of satinwood, holly, and rosewood, and beveled-glass mirrors. The *Atlantic* was also the first ship to acknowledge that great American indulgence, smoking. Previously smokers had to be content with a section of grating near the bow, where they nestled among winches and anchor cables and could expect to be regularly doused with spray. The *Atlantic* accommodated them in a small "outhouse" on deck, unpretentious and unadorned but the prototype of a quintessential male retreat aboard ships for decades to come.

The Collins liners were a triumph. Completing the run from Liverpool to New York in 10 days, 16 hours, the *Atlantic* took the speed record, only to be bested by her own sister, *Pacific*, in April 1852, with a run of 9 days, 20 hours. American journalists crowed—in an early echo of the Kaiser's pledge—that they had "wrested the Tyrian trident from Britain's grasp" once and for all. "Speed!" the anglophobe Senator Bayard bellowed. "Speed against which these British can never hope to compete. Speed of such magnitude as the Government of Britain and its chosen instrument, this man Cunard, never visualized or could ever hope to achieve against America!"

But the wave was cresting. Collins Line had built its reputation on speed and luxury over all other considerations, so it was not surprising that its newest and grandest vessel, the *Arctic*, should find herself steaming full ahead through heavy fog off the Grand Banks one September afternoon in 1854 with a shipload of passengers eager to reach New York. Somewhere in the fog the *Arctic* collided with a small French steamer, the *Vesta*. The smaller ship lanced her bow into the *Arctic*'s hull, sustaining considerable damage but mortally wounding the *Arctic*. Panic set in among the crew, who commandeered the few lifeboats and left the passengers of the *Arctic*, and her captain, to fend for themselves. Nearly all drowned, including several people prominent in East Coast society. But for Edward Knight Collins the most damning names on the victim list were those of his own wife, son, and daughter, and seven members of the Brown family, which had partnered with Collins in the creation of his ships.

Two years later, the *Pacific* disappeared without a trace, all aboard presumed lost. She had last been spotted by the Cunard ship *Persia* heading into a field of ice. Collins, in desperation, abandoned all pretensions of glory and inserted new advertisements for his ships, stressing "improved watertight bulkheads" and promising that "to avoid danger from ice, [Collins ships] will not cross the Banks north of 42 degrees until after the first of August." He had learned his lesson, but it was too late. The *Adriatic*, finest of all the Collins liners, was a Jonah ship even before her keel touched the water. The loss of her elder sisters hung over her like a black pall. On her maiden voyage in 1858 she sailed with only ten cabins occupied. Months later Congress withdrew its subsidy. The surviving liners were auctioned off at their piers, the

Atlantic and *Baltic* finding ignominious work as troop transports, the lovely *Adriatic* sailing under the British flag for Lever Line until 1885. The Collins Line was finished, as were America's dreams of supremacy on the Atlantic.

Cunard emerged from the fracas more powerful than ever. The same year Collins's liners ended up on the auction block, Samuel Cunard was knighted. Sir Samuel's dictum on safety had been vindicated, and the line would proudly boast at the turn of the century that it "had never lost a life." Amazingly, this record still stands today, excepting the lives lost through enemy action on board the *Lusitania* and one unfortunate woman who perished during a storm on board the *Queen Mary* due to a combination of seasickness and fright. But the brief, meteoric history of the Collins Line had also provided Cunard with another useful lesson: safety might be the key, but luxury and speed were valuable commodities. A shipping line that struck a successful balance among the three could count on winning the lion's share of passenger traffic. Even before Collins's ultimate fall from grace, Cunard captains were taking a leaf from his book. Though stringently warned by the company to "ever have regard to safety before speed," the captains had already begun to engage their American rivals in friendly—though spirited—races. The *Persia* was doing just that when the *Pacific* disappeared. Sir Samuel thoroughly disapproved of the practice but was powerless to stop it. For the last three decades of the nineteenth century, British shipowners spurred their fleets like thoroughbreds, each hoping to best the other's time. The race for the Atlantic became a sort of yachting cup for liners, governed by as many rules and codes of conduct, yet indisputably British. The collapse of Collins's line left the field to his British rivals; the lovely Inman liners, the sleek White Star fleet, and the irrepressible Cunard ships continued to challenge one another in an ongoing contest for the fastest passage from Queenstown, Ireland, to Sandy Hook, New Jersey, at the entrance to New York Harbor.

Ironically, even as the race intensified, the Cunard Line continued to pay lip service to its founder's cautious motto. Some even went so far as to deny the very existence of an Atlantic race. "I do not believe," said Cunard chairman David Jardine in 1890, "that either on our Cunard steamers or on those of any other Line which sail from Liverpool there is such a thing as racing. . . . So far as Cunard commanders and engineers are concerned they are instructed that . . . they are not to recognize the fact that there are any other steamers on the Atlantic. I believe it is the same in other companies, for the responsibility is too great to allow any racing to be run."

This was wishful thinking at best. As Cunard's chairman, Jardine must have turned a very blind eye to the fact that, whatever memoranda might be issued from the head office, Cunard commanders were zealously committed to keeping the title for speed in company hands. As for Jardine's earnest declaration that other lines felt as he did, it was utter balderdash, and he knew it. Just a month after his pronouncement, the Inman liner *City of New York* and White Star liner *Teutonic* departed simultaneously from Liverpool in an all-out dash across the Atlantic. For almost a week the two ships steamed within sight of one another, and eager passengers crowded the rails to shake their fists derisively at their opponents. The *Teutonic* won by a thin margin of four hours.

The fact is that even after Collins failed the public would flock to the fastest ship—just as it would the newest restaurant or most modern hotel. Fast ships were good business. So, in its own way, was luxury. By emphasizing both, the Collins Line effected a profound transformation in the way the ocean crossing was regarded. Before its advent, passage on the Atlantic was a trial to be endured. Going to sea was still, as Dr. Johnson had once described it, "like going to prison, with the chance of being drowned." But once the *Atlantic* and her sisters introduced resort amenities to their ships, the crossing was transformed into an integral part of the travel experience. Transatlantic travel became *fun*. The comedian Ed Wynn would later deadpan: "Say, when you go to Europe, be sure not to miss the boat trip!" Ships ceased to be mere means of conveyance, and a new expression was introduced into the Atlantic lexicon: "ocean liner." Originally, "liner" simply referred to the "line" between embarkation and destination, as in Southampton–New York. But in the latter part of the nineteenth century, the word took on a unique significance: liners became synonymous with floating hotels, evoking an image of grace, service, luxury, and speed. Cunard, almost against its own will, began to produce ships reflecting this new policy.

The evolution of the Cunard Line from a staid, dependable, unimaginative firm into a maritime colossus was greatly aided by the death, in the late 1860s, of Sir Samuel himself. While his keen business acumen had preserved the company through wars, depressions, and the ravages of the indifferent sea, his penny-pinching frugality had become something of a hindrance. With the advent of iron hulls and watertight bulkheads, as well as the promulgation of new safety regulations prohibiting masters from recklessly endangering their ships, safety was no longer the primary concern on the Atlantic. The White Star and Inman Lines, eager to capitalize on Collins's failures (while shamelessly copying his successes), introduced ships that rivaled each other in size, speed, and gold leaf. And the Cunard Line, freed from its founder's stern Calvinist disapproval, responded with the *Servia*.

Hyperbole is as endemic to the unveiling of a new ship as to a presidential election, and just as pointless. Each new vessel will be larger, faster, and grander than those preceding it; each will have a new array of whizbang gadgets, whether elevators, barber's chairs, shooting galleries, or wireless stations. Each company claimed their latest to be the "best ever," but in its effect on shipbuilding as a whole, and on history itself, the *Servia* was indeed a singular ship. Though neither the fastest nor largest on the Atlantic (the latter distinction still belonged to the hapless *Great Eastern*, by then a shoreside amusement gallery advertising the Bon Marché along her massive flanks), the *Servia* was what is known as a "transitional" vessel. In this case, the transition was from the spartan simplicity of the *Britannia* to the gilded luxe of the *Mauretania*, *Lusitania*, and every ocean liner to follow. Cunard had taken Collins's example to heart; *Servia* was "an enormous but shapely mass of steel," her interiors tricked out in columns and gold brocade and boasting a novelty that would not become the industry standard for another eighty years: private lavatories. True, only a small fraction of her First Class passengers enjoyed them (the rest continued to jostle over communal sinks, as they would for decades to come), but it was a significant advance all the same. One year later the *Servia* was joined by a sister ship *Ausonia*, and the two began a weekly service between Liverpool and New York that quickly gained the reputation

for being as speedy, safe, and regular as the 4:15 train from Padding-
ton Station.

The *Servia* and *Ausonia* also instituted a second Cunard tradition: building ships in pairs. Collins's liners could not truly be called
"sisters," as each one was in fact an improvement (or, at least, an em-
bellishment) of the last. It might have been canny Sir Samuel himself
who came up with the idea, for it was worthy of him: a pair of identical ships, servicing the same route and becoming interchangeable in
the public mind. Thus the Cunard sisters fostered the illusion of being in two places at once: while one was at sea, the other was loading
coal and passengers. They always seemed to be in their docks, waiting
for passengers with the same comfortable regularity of a seaside ferry.
The *Servia* and *Ausonia* were the first in a long line of illustrious
Cunard sister ships that would include the *Caronia* and *Carmania*,
Mauretania and *Lusitania*, and, of course, *Queen Mary* and *Queen
Elizabeth*. This tradition of sister ships would continue until the mid-
twentieth century.

It was precisely Cunard's commitment to sister ships that would
encourage its rivals to think in terms of *trios*, resulting in the *Imperator*, *Vaterland*, and *Bismarck* of Hamburg-Amerika and—most notorious of all—White Star's *Olympic*, *Titanic*, and *Brittanic*.

The next Cunard sisters to appear on the transatlantic run were the
Umbria and *Etruria* of 1884 and 1885. They were unremarkable in
every way except that they were the last major ocean liners to be
equipped with auxiliary sails and single screws. Of more interest than
the ships themselves was the manner in which they were advertised.
Shortly after their appearance, Cunard published a small booklet entitled *An Aristocrat of the Atlantic*, allegedly offering advice to young,
socially conscious ladies seeking passage. In fact it was a shameless piece
of industry fluff, striking the same themes of snobbery and indulgence
that the line's four-color glossy brochures do today. "The Cunard," it
sniffed, "has something. It has a name. Half the pleasure of doing a
thing really well consists in letting the other people—the people who
are not doing the thing at all but would like to if they could—know
that one is enjoying the very best that can be had." Crossing the Atlantic was no longer a voyage, much less an adventure—it was a social

statement. And, in case any of the rich Midwestern rubes should still miss the point, the pamphlet went on to suggest that the material used for the sofacovers (described frothily as a "sea-green Genoese") was worthy of being worn as an evening gown—the image springs to mind of Scarlett O'Hara dressed in her drawing room draperies.

There was no question that Cunard had "arrived." By the late nineteenth century the company was utterly supreme on the Atlantic, turning out a pair of magnificent liners every few years that swept up the Blue Riband, the accolades of the press, and—most importantly— the lion's share of the passenger traffic. The early peak came with the construction, in 1893, of the *Campania* and *Lucania*.

The first and most obvious point of note about both ships was that they were surpassingly ugly. In an age when graceful, swanlike clippers still sailed back and forth across the oceans, most steamship designers copied them. Funnels were concealed in a maze of yacht-like rigging; reciprocal engines lay hidden within long-stemmed clipper hulls. The Inman liners *City of Rome*, *City of Paris*, and *City of New York* were the most successful examples of this hybrid policy. Though far larger than any clipper ship, and carrying an extra layer of cream-painted superstructure, they crowded their funnels into a crisp trio far forward, leaving a long transom stern to fan out behind. Indeed, they are still remembered as among the most beautiful ships ever to cross the Atlantic. In marked contrast, the *Campania* and *Lucania* were living embodiments of "function over form." Stubby, squat vessels with layers of white wedding-cake decks and a pair of massive orange funnels grossly out of proportion with the rest of the ship, they had all the aesthetic appeal of a municipal gasworks. Their appearance was vaguely reminiscent of the White Star liner *Teutonic* in that they too dispensed with auxiliary sails, but they had none of that vessel's low-slung grace. Their closest cousin, in fact, was the Royal Navy flagship *Renown*, a 12,350-ton monster with four 10-inch guns and a plethora of small arms. The unlikely kinship between them was borne out when the *Campania* and *Renown* appeared together at the naval review at Spithead in 1897: both vessels shared crisp black hulls with red boottopping, white superstructures, twin funnels, and a massive chunk of hull that rose out of the water with sheer vertical doughtiness and

not the slightest hint of a rake. It was no accident that the *Campania*
had been designed as a possible adjunct to the Royal Navy; she radiated
British power from every rivet.

If the *Campania*'s exterior evoked stuffy images of Britain's naval
might, her interior spaces were the embodiment of Victorian largesse.
Their purpose, one Cunard advertisement suggested, was to foster the
illusion that passengers were not, in fact, aboard a ship at all: wealthy
travelers could, for up to six hundred dollars a day, enjoy the privilege
"of seeing nothing at all that has to do with a ship, not even the sea." As
with the *Etruria*, Cunard's brochures again provided a tangible yardstick of contemporary mores and class divisions. Weighing in at a
whopping 108 pages of hyperbole and puffery, the *Campania*'s was
nothing less than a Homeric ode. It covered everything from the
rosette-shaped electric lights in the reading room to the enormous crystal dome suspended over the First Class restaurant. Particular attention,
however, was paid to the ladies' accommodations. Women passengers
were a relative novelty, their presence aboard ship being the surest
indication that Atlantic crossings had indeed ceased to be masculine
adventures. As if in recognition of the perceived delicacy of these new
passengers, the company promised to transport them with the same
tender care as would be accorded a priceless piece of Dresden china.
In the *Campania*, ladies traveling in First Class enjoyed their own private saloon, decorated in silks and cushions, which men could enter
only with special permission. Why any man would seek admittance to
this feminine snuggery is not revealed, and indeed the brochure seems
to suggest that it exists precisely to rescue fleeing Daphne from her lust-
ful pursuers: "It is a club house and boudoir combined; if my lady has
a nervous headache, or wishes to escape the importunities of an ardent
but obtrusive admirer, or if she wants to read in quiet, or to gossip, or
to fritter her time away in dolce far niente she steals in here, and here
is sanctuary." The total effect of *Campania*'s First Class interiors was,
according to Cunard, a "silent sermon in good taste." Concerning
Steerage accommodations the brochure has exactly one sentence, pronouncing them to be in every way excellent.

Yet if the *Campania* marked the height of the Cunard Line in the
nineteenth century, she was also its downfall. The 1897 naval review

at Spithead was in many respects a last gathering of the dinosaurs: great, coal-burning, piston-driven behemoths with angular lines and ponderous, slouchy gaits. Just as the new *Dreadnought* class of battleships would soon render the *Renown* and her sisters obsolete, so too would a new generation of German passenger liners emerge to strike at the very heart of Britannia's mercantile empire.

-2-

"The Delightfulest Ship I Ever Saw"

THE INSTITUTE OF NAVAL ARCHITECTS, A BRITISH ORGANIZATION, HELD its first meetings in Germany late in 1896. The choice of location and the timing were of the utmost importance. Germany possessed the second largest merchant fleet in the world, but had no ocean greyhounds. The largest vessel it could boast was the *Fürst Bismarck*, which at 8,870 gross tons was only slightly more than half the size of the *Campania* and *Lucania*. Why were the architects suddenly so interested in Germany? In fact, they were not only interested, but nervous as well. The Earl of

Hopetown's inaugural speech was almost a plaintive bleat. "The British people and the German people," he told the international assembly, "divide the honor of being the two greatest commercial races of the world. We earnestly pray that it may always remain a friendly and peaceful rivalry. We regard you as cousins; the two nations are descended from the same stock; their languages are derived from the same root, and have a common origin. We have always been allies in the past. . . . Surely the world is large enough to hold us both."

What sudden anxiety could have prompted such cloying claims of brotherhood from the serene, supercilious English? The answer lay not far away, rising on the stocks in a Stettin shipyard. For even as the *Campania* appeared to the tumultuous sounds of cheers and brass bands at Spithead in June of 1897, the death knell of English supremacy on the Atlantic had already been rung. One month earlier, on May 3, the glistening black hull of the *Kaiser Wilhelm der Grosse* had slid from the ways into the churning waters of Bremerhaven. A great cry went up on shore, and the Kaiser himself, resplendent in an admiral's uniform, beamed with paternal pride. The ship that bore his grandfather's name had only one purpose: to surpass Cunard in every way, once and for all, and in so doing tweak the tail of the British lion.

The Kaiser's fervent desire for German supremacy in this race was like a seedling that quite accidentally finds itself in fertile ground. Had German passenger lines not been uniquely positioned to accomplish his demand—as well as profit from it—Germany might well have had to look elsewhere to assert her new imperial stature. As it was, however, the Kaiser's anglophobic competitive streak exhibited itself within a much larger social dynamic of immigration, trade, and empire.

German and British shipping companies had long enjoyed a relationship that was both cordial and mutually profitable. The Germans, lacking their own massive shipyards, frequently ordered liners from the same British builders that constructed vessels for White Star, Inman, and Cunard. At sea, the ships treated each other with a time-honored respect, even gallantry. In 1889 the German ship *Fulda* rescued the 824 passengers and crew of Cunard's *Oregon* after she was struck by a schooner. Cunard graciously asked what compensation they could provide the German firm for its services, and received the good-natured reply, "Highly gratified having been instrumental in saving so many lives. No claim." Nevertheless, the British would soon be able to pay them back in kind; four years later, as the *Fulda*'s fleet-mate *Eider* lay stranded in fog off the Isle of Wight, all aboard were taken ashore by British lifeboatmen. Kaiser Wilhelm, in a rare display of good grace, sent gold watches to each man and £200 to the Lifeboat Institute.

The German companies had never been a serious threat to Cunard, not because they were insignificant, but because their fleets were too spread out. Germany's nationalistic quest for its "place in the sun" decreed that a large portion of its merchant fleet be scattered about the globe, servicing each and all of its imperial outposts. German companies of any size and prestige were expected to cover *all* possible routes. Hence the grandiose motto of Hamburg-Amerika Lines: *Mein Feld Ist die Welt*—My Scope Is the World. England had a similar web of colonial trade routes, but with one crucial difference: individual British firms catered to specific areas—Cunard on the Atlantic, P & O in the Far East, and so on. The Atlantic had never been a priority for the Germans, and the vast majority of their traffic on it was reserved not for First Class, but for Steerage.

This policy was dictated not only by nineteenth-century Germany's new nationalism, but by the second great social force at work in Germany, as well as in the rest of Europe: emigration to the West. Various factors motivated the great exodus of Eastern Europeans to America in the nineteenth century, the most common being economic hardship and political unrest. Just as warring Germanic tribes had once pushed each other farther and farther toward the western shores of the Continent in the declining days of the Roman Empire, so now did half a century of intermittent wars, famines, nascent revolutions, and mass industrialization drive a new generation of their descendants right into the sea. From Austria-Hungary, Russia, Scandinavia, and the Balkans, primitive dirt roads and major thoroughfares were dotted with the caravans of the displaced, all hopeful, all heading west. Among the major European ports, including Rotterdam, Le Havre, and Antwerp, the German cities of Hamburg and Bremen were both the most accessible and most logical terminals for this mass influx of one-way travelers.

Though smaller companies flourished in the flush of emigrant traffic, Bremen and Hamburg could each claim its own major passenger firm. In Bremen, it was the venerable Norddeutscher Lloyd, boasting a glowing endorsement from no less a personage than American author Samuel Clemens (Mark Twain). Traveling aboard the *Havel* in 1892, Clemens wrote to a friend: "This is the delightfulest ship I ever saw. . . . If I were going to write a book I think I would try to get my family's leave to take a room in the *Havel* and ferry back and forth till the book was finished." So impressed was he with Norddeutscher Lloyd's flagship that he later published an essay, "The Modern Steamer and the Obsolete Steamer," which lauded the remarkable technological innovations the Germans had introduced and compared their ships favorably with the "dull, plain, graceless, gloomy and horribly depressing" ships of only a decade before. The miserable vessel Clemens so thoroughly castigated was the little *Batavia*, of the Cunard Line.

From Hamburg emerged a second, much smaller firm bearing the ponderous name Hamburg-Amerikanische-Paketfarht-Aktien-Gesellschaft, which was frequently—and mercifully—shortened to its initials, HAPAG, or to the more euphonious Hamburg-Amerika Line. Unlike the aristocratic Lloyd, Hamburg-Amerika cared little for the luxury trade. Its ships were small, dingy, cramped, and profitable. Though Bremen had been the first to capitalize on the burgeoning emigrant business, the canny directors of their Hamburg rival were not slow to follow. For several reasons, most of them geographic and many relating to the routes of nineteenth-century railways, Hamburg had a slight logistical edge over Bremen for attracting emigrants to the West. Both cities—and both companies—shamelessly solicited customers, and neither was above accepting a well-placed bribe. Long-standing contracts between shipping agents and many Central European governments guaranteed specific numbers of healthy, serviceable emigrants to fill the ships' holds every year, in much the same way as a crop is delivered to market or—more realistically—slaves to the auction block.

Passage from a German city was not the only way Germans profited from the emigrant boom. Even as shipping agents of the Norddeutscher Lloyd and Hamburg-Amerika lines courted passengers, other German agents were busily recruiting them for cross-Channel passage to Liverpool and onto the ships of the Cunard and White Star lines. This so-called indirect traffic siphoned a considerable portion of the German companies' business; not surprisingly, an acrimonious relationship developed between pro-British and pro-German agents in

Hamburg and Bremen. In marked contrast to the genteel atmosphere
at Cowes, these agents frequently resorted to threats, curses, even fist-
fights, and the police forces of both cities were constantly called in to
protect the emigrants of one group from solicitation—or outright
snatching—by the other. Though resembling nothing so much as gang
warfare, these seemingly trivial brawls were perhaps the first harbinger
of the deadly competitiveness between the British and German passenger lines.

Considering the state of German passenger trade in the late nineteenth century, the Kaiser's offhand remark on the deck of the *Teutonic* that "we must have some of these" carried enormous implications for the German firms commissioned to fulfill the task. Competing
with the British on their own turf meant playing by their rules. First,
it called for a massive reshuffling of the German passenger fleets, shift-
ing from an emphasis on far-flung trade routes to a centralized focus on
the North Atlantic. The companies' symbolic role as links between the
mother country and her dominions and trade partners would not be
abandoned, but it would be subordinated. From now on, they were
rivals not of each other, but of Cunard. Even as the governments of
Britain and Germany made lasting pledges of peace, and German
diplomats assured their British colleagues that the Kaiser's naval fleet
would be used only to defend Germany's imperial possessions, the
directors of Hamburg-Amerika and Norddeutscher Lloyd had been
ordered to forget about the empire and concentrate on England.

This radical shift in policy also meant a transformation in the ships
themselves. Hamburg and Bremen could no longer be content with
their ugly, serviceable cash cows, nor could they gear their marketing
strategy primarily toward the emigrant trade. To wrest glory from the
British, the Germans had to produce a true wonder, a ship that would be
fast—not merely fast, but the fastest. Nothing less would win the Blue
Riband. It had to be the largest—not by a margin of a mere few hundred
tons, but by so much that it would send British naval architects reel-
ing. It had to be the most luxurious—promising delights and diver-
sions that would win the millionaires over from Cunard, with all its
silk cushions and gushy prose. Finally, it had to settle the matter of indirect traffic once and for all. A supership leaving from either Bremen or
Hamburg—or preferably both—would obviate the need to ferry pas-

sengers across the Channel. She would be an immensely reassuring sight to the unwashed hordes deposited at her dock, sleek and black with massive funnels and the promise of a clean, safe passage to the New World.

Yet above all else, one thing was abundantly clear: the ship must be built in Germany. This was reaffirmed by the Kaiser himself, who scorned the notion of racing a British-built ship against British-built competitors. The German vessel must be an embodiment of Germany herself: her greatness, her beauty, her technological prowess. It was the first time in history that the creation of a ship was unabashedly linked, through nationalistic fervor, to the nation that produced her. Other ships had borne names like *Great Britain*, *America*, and *France*, but while each might be hailed as a credit to its progenitors, none was explicitly conceived as their floating embodiment. None, moreover, enjoyed the personal sponsorship of its country's leader. The Kaiser, indulging in a rare metaphysical flight of fancy, made his feelings quite plain: "Any man," he declared, referring of course to himself, "who, standing on the deck of a ship with the starlit firmament of the Almighty as his canopy and the boundless seas as the only object of his vision, takes occasion to question his conscience, to weigh his responsibilities, and to contrast them with his inclination to do good and keep in the path of righteousness, will not hesitate to pronounce a sea voyage a salutary thing for himself and those depending on him."

Norddeutscher Lloyd, commissioned with the task of creating a vessel that would, at the same time, be a successful commercial enterprise, a mechanical wonder, an embodiment of German culture and predominance, and a catalyst for His Imperial Majesty's royal conscience, came up with a brilliant solution—they passed the buck. The deal they offered German shipyards was simple and sublime: build us the greatest, fastest, and most beautiful ship on the Atlantic, and we'll pay whatever it costs; fail, and you can keep her. It was just the sort of imperious nonsense that the Kaiser himself might have authored— indeed, though there is no proof of it, there's good reason to believe that the idea was his. In any event, the challenge was taken up by two shipyards: Schichau Werke of Danzig, and Vulcan Werke of Stettin.

Neither company had ever constructed a major transatlantic liner. Both had been content with producing modest, ferry-like ships with large holds for cattle, grain, or emigrants. The largest vessel produced by Vulcan was the *Fürst Bismarck*, of 1890, already mentioned. She was predominantly a cargo ship, with only one-third of her hold devoted to passengers who did not object to barracks-like accommodations. Schichau's record was even less impressive. In fact, the history of both firms was woefully short: less than a decade before, Germany had still been ordering ships from Scotland. As the Kaiser's interest in maritime matters grew after 1889, the yards began to import English and Scottish technicians—at ridiculously inflated salaries—to train their German counterparts. Once the Germans had absorbed this knowledge, the Scots were thanked kindly and sent home. By the mid-1890s, when Lloyd's challenge emerged, both yards felt confident that they could beat the British at their own game.

The Schichau yard worked mightily and in two years delivered the *Kaiser Friedrich*. She looked every inch a champion with a massive hull nearly 700 feet long, topped with three enormous funnels. Her interiors were designed by Johannes Poppe, the preeminent German interior designer of the time, and featured a pastiche of borrowed styles. The *Friedrich* was the first German ship to emulate the British in taking shoreside luxury to sea; her interior spaces included everything from a central atrium rising three decks, to a great glass dome, to an icecream fountain off the First Class promenade. She even did the British one better: while the *Campania*'s interiors attempted to transport a gentleman's country estate to sea, the Germans tried to recreate an entire Wagnerian castle. The results were mixed. "German decorative art," one Englishman sniffed, "is in a particularly happy position to supply all that is necessary to make a steel tank resemble a palace."

In her appearance, the *Kaiser Friedrich* was a trendsetter. In everything else, she was an utter catastrophe. The transatlantic record held by the *Campania* was just over six days at an average speed of 21 knots. The *Friedrich*'s builders had promised a service speed of 22 knots, which would easily ensure her the Blue Riband. Yet her engines, capable of producing revolutions of 24,000 horsepower, could barely deliver 17 knots. On her first voyage, the *Kaiser Friedrich* arrived off the Fire Island lightship outside New York harbor in 7 days, 11 hours. On her return, she took 9 days, 2 hours, and 30 minutes. Schichau, in desperation, returned her to Danzig for intensive alterations. Three months later they tried again. With engines clanging furiously and the entire ship rattling like a demented freight car, the needle slowly crept up to 20 knots. There it remained. When the unfortunate, magnificent *Kaiser Friedrich* arrived in Germany, Norddeutscher Lloyd sent her back to Danzig with a note: "Declined, with thanks."

It was an utter humiliation for Schichau, for Germany, and for the Kaiser. Every Englishman in his club chuckled richly over the morning paper, delighting in the Germans' failed attempt to best the mighty Cunard line. Worse still, a legal dispute emerged between the yard and Norddeutscher Lloyd over proper ownership and disposal of the worthless vessel. At one time the *Kaiser Friedrich* was chartered to Lloyd's rivals, the Hamburg-Amerika line, while she continued to limp across the Atlantic at miserable speeds. Even the smaller, more modest Hamburg-Amerika became disgusted with her, and she was returned again to the murk of her dock in Hamburg. There she sat, unused and neglected, for fifteen years. If a ship could have a soul, hers must certainly have suffered as she watched bigger, faster cousins sail past, contenders in a race she had lost. And even if not, it still must have been galling for all Germans, from the Kaiser on down, to be continually reminded of their first, aborted, attempt. Finally in 1912—after the *Titanic* had disappeared into the cold waters of the North Atlantic and as the Hamburg-Amerika liner *Imperator* lay near completion in her dry dock and Germany seemed again triumphant—the *Kaiser Friedrich* was given one last chance. Leased to the newly formed French Sud Atlantique line, she was refurbished and placed on the run between Le Havre and Brazil, with a Gallic red rooster painted on each of her three buff funnels. Yet her reprieve lasted less than a year, and she was again laid up, now in Bordeaux. Just two years later, in March 1915 the French government requisitioned her as a troopship. Her decks were fitted with 5.5-inch guns, and—looking slightly ridiculous in her new guise—she was sent to the Mediterranean. In one of the many ironies of an ironic war, she was torpedoed and sunk in November 1916 by the same country that had built her just twenty years before.

The fate of the *Kaiser Friedrich*, though tragic, was not surprising. Despite coaching by the British, German engineers could hardly have been expected to absorb three centuries of shipbuilding in two years. If the *Kaiser Friedrich* symbolized anything, it was that a mere imperial command could not itself will the impossible into reality. The ship's sorry history should have served as a lesson for the cocky emperor, but it did not. For while the Schichau company fell victim to the inevitable, the Vulcans produced a miracle: the *Kaiser Wilhelm der Grosse*.

"A Certain Amount of Resentment"

One historian has described the *Kaiser Wilhelm der Grosse* as "nothing short of a sea-going boast," and that about sums her up. She was long and lean, all muscle and no flab. The hull seemed stretched taut like a rubber band, with the superstructure adding to rather than detracting from an overall sense of determination and speed. Even made fast to her wharf, she looked as though she was about to spring. Inside, her interiors were so lavish (overbearing, some thought) that they were given their own sarcastic moniker: "late North German Lloyd." In essence, as one American put it, this meant "two of everything but the kitchen range, then gilded."

But by far the most notable innovation aboard the *Kaiser Wilhelm der Grosse* was her funnels. She carried four of them, a number not equaled since the *Great Eastern* had gone to sea with five slender stovepipes in the mid-1860s. The *Kaiser*'s were not stovepipes, but massive chutes painted in the distinctive mustard yellow of Norddeutscher Lloyd, towering over the boat deck at a slightly jaunty angle. These funnels were her calling card, for no other ship had anything to compare with them. Whether on company brochures, in newspaper photographs or soap advertisements, they made her instantly recognizable. And so began a decade-long squabble among German and British ships about the most tangible yardstick of the competition between them— the funnel wars. Funnels are simply the smokestacks through which exhaust from the engines is vented. Their shape and height are dictated by the necessity to prevent smoke from engulfing the upper decks and harassing the passengers (which is exactly what happened when the *Bremen*, of 1929, sacrificed physics for aesthetics and went to sea with two squat little funnels that emitted smoke that nearly suffocated passengers in a billowing oily cloud until they were eventually raised). Almost from their first appearance on the Atlantic, funnels became the most easily distinguishable marker of ships and companies, because their height, color, and shape were the first aspects of a ship that could be recognized on the horizon. A ship's funnels were as distinctive as the color of someone's hair: painted in company hues—HAPAG yellow, Inman black, White Star beige, Cunard's distinctive reddish-brown—they announced their ships and symbolized their lines. Similarly, their shape, number, and placement distinguished a ship at once and made her unique. Once, as the *Queen Mary* made her way toward the Rock of Gibraltar, a signalman radioed her, "What ship? What ship?" The *Mary*, whose trio of raked, massive red-and-black funnels made her utterly unmistakable, radioed back incredulously, "What rock? What rock?"

Sometime in the mid-1890s, an unnamed German engineer realized the symbolic power of these ungainly smokestacks. Few ships needed more than two; most were content with one. Yet by the early years of the twentieth century, the number of funnels a ship had became somehow synonymous with her size, speed, even safety. Far from being seen as a necessary if unsightly addition to marine architecture, a ship's funnels became her cynosure. Thus the *Kaiser Wilhelm der Grosse* went to sea with four great yellow funnels, sharply raked and grouped in two pairs, forward and aft. It was a pattern the Germans would continue on the *Deutschland, Kronprinz Wilhelm, Kronprinzessin Cecilie*, and *Kaiser Wilhelm II*. As these German ships appeared one after the other, the British began to feel deprived of funnels. The first drawings for the Cunard superliners *Mauretania* and *Lusitania* depicted them with three funnels, yet the finished ships carried four. White Star's *Olympic* and *Titanic* also had four, but one was a mere dummy, an empty shell for miscellaneous machinery. By then the fixation on funnels as symbols of virility was so entrenched that no great Atlantic challenger would think of appearing with fewer than four. And so powerful was this symbolism that some emigrant passengers embarking on the new, three-funneled *Imperator* of 1913 objected and indignantly waved advertisements for the much smaller, older, and slower—but four-funneled—*Deutschland*.

The *Kaiser Wilhelm der Grosse* had been built for two purposes: grandeur and speed. The magnitude of the former was plainly apparent even as she took shape in the fitting yard. It seemed almost as though the entire ship had been designed merely to embarrass the British. Her public rooms were bigger, rising three decks rather than two. Where the

British would be content with a single painting on the aft wall of the First Class Lounge, the Germans papered theirs with copies of the great masters. Even the windows were fitted out in stained glass etched with nautical scenes. Whereas the British had tried to convey a sense of comfort and familiarity to their vessels, the Germans aimed to stun their passengers into God-fearing awe.

The second objective, speed, was harder won. For months engineers had fine-tuned her engines; the results of her sea trials were a closely held company secret. It was only on her maiden voyage that the real power of the *Kaiser Wilhelm der Grosse* became plain for all to see. She rushed across the Atlantic at an average speed of 21 knots, in 5 days, 22 hours, and 30 minutes—the fastest maiden voyage yet. On her return trip, incredibly, she bested her own time. It was impressive, but not fast enough to catch the *Lucania*. The Cunard ship still held the speed record, set during a westbound passage in October of 1894. The *Kaiser Wilhelm der Grosse* returned to Vulcan for extensive tinkering on her engines. When she came back some weeks later, her average speed had increased to 22.35 knots. Better, but not yet perfect, so more tinkering at Stettin followed. Finally, in May of 1898, a full year after the liner's maiden voyage, she was ready. Supplied with extra coal and coaxed to the very limit by her engineers, the *Kaiser Wilhelm der Grosse* streaked across the Atlantic almost six hours under the *Lucania*'s record. Jubilant celebrations erupted throughout Germany. In Bremen, flags fluttered gaily over the North German Lloyd offices, and their managing director received a steady stream of congratulations, every inch the proud father of a champion. But the happiest man in Germany was Kaiser Wilhelm II. For everyone else, the *Kaiser*'s record was an immense Teutonic achievement. For him, it was revenge. It was as though Cowes had never happened. He had been beaten at yacht racing, again and again, by his smug, self-satisfied cousins, whose casual, all-in-good-fun demeanor made each failure all the more damning. But here was a 14,349-ton megaship that had snatched the speed record from right under the British upturned nose! The man nobody liked could claim his vengeance against them all, and he reveled in their discomfiture.

And the British were discomfited. The year 1897 was *their* year, the year of their queen's Diamond Jubilee, the year when the greatest fleet in the history of the world assembled at Spithead to celebrate its own magnificence. And yet here, into the melee, came a German usurper who—like the Kaiser at Cowes—spoiled all the fun. Social chronicler Humfrey Jordan describes the British mood best: "In that jubilee year," he writes, "England was not feeling modest. She despised foreigners without troubling to conceal the fact; she recognized herself, with complete assurance, as a great nation, the head of a mighty empire, the ruler of the seas. But, with the jubilee mood still warming her citizens to a fine self-satisfaction in being Britons, England lost, and lost most decisively, the speed record of the Atlantic ferry to a German ship. The *Kaiser Wilhelm der Grosse* was a nasty blow to British shipping; her triumphant appearance on the Atlantic came at a moment peculiarly unacceptable to the English public."

The first storm cloud appeared in the *Daily Telegraph* on May 8, 1898. Buried in the back pages, a small notice simply read, "By running 580 knots [nautical miles] on the last day of her westward Atlantic voyage the *Kaiser Wilhelm der Grosse* has won the blue ribbon of ocean steaming. As the westward day represents 25 hours, her average steaming per hour was a trifle over 23 knots." The *Telegraph*'s detached prose was revealing. By drawing attention to the single day's run at the end of the voyage, the notice subtly suggested that the German ship won by a fluke, a single burst of lucky speed. By terming the result of her superior engines a "trifle" over the service speed of the Cunard ships, it suggested that they were merely being held in reserve. Surely the *Lucania* would take back what was rightfully hers the next time she sailed.

But the *Kaiser Wilhelm der Grosse* was not a fluke. In the next two years, she clung tenaciously to the Blue Riband, bettering her own records in the process. Her engines, capable of producing an unheard of 28,000 horsepower, drove the ship faster and longer than her rivals. The Atlantic passage was not a sprint, but a marathon, and in the six-day run from one coast to the other smooth reliability mattered more than brief bursts of speed. The German shipyard, with relatively little experience at constructing ocean greyhounds, had nevertheless conceived engines that consistently outpaced their traditionally superior British rivals. By August 1900 the London *Times* was forced to admit what had become all too obvious to the Cunard Line. "When the *Kaiser Wilhelm der Grosse* made her first appearance," its correspondent wrote, "it was hinted that she was being driven for all she was worth and that in consequence she was being shaken to pieces and could not possibly keep up her rate of speed. Events have falsified this anticipation. She has throughout maintained the promise of her early voyages and has made uniformly rapid and safe passages."

It was merely the first blow of many for Great Britain. Three years after the *Kaiser Wilhelm der Grosse*, Hamburg-Amerika lines presented their own flagship, the *Deutschland*, hoping that the ship would catapult the smaller, more modest Hamburg firm into the big time. To run in direct competition with North German Lloyd, vastly superior in both its fleet and its funding, was to court financial ruin; across the Atlantic, American tycoons pitted their railways against one another in duels to the death. Thus, with so much at stake, HAPAG was taking no chances. Company chairman Albert Ballin had gone to the same shipyard that had built their rival's flagship, Vulcan Werke of Stettin, and offered them a simple proposal: build us a ship that will beat the *Kaiser Wilhelm der Grosse*. It was an interesting challenge, and one that the Stettin builders accepted without hesitation. In almost every respect, the finished product was a slightly larger, slightly faster version of the *Kaiser:* seen side by side, they were scarcely distinguishable from one another. Construction was completed at lightning speed, and in a remarkable five months (construction generally took a little over a year) the *Deutschland* was ready. Her maiden voyage was scheduled for July 4, 1900, and the date had more than one symbolic meaning. Besides being America's Independence Day, it also marked the sixtieth anniversary of the maiden voyage of Cunard's first liner, the *Britannia*.

The inaugural season of the *Deutschland* was a triumph for her owners, her builders, and the German people. In August of 1900 she took the Blue Riband from the *Kaiser Wilhelm der Grosse* and did not relinquish it for another three years. But it was not for want of competition. North German Lloyd line, smarting at the defeat, subtly encouraged the *Kaiser*'s master to boost his ship's speed. HAPAG showed no willingness to back down, and soon the makings of a race were about. In early September, the two ships left New York at the same time, bound for Plymouth. It was abundantly clear as the liners departed within sight of each other that this was not mere coincidence. One commentator on board the *Deutschland* recorded that "everyone knew that Captain Albers of the *Deutschland* and Captain Engelhart of the *Kaiser Wilhelm der Grosse* were bent on showing the best their ships could do, although both commanders denied that there was to be a set race." For the first three days the ships were some miles apart, the *Kaiser Wilhelm der Grosse* taking an early lead. On the third evening, the *Deutschland* made to close the distance. "All night the *Deutschland* tore through the water at full speed making over 23 knots," wrote the passenger, "and at five o'clock the next morning the 'Kaiser' was sighted." From then on, the two Germans ran at dead heat. The scene of the ensuing chase reads like a sea adventure from the Napoleonic wars:

> There was a stampede for the decks and hour by hour the excited passengers and crew kept their eyes on the chase. The *Deutschland* slowly but surely overtook her rival. In the early hours breakfast was neglected. As midday drew near and the "Kaiser" was more closely approached all thought of dinner was abandoned.

> At 11:30 A.M., cheers rang over the water for the *Deutschland* yard by yard had lessened the distance and drawn level with the galloping Norddeutscher. Four miles apart, nose level with nose, the great liners struggled for the lead. It was the *Deutschland*'s day. In one hour's time she was well ahead. By nightfall the "Kaiser" was out of sight behind and she never saw the *Deutschland* again.

The *Deutschland* was now acclaimed as the biggest, fastest, most magnificent liner the world had ever seen. But victory came at a price. The *Deutschland* had sacrificed too much for that extra ounce of speed. An otherwise lovely ship, she vibrated so badly during her inaugural voyages that many passengers—including some high above in First Class—found their cabins uninhabitable. Steerage, which was located just above the engines, was a minor sort of hell. Even in a calm sea, the *Deutschland* rolled and shook horribly as the force of her quadruple-expansion steam engines and twin screws beat mercilessly upon the ship's frame. The shaking was so pronounced that it utterly negated the sybaritic delights the vessel had to offer, which included a gymnasium and the First Class veranda café. Traveling aboard the *Deutschland* was like staying in the Ritz-Carlton during a 5.0 earthquake.

After five years of headache, the directors of Hamburg-Amerika had learned their lesson. Never again would they attempt to produce a speed demon; the company gracefully left the field to its Bremerhaven competitors and turned instead to creating the largest and most sumptuous ships on the Atlantic. Luxury became the watchword. In line with this new policy, in 1910 the *Deutschland* was withdrawn from transatlantic service and sent back to her builders in Stettin. There, over the course of an entire year, she received as thorough a conversion as any ever attempted, and emerged in the summer season of 1911 as the *Viktoria Luise*. White-painted, with topiary in the lounges and her officers decked out in summer whites, she became the first, and for quite some time the largest, ship built specifically for cruises. Sent on holiday excursions to the Mediterranean, Caribbean, and Scandinavia, she pioneered routes that became the hallmark of cruises for the next century. With her engines running at only half-strength, and carrying less than a quarter of her original passenger load, her interiors in all their lavishness were finally appreciated. She became the most successful cruise ship in the world, gaining that invaluable title of "millionaires' boat."

The *Deutschland*'s faults, though painfully obvious, were not singular. Curiously, from the *Kaiser Friedrich* of 1897 to the *Vaterland* of 1913, every German ship had an Achilles heel. For some it was speed; for most it was stability. The *Kaiser Wilhelm der Grosse*, for example, rolled like a drunk. "Rolling Billy," as she came to be known, cost her owners a small fortune in replacement china after almost every voyage. This problem would only be magnified as the German ships grew bigger, culminating finally in the *Imperator*, a vessel so clumsy and awkward that she sailed almost constantly at a slight list. Why did the German ships have so many faults? One possible explanation is that despite the phenomenal success of the *Kaiser Wilhelm der Grosse* and her descendants, the German designers still had not quite caught up with the shipbuilding acumen of their British rivals. While effort, trials, and sheer bravado might produce the fastest ship in the world, only experience could produce one that was also stable, comfortable, and easy to manage. The German ships of the early twentieth century were like thoroughbred horses running their first race: fast, sleek, and beautiful, yet still inexperienced and temperamental.

In spite of these shortcomings, the race continued. The White Star

Line, which had seemed a poor cousin to Cunard during the reign of the *Campania* and *Lucania*, stunned the world with the sudden appearance of its own champion, the *Oceanic* of 1900. Though she would never beat the Germans' speed records, she was—at 17,272 tons—slightly larger than the 16,502-ton *Deutschland*. Her interiors, likewise, did the German ship one better—not least because they did not rattle like a Coney Island roller coaster. The *Oceanic* could also claim the distinction of being the longest ship afloat, the first to exceed 700 feet from stem to stern. For the crestfallen Germans, it was the *Teutonic* all over again. Their newest entry, the *Kronprinz Wilhelm*, due for delivery in 1901, weighed in at a disappointing 14,908 tons. Built for Norddeutscher Lloyd with the express purpose of winning back the Blue Riband from Hamburg-Amerika, she never quite succeeded.

Pausing to mark the turn of the century, one might almost compare the situation to a freeze-frame photograph. At that exact second, the British still held the title of world's largest ship, while the Germans held the record for the world's fastest. But it was all ephemeral, a fleeting moment that would pass in the shutter's millisecond click before normal time resumed again. For already on the ways was a new competitor, the *Kaiser Wilhelm II* of Norddeutscher Lloyd, that would seize both titles; already the directors of the Cunard and White Star lines were meeting in their boardrooms in Southampton and Liverpool, debating how best to challenge this new German menace.

Then, in early 1901, as if to punctuate the transition from one century to the next, Queen Victoria died. It was not an unexpected occurrence, for the Queen's health had been declining steadily since her Jubilee in 1897. Rheumatism had confined her to a wheelchair, and her eyesight, which had been excellent until her eighties, began to fail. She complained of pains throughout her body and even her memory—the hallmark of her character—had become erratic. The death of her son Prince Alfred from cancer in July of 1898 sent the Queen into a deep depression from which she never quite emerged. She then received news that her daughter Victoria, Dowager Empress of Germany and mother of the Kaiser, had the same ailment. "Vicky" was her mother's favorite, a bright, opinionated woman much as the Queen herself had once been. Throughout her long "exile" in Germany, the younger Victoria had watched with chagrin as her son grew more and more remote from both her and England. Now she was almost a living ghost, cut off from an increasingly anglophobic court, and receiving little more than cold courtesy from her son's new nationalistic confidantes.

On January 13, 1901, the Queen made her last entry in her diary and went to bed. The following day, for the first time in nearly seventy years, she was too exhausted to write. Once the inevitable became clear three days later, the family was summoned.

The most surprising response came from Kaiser Wilhelm himself. Caught in the middle of a celebration marking the bicentennial of the Kingdom of Prussia, he had just finished delivering a speech in which he promised to make the German navy "as mighty an instrument" as her army. Handed a telegram informing him of his grandmother's condition, he hurriedly canceled all appointments, called off the celebration, and booked passage on the Flushing–Dover mail boat for that very evening. His aides were shocked—and more than a little disturbed—by this sudden burst of filial obligation. They had, after all, spent the last several years carefully constructing a general feeling of public animosity toward the British, which the Kaiser's race across the Channel might seriously undermine. It was, they agreed quietly, a hell of a time for Wilhelm to remember suddenly that he was half English.

But the Kaiser pressed on, undaunted. His behavior over the next few days was unprecedented, marking a genuine wellspring of affection between the brash young monarch and his ancient, stolidly British grandmama. First was his extraordinary wish (from a man who had once demanded that he be called "Your Imperial Majesty" at all times) to be treated not as the Kaiser, but as a concerned grandson: "I have duly informed the Prince of Wales," he told Chancellor von Bülow, "begging him at the same time that *no notice* whatever is to be taken of me in my capacity as Emperor and that I come as a grandson. . . . I suppose the petticoats who are fencing off poor Grandmama from the world—and I often fear from me—will kick up a row when they hear of my coming. But I don't care, for what I do is my duty, the more so as it is this unparalleled Grandmama, as none ever existed before." Then there was his behavior at Osborne House, the Queen's residence. He was quite right in distrusting the behavior of the "petticoats," his English aunts Beatrice, Louise, and Helena. But after an initial display of peevishness, even they were overcome by his genuine display of grief. As the queen sank into darkness on Sunday, January 22, there were three figures by her side. The Prince of Wales knelt over her, while her head was supported on one side by her doctor, James Reid, and on the other by Kaiser Wilhelm II.

Wilhelm's behavior so impressed the family that it seemed for the moment as though the last ten years, from the incendiary Kruger Telegram to the more recent aggressive German Navy Laws, had never happened. He measured the Queen's body for her coffin before her sons the new King and Prince Arthur lifted her in. Wilhelm would later remark wonderingly, "She was so little—and so light." As Bertie left for London to be proclaimed King Edward VII, Wilhelm took charge of Osborne House, remaining there for almost two weeks. During this brief flush of détente, King Edward worked quickly to remind the Kaiser of his British heritage. In short order the Kaiser became a Field Marshal of the British Army, and his son received the Order of the Garter, among whose notable recipients had been Lord Nelson. It might have been genuine gratification, or good politics, that led the new King to remark of his nephew: "William's touching and simple demeanor, up to the last, will never be forgotten by me or anyone."

But it was not to last. Though Victoria's death had been a cause of genuine sorrow for the Kaiser, it also removed the last restraining bolt on his animosity toward the British. While Victoria was Queen, the Kaiser's loyalties had remained divided; Victoria was a living symbol of England—of its doughtiness, prejudice, insularity, tenacity, and undaunted courage—all qualities that the Kaiser despised and envied. Yet she was also his grandmother, the woman who could treat his imperial affectations as childish braggadocio and still retain for him an affectionate love and concern. Had Queen Victoria lived forever, the sullen voices of Wilhelm's pan-Germanic advisors would always have had a powerful counterpoint. But she did not, and King Edward could never fill that role. Affection between the two men was forced, and too many years of competition—mostly from Wilhelm's side—had severed any real familial bonds. While Victoria would always be "Grandmama" in Wilhelm's eyes, King Edward was "Bertie," the smug and self-satisfied figure on the Royal Yacht Squadron club lawn. When the

Kaiser returned to Germany, he embarked again on his quest for universal German superiority with renewed vigor.

The first and most compelling manifestation of this policy was the *Kaiser Wilhelm II* of 1903. It was perhaps inevitable, considering that Wilhelm's grandfather, father, mother, wife, and son all had ships named in their honor, that the greatest should be named after the Kaiser himself. Once again Wilhelm stood godfather to a monstrous German liner, presiding over the launching with an air of immense self-satisfaction. For an egoist like him, there could have been few experiences more gratifying than watching an immense wall of steel bearing his name plunge stern first into the harbor, to the accompaniment of cheers. The honor of having a ship bear one's name is so great that it is almost always bestowed posthumously. This is so ingrained in the public psyche that when, in the 1930s, the Italian Line proposed to name its newest ship *Dux* in honor of *Il Duce*, Benito Mussolini uncharacteristically demurred. But the German Kaiser knew no such restraint. The Emperor's sponsorship was nowhere more apparent than in the First Class dining saloon, which featured a life-size portrait of the man himself, framed with "allegoric figures of Loyalty and Sagacity," as well as dimpled cherubs that somehow represented—though it is hard to imagine how—the Trades, Commerce, and Shipping. The whole business was supported by four gilded ornamental eagles.

The *Kaiser Wilhelm II* succeeded where her near sister, the *Kronprinz Wilhelm*, had failed. But in all respects she was very much a "serviceable" ship, not a trendsetter. At 19,361 gross tons she beat out the *Oceanic* as the largest liner afloat, though the difference was negligible. She also snatched the Blue Riband from the beleaguered *Deutschland*, though again her speed record was only slightly better. Even her interiors, though they were predictably lavish, were little better than those of the earlier German liners. Nevertheless, the new *Kaiser* was a much better ship all around than either the *Deutschland* or *Kaiser Wilhelm der Grosse*. She held herself better in a heavy sea, and the vibration of her engines was considerably more muted. Thus the *Kaiser Wilhelm II* wasn't a revolutionary, but rather the refined product of several prototypes, borrowing their strengths but sharing none of their awkwardness.

Above all, the *Kaiser Wilhelm II* was undeniable proof that German shipbuilding had left its infancy. The Germans had established something almost like an assembly line for ocean liners, producing a new 19,000-ton ship every two years that was in every respect an improvement over the previous model. These ships were not only larger and faster than their British counterparts, but also provided a level of service that far exceeded the expectations of passengers. The stuffiness and propriety of the *Campania* were replaced by a general attitude of bonhomie and rigorous fun aboard the *Kaiser Wilhelm II*. The German preoccupation with *mens sana in corpore sano*—a sound mind in a sound body—revealed itself in a predilection for deck games, vigorous walks around the Boat Deck, and athletic contests. German brochures touted the sea voyage as being salutary for the health, an attitude that contrasted sharply with the apparent aim of Cunard to remove its passengers from any suggestion of the sea at all. Recalling to mind the *Campania*'s thoughtful provisions for aristocratic ladies engaged in languorous "dolce far niente," one social correspondent spelled out the difference on the German ships: "On the German steamers," she wrote, "it is considered no breach of etiquette for a woman to go after dinner with a man friend, or with her chaperon, or husband, or brother to the smoking room and enjoy her coffee, but on the English, French, and American liners, this custom is not in vogue and must not be enforced by even the most innocently gay and adventuresome young lady." Thus any young woman of "adventuresome" spirit, reading between the lines, would immediately book passage on a German steamer.

"In a word," said one British journalist, "the Germans have got rid of a good deal of that rigidity in the matter of life on shipboard which too often seems a sort of inevitable byproduct of British ownership. The explanation is, perhaps, that we have played the game on certain lines for so many years, and with such marked success, that anything which does not quite conform to tradition is perforce regarded with a certain amount of resentment."

Thus 1903 was a banner year for German shipping, and for Germany herself. From the Norddeutscher Lloyd docks at Bremen, the *Kaiser Wilhelm der Grosse*, *Kronprinz Wilhelm*, and *Kaiser Wilhelm II* had swiftly and surely wrested control of the Atlantic from British hands. The *Kaiser Wilhelm der Grosse* alone, though the smallest and oldest of the three, had garnered 24 percent of all passenger revenue.

She also became, in 1900, the first ocean liner to be equipped with a wireless set, a device that, before the loss of the *Titanic*, was regarded more as a novelty for passengers than a lifesaving apparatus. The German ships, even the noisy *Deutschland*, were the technological wonders of the age, leagues ahead of Cunard and White Star both figuratively and actually. "It is little less than remarkable," the same journalist commented, "that a nation which in the eighties was more or less dependent on this country for the construction of her mail ships should have so rapidly developed her shipbuilding talents that she now produces a vessel which is the largest in the world and which in point of speed promises to equal any steamship yet afloat. . . . [T]here are features about the *Kaiser Wilhelm II* which represent an approach to luxury in voyaging which has as yet been unattained."

It was then, at their moment of triumph, that an unseen hand suddenly rose up and nearly dashed the cup from the Germans' lips. This intervention came not from England, but from that most unlikely of competitors, the United States. The ghost of Edward Knight Collins and his dream of American supremacy on the Atlantic had found a new champion in the bulbous-nosed billionaire J. Pierpont Morgan. Germany and Britain had battled for control over the Atlantic; Morgan would simply try to buy it whole.

-3-

Morgan's Gambit

JOHN PIERPONT MORGAN STOOD OUTSIDE THE RECEPTION ROOM OF Buckingham Palace, nervously fingering his silver-hilted sword. The sixty-four-year-old man, whose austere, granite dignity normally made him as formidable and unapproachable as his banks, was dressed from head to foot in a bizarre courtier's costume that resembled nothing so much as the one Gainsborough's "Blue Boy" wore. His paunch was concealed within a velvet tunic lined with silver buttons; silk stockings encased his meager calves. On his feet he wore a pair of outrageous opera pumps. It was the sort of outfit Little Lord Fauntleroy might wear for a summer's afternoon in the park, and upon seeing it one could almost imagine old J.P.'s bald pate capped in a broad-brimmed straw hat, with a lollypop sticking out from under his moustache.

But it was the sword that worried him the most. Protocol dictated that proper court dress include a ceremonial sword, just as it had mandated the silver buttons and the opera pumps. J. P. Morgan, whose anxiety about doing the "wrong thing" outweighed even his own mountainous dignity, accepted the sword, even though the weight bothered him, making him feel lopsided. He was terrified that he would stumble over it as he made his way across the crowded room to greet King Edward VII. This fear was not occasioned by any awe of the King; Morgan had met other kings, and his wife had once joked that she would rather be the Princess of Rails than the Princess of Wales. But Morgan viewed the ensuing spectacle as the introduction of one monarch to another, and thus his performance would be scrutinized just as carefully as Edward's. There was some truth to this, as J. P. Morgan was perhaps the only man in the new twentieth century whose unbounded egotism was borne out by reality. In 1902 he stood at the zenith of his power, at a time when kings and emperors begged for his favors and the President of the United States consulted him almost weekly on the American economy.

Moments later, the doors opened. His Majesty, soon to be crowned, stood at the far end of the long corridor, a gauntlet J.P. had to walk. The sword clanking uncomfortably against his side, he traversed the marble pathway without incident. The King received him warmly, greeting him with just the right touch of polite informality that indicated an exchange among equals.

"A Wonderful Man"

The passions that drove J. Pierpont Morgan to take on the Atlantic Ocean were as varied and contradictory as the man himself. But first and foremost among them was his mania for collecting: art, real estate, furnishings, women, railroads. He pursued each with the blunt purposefulness of a rhinoceros: head down, nostrils flared, and charging. He bought whole collections at a time, cleaned art dealers out of their stocks, left agents standing open-mouthed as he rampaged through their shops, saying only "How much," "Too much," or "I'll have it." One might understand this mad dash to acquire in a self-made man anxious to impress his wealth upon the world, but J. P. Morgan was born rich. The son of Junius Spencer Morgan, he came of age in a series of expensive European schools, while his father consolidated his business empire in banking. An early picture of Morgan shows him in his schoolboy uniform at Göttingen, Germany: capped in a broad sailor's hat with a gathered silk bow tie at his throat, sixteen-year-old Pierpont displays an almost feminine attractiveness. He has high cheekbones, his eyes flashing dark and set slightly close together, his mouth curved into a pleasing smile.

But the dashing young J. P. Morgan of 1853 was a distant and perhaps painful memory to the old man of 1902. For time had not only aged Morgan, it had ravaged him. It was as though nature, the only force on earth that J. P. Morgan could not control, combine, or coerce, had taken its revenge upon his very face. An early skin disease resulted in periodic rashes that disfigured him as he aged, covering his face and body with ugly red splotches. As time wore on, the disease abandoned the rest of him and focused on his nose, which seemed, like the portrait of Dorian Gray, to grow larger, redder, and more horrible as the fortunes of its owner progressed. Contemporary descriptions likened it to "an overripe pomegranate" or "a squashed strawberry." At first this disfigurement caused Morgan considerable embarrassment and shame. Later, as he became a force to be reckoned with, he externalized the embarrassment and made his nose a challenge to all comers. The walls of J. P. Morgan's office were glass, opening directly onto the main banking floor of the House of Morgan. He sat behind an enormous desk like a waxwork diorama in Madame Toussaud's. He had, in effect, placed himself in a cage and opened the zoo. But the walls might as well have had one-way mirrors, for while Morgan often peered out into the teeming hub of his financial empire, his gaze was never returned. When he spoke, he thrust his nose forward like a banner before a conquering army—and all but the most brazen spectators fled before it.

Yet if Morgan's nose was a banner, it was also a flytrap: it drew in and fascinated observers, and then they were subjected to the cold torture of the chilly eyes above it. James Henry Duveen, the famous art dealer, wrote of his first experience with Morgan:

> I had heard of Morgan's disfigurement, but was not
> prepared at all for what I saw. No nose in caricature ever
> assumed such gigantic proportions or presented such
> appalling excrescences. If I did not gasp, I must have
> changed color. Morgan noticed this, and his small, piercing

eyes transfixed me with a malicious stare. I sensed that he
noticed my feelings of pity, and for some seconds which
seemed like centuries we stood opposite each other without
saying a word. I could not utter a sound, and when at last I
managed to open my mouth I could only produce a raucous
cough.

But by the turn of the century, Morgan's nose had become so integral a facet of the man's image that he himself began to cultivate it. It
was his badge of office, the symbol of his wealth and omnipotence.
Music hall ditties rhapsodized about it, and political cartoonists
delighted in depicting it in various allegorical forms. Morgan himself
remarked with rare humor that his nose was "part of the American business structure."

Strangely enough, Morgan's nose did little to discourage the entourage of women who flocked around him, potent evidence that
power is truly the greatest aphrodisiac. But reading the diaries of some
of these ladies reveals a curious fact: rather than merely being dazzled by
his millions, most were fascinated by the sheer magnitude of Morgan's
personality. Lady Victoria Sackville-West, who became a favorite mistress of Morgan's, recorded that during one intimate moment with
him she was simply overwhelmed:

> I had a long talk with him in the garden. He told me many
> of the bothers of being very rich, but that the great thing
> to have was personality, which he has to an infinite degree.
> He has a wonderful personality, I have not met anyone
> as attractive . . . he is full of life and energy; a wonderful
> man.

True, not all women were as enamored of him as Lady Victoria,
and just as his collection of art included a number of forgeries, so too
did his collection of conquests include several unabashed gold diggers.
One aristocratic Englishwoman, deep in debt, collected £15,000 and
a promise to pay the remaining £185,000, but demurred; "I just cannot
bear the thought of being kissed by that nose," she lamented. Morgan
was an ardent lover, but hardly a skillful one. He was fumbling and lust-
ful, his lecherous impulses grating uncomfortably against his reserve.
"I hope you don't mind," he whispered to one woman, as without any
warning he seized her in his arms and kissed her. Morgan's European

holidays aboard his magnificent yacht *Corsair* had a Lucullan splendor about them, as agents on the Continent scrambled to fulfill his wants. While art dealers scoured manor houses for *objets d'art* to add to his collection, procurers of a different sort made sure that a steady stream of feminine company traversed the yacht's gangplank. Morgan consorted with duchesses, actresses, debutantes, society ladies, and whores. His tastes ran the gamut from virginal to matronly; of the latter, one sour critic commented that "Morgan not only collects old masters, he also collects old mistresses." Through it all, J.P. remained masterfully aloof. Had his misadventures occurred a century later, his reputation would have rivaled that of the Kennedys. But the tact of the press of that time kept Morgan's baser impulses out of the public eye; there was also fear of the terrible weight of his wrath should his name appear. Morgan believed in a strict separation of business from pleasure. When reports of steel magnate Charles M. Schwab's elephantine dalliances in Monte Carlo hit the papers, J.P. was white with fury. Schwab, who owed his position to the Morgan trust, appeared contrite as the old man vented his rage, accusing him of besmirching the House of Morgan. "But all I did," the penitent rejoined, "was what you have been doing behind locked doors for years."

"That, sir," said Morgan coldly, "is what doors are for."

Morgan was no less ardent or blunt in his aesthetic acquisitions. His first collection was a symbolist's delight: broken bits of stained glass that had fallen from Europe's cathedrals and which the adolescent J.P. snatched up greedily, storing them in large bins for future use. As he matured, his tastes developed. His father was a great collector, and the younger Morgan began to compete first with the man and later, after a startled horse threw the elderly patriarch from his carriage onto the cobblestones below, with his memory. Instructed by some of the greatest authorities of the age, and sobered by the omnipresent threat of fraud, J.P. became a formidable expert in his own right. Yet though he might have possessed the knowledge, he would never achieve the subtlety and discrimination of a true connoisseur. While other American millionaires spent their summers sorting minutely through the gilded detritus of the Old World, Morgan, characteristically, bought whole collections—even whole houses—at a time. "What's the use of buying one little piece?" he would remark disdainfully.

But Morgan's artistic voraciousness nearly cost him his dearly won friendships with England and Germany. Shortly after his coronation, King Edward asked and was permitted to view the Morgan collection on private display in Morgan's London home at Prince's Gate. The King, though awed by the breadth of Morgan's acquisitions, was dismayed to see one of his favorite portraits, Lawrence's of the Countess of Derby, hung in a room with a depressingly low ceiling. When His Majesty ventured to ask why this lovely painting had been relegated to such inauspicious surroundings, Morgan was brusque. "Because I like it there, sir," he growled. The King, highly affronted, viewed the remainder of the collection in silence.

Morgan's gaffe with the Kaiser was even more potentially damaging. For Kaiser Wilhelm, among his many other pursuits, was an enthusiastic art collector himself. He rationalized the expenditure, as he did his navy and merchant fleet, on the grounds that by restoring these treasures to Germany he was adding to the glorious culture—and therefore the national prestige—of the German people. It was perhaps inevitable that Morgan, with his single-minded thirst for acquisitions, would eventually trip over imperial pretensions. Finally he did, in the unfortunate person of Wilhelm von Bode, the art appraiser. Though employed by the House of Morgan, he was still a German and, as such, proudly of service to His Imperial Majesty and whatever taste the Kaiser chose to indulge. The bone of contention was a particularly promising collection offered by the widow of German financier Oscar Hainauer. Von Bode, acting on instructions from the Kaiser, submitted a bid. Morgan—either unaware of or indifferent to the presence behind von Bode—promptly offered three times as much. The Kaiser was enraged, and demanded of his chancellor that a decree be issued preventing the export of any works of art, German or otherwise, in German collections. Von Bode intervened, timorously reminding Wilhelm that if this decree were enforced other nations might follow suit, and the entire free market of art exchange would, in effect, come crashing down around their ears. The Kaiser, still fuming, submitted to necessity. The Hainauer collection was duly crated and shipped to the Southampton docks, where it joined similar treasures from England, France, Holland, and the rest of Europe on their journey to the New World.

"*I Owe the Public Nothing*"

It's Morgan's, it's Morgan's,
The great financial gorgon!
Get off that spot,
We're keeping it hot,
That seat is reserved for Morgan!

It is a commonly held axiom that no one man can own the world. Yet J. Pierpont Morgan came close. By 1901 he stood at the pinnacle of a financial empire that has never been equaled, rarely even rivaled. It is difficult for us, living in an age of Bill Gates and Ted Turner, to conceive of the power that Morgan held absolutely. And it was not merely his fortune: Though certainly the richest man of his time, Morgan's net worth would have paled in comparison to the moguls of today. Nor did he hold any official government title, such as would have justified the vast control he exercised over the American economy. It was, rather, the unique circumstances of early-twentieth-century capitalism that allowed a man like Morgan to attain political power commensurate with his financial position, to exercise influence outside the accustomed realm of the business community, and to transcend his fellow plutocrats. J. P. Morgan was more than a pillar of American business; he was practically a branch of the American government. He regarded the American economy as a personal trust, and ran it accordingly. Presidents did not merely ask his advice; they sought his consent. For Morgan, unlike the president, could either plunge the American economy into a panic of depression, as he did inadvertently in 1901, or save it through a personal loan, as he would do several years later.

In the early twentieth century business and politics were very much personal affairs. In both, power lay in the hands of a select group of individuals. Harriman, Carnegie, Rockefeller, Vanderbilt, Hill, and Morgan controlled industry and transportation, just as Mark Hanna, Tom Platt, and a very few others controlled the American political machine. Predictably, both groups commingled everywhere: in private clubs, in the summer colonies of Newport and Long Island, in hotels on the Continent, in ships crossing the Atlantic. Occupying center stage in this brief golden age of the robber barons—a period spanning only three decades, from the first great fortunes made in the aftermath of the Civil War to the first successful antitrust suits and the rise of organized labor in the early 1900s—J. P. Morgan was able to parlay his immense fortune and singular character into a position of near omnipotence. In another age, he could have been a Pericles or even an Augustus, so strong was the personality cult surrounding him.

Yet Morgan remained magnificently indifferent to political power. He was quite willing to let the politicians worry about how to feed the American poor, school their children, and subsidize their crops. Morgan regarded himself as a businessman, concerned solely with the bottom line. Public accountability was as alien a concept to him as public acclaim; "I owe the public nothing," he famously remarked. Yet Morgan understood implicitly the responsibilities inherent in ownership and employment. He did not share the sentiments of notorious coal baron George F. Baer that laborers were like little children left in the care of benevolent, Christ-like employers, and he did recognize that he and his fellows could not simply act with total disregard for the public good. Happily for him, J. P. Morgan saw his interests and those of the public as one and the same. So, when Morgan set out to buy the world, he accepted the dubious responsibility of running it as a necessary evil.

"Of all forms of tyranny," Theodore Roosevelt wrote in his autobiography, "the least attractive and the most vulgar is the tyranny of mere wealth, the tyranny of plutocracy," and there's little doubt to whom Roosevelt was referring. When he assumed the Presidency in 1901 after an assassin's bullet claimed the life of William McKinley, Roosevelt saw only one true challenge to his power. In a single afternoon only seven months before, J. P. Morgan had become the most powerful man on earth. On that day, February 15, 1900, sixty-six-year-old Andrew Carnegie agreed to sell his shares in Carnegie Steel to sixty-four-year-old Morgan. The selling price of $420 million had actually been hammered out some weeks earlier by Morgan and Charles Schwab. The whole matter was conducted so informally that one can scarcely grasp its importance. It had begun with a tentative offer brokered through Schwab, indicating to Morgan that the elderly Scotsman—who by now had become so enamored of his philanthropic role that he began to fashion himself as a sort of generous county laird *extraordinaire*—was willing to sell, for the right price. "Well," said Morgan, with studied indifference, "if Andy wants to sell, I'll buy. Go and find his price." The whole deal, possibly the greatest financial transaction of the century, was concluded within two weeks. Schwab presented Morgan with a few penciled figures on a sheet, to which Morgan responded, "I accept." Shortly thereafter Morgan took the unprecedented step of calling on Carnegie in person (his cardinal rule was for all business to be transacted in his own office—a sort of home-court advantage that he found invaluable). The two men met for scarcely fifteen minutes, then Morgan stood, extended his hand, and said "Mr. Carnegie, I want to congratulate you on becoming the richest man in the world." And that was that.

The acquisition of Carnegie Steel cleared the path for an even greater enterprise, the Northern Securities Railroad trust. J. P. Morgan & Co. had made its fortune on the rails, capitalizing on the meteoric expansion of railway lines between the major industrial hubs of the Northeast and the burgeoning mining and logging communities of the West. Now Carnegie Steel was supplying the tracks upon which Morgan's trains traveled—a wonderful arrangement for Morgan, and entirely in line with his vision of the new United States. For Morgan's monopolistic practices pursued not merely greater profit, but a utopian goal: the complete and total elimination of competition in American business. Morgan believed himself a visionary, and the vision he held most dear was of a United States totally unfettered by—as he saw it—wasteful and retrograde sniping among rival companies. In that, Morgan was not altogether wrong. The great fortunes that had sprung up in the aftermath of the Civil War had not, as once anticipated, melded into a coherent and harmonious aristocracy. Instead, industrial czars had engaged in fierce and often mutually destructive wars: buying each other out, sabotaging each other's businesses, forming combines and alliances for the sole purpose of frustrating one another's plans. Sometimes business feuds became personal, as when Jim Fisk and Jay Gould deliberately and maliciously destroyed the fortunes of several rivals—leading these unfortunate men to ruin, dipsomania, and even suicide. Morgan, whose own fortune was owed to methods such as these, found the whole situation utterly deplorable. It was, to him, akin to the natural Hobbesian state of anarchy that preceded the advent of law and order. And Morgan never doubted his role as lawgiver. Even as the House of Morgan voraciously absorbed nearly every sizable railway in the country, Morgan insisted that his aim was merely to "secure perfect and permanent harmony in the larger lines of this industry," and not—heaven forbid—"to create any monopoly or trust, or in any way antagonize any principle or policy of the law."

Perhaps the most astonishing aspect of this humbuggery was that Morgan himself believed it. Here was no Janus-faced plutocrat hoodwinking the multitudes: Morgan maintained to the end of his life that his only aim was to leave his nation with a solid, permanent foundation in industry and transport. If his creed had a name, it might have been the oxymoronic one "private socialism": all the components of industry working in perfect tandem under the benevolent despotism of a single corporation, upon which sat a single figure—J. P. Morgan. The turn of the century, which has frequently been termed a "golden age" for capitalism, was in fact nothing of the sort. The true golden age had withered and died over a decade before, when Morgan, Carnegie, and Rockefeller consolidated their empires and absorbed all the lesser satellites of their respective industries. Now that Carnegie Steel was furnishing Morgan rails, J.P. felt that his long-cherished dream of coast-to-coast uniformity was within reach. Until that time, competition among the railways had resulted in a mess of differing gauges, prices, and timetables for trains across the United States. Now, under Morgan, gauges and prices were made uniform.

The last gasp of *laissez-faire* competition came only months after the purchase of Carnegie Steel. The Morgan trust had been locked in negotiations for the purchase of the Burlington Railway line, one of the few remaining companies not yet in the fold. Rival entrepreneur Edward Harriman executed an unusual gambit: rather than fight over the Burlington, he attempted to acquire a controlling interest in its parent company, Northern Pacific Railways. This precipitated a brief but damaging panic on May 9, 1901, as Morgan and Harriman struggled for control of America's rails. Morgan emerged triumphant but bloodied. It was this experience that led him and his partner, James Hill, to envision an even larger trust to serve as a financial citadel against the likes of Harriman. They named this new supertrust the Northern Securities Company. Thus, just as U.S. Steel (formerly Carnegie Steel) became indispensable to American industry, the Northern Securities trust assumed virtual control over American transportation.

Flushed with success, Morgan was supremely complacent. He had achieved what earlier tycoons believed impossible: complete control over every link in the chain of American business. His steel formed the rails of his railway line, which carried the weight of his trains, which then moved goods and passengers across vast expanses of what was quickly becoming *his* nation. But this glorious procession stopped abruptly, frustratingly, at the easternmost and westernmost terminals—the Atlantic and Pacific Oceans. There he was once again at the mercy of rivals—and foreign rivals at that. The smooth workings of his financial machine were halted; it was almost as though his trains passed over the Brooklyn Bridge and hurtled into oblivion. But his Continental acquisitions had awakened in Morgan a new sense of the possible. He had looked long and hard at the Old World and found it basically wanting. Revolution, war, famine, and empire-building had taken their toll on the monarchies and left the Continent of Europe dangerously unstable. Germany and France were politically uncertain. Italy was anyone's guess. Even staid, sober Britain seemed to be abandoning herself to a senseless struggle with imperial Germany. Order and logic were impossible over there, and without them no permanent deals could be reached. Nowhere was this more apparent than on the North Atlantic, where British and German lines had been at each other's throats for years. Morgan, a pragmatist, saw only one solution.

He would buy them all.

"Morganizing" the Atlantic

The idea came to him first on a transatlantic voyage in 1893. Comfortably ensconced in the smoking room of a British liner, he was asked by a colleague whether it would be possible to bring together the rival companies on the Atlantic into a single trust—to create, as it were, an Atlantic combine. Morgan, master of the understatement, pondered this for a moment. "Ought to be," he mused.

But he could not afford to be hasty. Morgan might have been the proverbial bull in the china shop in his private affairs, but in business he was subtlety itself. It would take almost a decade before the climate

was right, and he was content to wait. In fact, Morgan was in his element, as the competition on the Atlantic mirrored that for the pre-
Morganized American railways. At the top, the British and Germans
battled it out for the lion's share of passenger traffic. There was no
clear victor; in 1900, the British had the largest ship in the world, the
Germans the fastest, and the shipyards of both nations were busily
constructing successors. On the periphery of this conflict were the
other Continental nations, most notably France and Holland, whose
entries—though undistinguished—still accounted for a respectable
portion of the transatlantic trade.

At the very bottom were the American lines. There were only two
of any consequence, the International Navigation Company of Philadelphia and the Atlantic Transport Company of Baltimore. Both were
in dreadful financial shape. They had unwisely engaged in a rate war
with the British, and lost badly. Their respective hubs, Philadelphia
and Baltimore, could not compete with the port of New York. Their
ships were small, badly serviced, and already quite dated. The mainstay
of both lines was the immigrant trade, and neither could muster the
panache, luxury, or speed to enter the competition for First Class
clientele.

Still, Morgan saw an opportunity. Given the right climate, both
companies could easily be made profitable. Morgan proposed to man-
ufacture that climate by removing or absorbing all potential competitors. Thus, to insure the predominance of his tiny American fleet, Morgan would buy the Atlantic itself. There was a manic brilliance in this,
an element of the fantastic that seems almost mythological. Yet there
was also at least a modicum of dollars-and-cents logic as well. Morgan's reasoning was based on three premises. First and foremost was
the concept, conceived by Morgan himself, of a "through bill of lading." If a single combine controlled both the Atlantic routes and the
American rails, it would be possible to ship goods from Liverpool
to Seattle for the same price as, say, from Chicago to New Orleans.
Efficiency, Morgan's watchword and obsession, would be increased a
thousandfold.

Second, Morgan harbored a very human desire to see the Stars
and Stripes fly over the Atlantic. This was not mere patriotism; Morgan
understood that the only common link between all the European lines

was that they serviced American ports. It was certainly inequitable—perhaps even unconscionable—that the nation receiving most of the traffic should have no control over it. American predominance on the Atlantic was, to Morgan, the natural and inevitable consequence of American ascendancy in business and trade. It was not merely disheartening to see American goods shipped by foreign competitors; it was needlessly wasteful. Rate wars between the various lines were hindering trade—and hurting the United States, as principal benefactor, most of all. J. P. Morgan could thus rationalize the Atlantic combine as a necessary and reasonable measure to ensure the free passage of goods. But this argument was specious at best; Julius Caesar might have justified the conquest of Gaul using the same logic.

Third, there was the question of immigration. Between 1820 and 1920, no less than 30 million passengers crossed the Atlantic, the vast majority of them immigrants. Unrestricted immigration reached its zenith after 1900, when a staggering one million people from nearly every nation on earth made the voyage each year. At the turn of the century, the flood of foreign labor landing on America's eastern shores was so great that even the most humble tramp steamers—including those of the International Navigation and Atlantic Transport companies—were booked to capacity. It was, in fact, virtually impossible *not* to make money; in 1900, there were more willing passengers than ships to accommodate them. But only two men fully understood the implications of this imbalance of supply and demand. One was Albert Ballin, head of Hamburg-Amerika Lines. The other was J. P. Morgan.

The problem, as Morgan saw it, was that rivalries among shipping lines obscured the basic truth: that there was more than enough business to go around. Instead of cooperating with one another and facilitating the transport of this limitless human cargo, competing national shipping lines were expending needless energy trying to woo—or filch—prospective customers from one another. It was akin to a railway war in which carloads of grain are allowed to spoil at the sidings because the competing lines can't agree on a timetable. Morgan had seen many such wars in his time and was anxious to check another on the North Atlantic. Yet he was not so naïve as to trust diplomacy or mutual accord, tactics that had never worked, even among like-minded American entrepreneurs; among nations, they were doomed to failure. In short, if the nations of Europe would not act in concert voluntarily, he would *force* them to do so.

Morgan also noticed an additional fact: immigrants, particularly those from Eastern Europe, invariably gravitated toward ships with American-sounding names. The reason was not hard to fathom: though in theory available to all, the privilege of citizenship was earned, not given. Vast processing centers at Ellis Island in New York harbor and elsewhere along the Eastern seaboard acted as siphons, and indeed a significant minority of immigrants were deemed "unsuitable" and returned to their point of origin. They could be turned away because of ill health, mental or physical defects, or doubtful political inclinations. For whatever reason—or for no reason at all—there was always the dreaded possibility of being refused. Thus, for those intending to make a new life in America, there was something obscurely comforting about making the voyage in ships bearing names like *America, Washington,* and *President Grant.* The names suggested that these passengers had, in some way, already been admitted (the French Line would later employ a similar tactic on eastbound patrons, claiming in their brochures, "France, you know, really begins at West Forty-fourth Street!"). Far better, they reasoned, to arrive in New York on a vessel like the *Washington* than on the *Leopoldina*! Dubious though this logic may have seemed to him, J. P. Morgan was the last man on earth to dispute market choices. He would, instead, capitalize on them. If America sold passages across the Atlantic, then American ships would have a natural advantage over their competition. He was prepared to bank on that advantage.

His first move was to acquire the International Navigation and American Transport lines in December 1900. He then purchased the venerable Inman Lines of Liverpool (whose vessels included the stately *City of New York*). Shortly following the sale, almost like door prizes, came the additional acquisitions of the tiny American Line and Belgian Red Star Line. Less than a year later he added the British Leyland Line, one of the largest (though not particularly glamorous) firms on the Atlantic, to his growing conglomerate. Morgan's tactics were as abrupt as they were effective. Once, when starting negotiations for the purchase of a small steel mill, he had arranged for the mill's executives to meet him at his office. They came girded for battle; the mill was worth at most $5 million, and they'd be lucky to get half. Just to put the arrogant Morgan in his place, they were going to start by asking $10 million. But before they could begin the great man himself raised his hand. "Now I don't want any talk from you men," he said, addressing them like errant junior clerks. "I know all about your plant and what it's worth; I haven't time for any haggling; I'm going to give you $20 million. Now take it or leave it." Thus, when the directors of the Leyland Line began to protest that they could not possibly sell—the honor of the firm, the duty to His Majesty's empire, et cetera, et cetera—he simply offered them $22.5 million in gold and told them where to sign. Explaining himself to his shareholders, Leyland's chairman said candidly that the American offer was so outrageous that he did not have the right, as a responsible businessman, to refuse.

Indeed, the exorbitant price paid for Leyland Lines was, in 1901, the subject of quiet amusement to the British public. "The vendors," said the *Annual Shipping Review* with sardonic restraint, "made an exceptionally good bargain—which it is probable the purchasers will soon find out." But the warning was there, for those who could see it: if Morgan could shell out princely sums to buy small shipping firms, what would prevent him from targeting something larger? Just as his initial purchase of little steel mills would lead to the purchase of Carnegie Steel—and the creation of the mammoth U.S. Steel—so too were these early acquisitions a mere hint of what was to come. Yet, despite a few questions asked in Parliament and a discreet rumbling in the London *Times,* the Leyland sale passed almost unnoticed by the government and people of Britain. So, in July 1901 when the board of directors of the venerable White Star Line announced that they, too, had submitted to Morgan's yoke, the response was unanimously one of shocked, indignant, vociferous outrage.

"Almost Like a Declaration of War"

Today the White Star Line is inextricably associated with its most famous progeny, the ill-starred *Titanic.* Yet before the advent of this legendary ship and her sisters, White Star was one of the most powerful and illustrious firms on the Atlantic, a worthy and equal rival to the mighty Cunard—and in many ways superior. The company enjoyed a history almost as long, having been founded in Liverpool in 1867 to carry the mails between Great Britain and New York. Unlike Cunard, however, White Star's safety record was far from spotless. On April 4, 1864, the *Royal Standard*—in a bizarre foreshadowing of later events— collided with an iceberg on the return leg of her maiden voyage; 546 people died when the *Atlantic* sank after striking Marrs Rock off Halifax in 1873; the *Naronic* disappeared without a trace in 1893; the *Germanic* was lost during a blizzard in 1899; the *Republic* foundered after a collision with another vessel in 1909. Yet despite this litany of catastrophes, the White Star Line was among the largest, most popular and most innovative firms at the turn of the century. It was White Star that introduced the *Teutonic,* the ship that had so delighted Kaiser Wilhelm in 1889 and thus begun the great race, and in 1901 it was White Star's *Oceanic* that was the world's largest liner.

Thus, in 1901, White Star was a glorious prize. It was also most emphatically not for sale. The company president, J. Bruce Ismay, had inherited the reins from his father, Thomas, only two years before. The autocratic and irascible Ismay senior was thought to be a genius in shipping circles, having raised his company from obscure origins to place it at the epicenter of the Atlantic trade. Thomas Ismay had hammered out a unique arrangement with the shipbuilding firm of Harland & Wolff whereby the firm would act as exclusive builder of every White Star vessel. Under this agreement, Harland & Wolff delivered a brand-new ocean greyhound to White Star almost annually from 1869 to 1912. The result was a fleet of the most luxurious and beautiful ships on the Atlantic. White Star, under Thomas Ismay's chairmanship, had eschewed the contest for speed and emphasized instead unparalleled luxury and size. The *Oceanic,* of 1899, was conceived along these lines. Never intended as a speed demon, she was a magnificent ship, with a 21-foot-diameter dome over the First Class restaurant and the finest library afloat. It was only at Thomas's death in 1899 that control of White Star passed to his son, Bruce. The younger Ismay, vain and pompous, was determined to best the memory of his late father; J. P. Morgan made short work of him.

Initially, Morgan put on a fine show of being convinced against his will. "I do not think favorably of entering the shipbuilding business," he said to his London partners in 1900. As if to underscore that sentiment, he instructed them in March of that year not to sponsor a White Star stock issue, and declined a loan that would have permitted the construction of several new ships. This was all so much smoke screen. Scarcely a few months later, after the Leyland Line had been absorbed, the Morgan combine declared itself the International Mercantile Marine Company. The carefully worded and deliberately bland announcement was, according to one account, "almost like a declaration of war." When Morgan began making overtures to White Star in 1901, about the time Queen Victoria sank into her last illness, the shipping world convulsed. Ismay and his partners flatly refused even to parlay with Morgan, and the financier responded in kind. Ignoring them magnificently, he turned his attention to the shareholders. In a confused, almost chaotic, scene at a shareholders' meeting in June 1901, Morgan's offer was accepted. The board, shoring up dignity in defeat, capitulated gracefully. Morgan acknowledged this by generously allowing them all to keep their chairs.

When the purchase of White Star became public, the outcry was fierce. It was almost as though the British people had awakened one day to find their entire merchant fleet utterly gone: the docks of Liverpool, Southampton, and Bristol forlorn and empty, the great shipping houses stripped of their furnishings, and the countless mooring buoys along the Channel bobbing listlessly in the wake. Newspapers decried the sale with uniform and nonpartisan fervor. Questions were asked in the House of Commons; Prime Minister Asquith responded that Morgan had already offered to explain his intentions to the government and stood ready to advise it on any further actions. The Commons's reaction to this was mixed.

Even more disturbing revelations were soon to come. Following his triumphant success with White Star in July 1901, Morgan quickly turned his attention to their erstwhile rivals, the German lines. Albert Ballin, Hamburg-Amerika Line chairman, passing through New York in late May 1901 on his way back from a business trip to the Orient, heard a rumor about White Star and immediately suspected the worst. On arriving in Germany he at once sent a memorandum to friends in the German government, among them the industrialist Prince Henckel-Donnersmarck, warning them of impending disaster should Morgan purchase the British company and then turn his attention to

Germany. It was a nightmare scenario, for if Morgan did look to Germany, his first action would certainly be to gain a controlling interest in Hamburg-Amerika. But if Morgan did not turn to Germany, things would be even worse, as Ballin feared—correctly—that he would then see his ships marginalized and excluded from the great international combine. England would thus gain predominance again on the Atlantic—though through American sponsorship—and Germany would be left with a dwindling share of a diminishing pie.

At this point an unlikely friendship served to remedy matters. Ballin was intimately acquainted with Lord Pirrie, the genial, puckish chairman of Harland & Wolff, having at one time ordered his ships from the Irish builder. Pirrie had also been a close friend of the late Thomas Ismay and now served as a sort of mentor to his son, Bruce. Ballin consulted Pirrie at once, and Pirrie then traveled to New York to meet J. P. Morgan himself. The news, which Ballin relayed back a week later, was not encouraging: Morgan did intend to buy White Star. But, he said, he had no intention of gaining a controlling interest in Hamburg-Amerika or North German Lloyd. Ballin didn't know whether to mourn or rejoice. His anxieties were increased when an associate of Pirrie's warned him that International Mercantile Marine (I.M.M.) was already consolidating preferential relationships with the largest railroads in America. When the news of the White Star purchase became public in June, Ballin—a man of mercurial temperament—was moved to despair. Yet, despite the strained circumstances, he could not help but be awed by his former nemesis. This was scarcely surprising, for the contrast between the two men could not have been greater. Morgan—tall, stately, taciturn—looked like the general's statue in *Don Giovanni* brought to life; Ballin, diminutive, dapper, bald, looked like nothing so much as an extremely well-dressed dormouse. Reporting back to Berlin, he described Morgan as "a man of whom it is said that he combines the possession of an enormous fortune with an intelligence that is simply astounding."

Ballin found the American financier surprisingly affable. Morgan confirmed Pirrie's report that he did not wish to buy a controlling interest in Hamburg-Amerika, but, Ballin countered, even if he did not purchase the firm directly, his combine would surely ruin them in the long term. Morgan agreed and proposed a compromise. He would purchase 51 percent of HAPAG and North German Lloyd, giving him de facto control but not a complete autocracy. Ballin would continue as company president, the ships would retain their German registry, the board would remain intact; nothing, in short would change— outwardly, that is. The predicted increase in profits of the newly formed combine would more than compensate for Morgan's considerable share. But most importantly, HAPAG would remain an autonomous company, whereas White Star (and, if also conquered, Cunard) would be under the direct supervision of I.M.M. and J. P. Morgan. It was more than Ballin had hoped for. In one stroke, he could achieve permanent German supremacy on the Atlantic. He hastened to deliver the good news to the Kaiser.

Yet here he encountered a snag. From almost every direction came vehement protests and official intransigence, just as it had in England. First were HAPAG's directors, who saw only the threat of the Morgan combine and could not be made to see the opportunity. Ballin quickly silenced opposition by threatening to resign as chairman. Appalled, the board capitulated. But Ballin's problems were only beginning. The Kaiser, receiving the report about the proposed combine, flew into a rage and summoned Ballin to his hunting lodge at Hubertsstock to account for himself. The scene was one of almost Wagnerian pretension. A "special carriage" took the HAPAG chairman from the train station for the two-hour trip into the deeply forested Hubertsstock, while outside the October air was cold and crisp. Arriving at the palatial lodge, Ballin learned that Metternich, Wilhelm's wily chancellor, had warned him that the practical effect of the Morgan combine would be to allow the Americans to purchase 20 million marks' worth of HAPAG shares. When he was finally confronted by his irate monarch, Ballin hastened to reassure him. His account of the conversation that followed is remarkable both for its clarity and for its very human portrait of the troubled Kaiser:

> During an after-dinner walk with the Kaiser . . . I explained the whole proposal in detail. I pointed out to the Kaiser that whereas the British lines engaged in the North Atlantic business were simply absorbed by the trust, the proposed agreement would leave the independence of the German lines intact. This made the Kaiser inquire what

was to become of North German Lloyd, and I had to
promise that I would see to it that the Lloyd would not be
exposed to any immediate danger arising out of the agreement, and that it would be given every opportunity of becoming a partner as well. The Kaiser then wanted to see
the actual text of the agreement as drafted in London.
When I produced it from my pocket we entered the room
adjacent to the entrance of the lodge, which happened to
be the small bedroom of Capt. Von Grumme, and there a
meeting, which lasted several hours, was held, the Kaiser
reading out loud every article of the agreement, and dis-
cussing every single item.

It is not difficult to envision the Kaiser perched on the end of von
Grumme's narrow bed, his querulous voice dripping scorn with every
syllable, as Metternich snickers, von Grumme fidgets, and Ballin wilts.
Yet after a very long time (Ballin euphemistically terms it "several
hours") the same realization that had struck Ballin almost at once
finally began to dawn on the Kaiser. This obstreperous American
might, he thought to himself, be the greatest thing ever to happen to
German shipping. If Morgan kept his word—and the full might of
Imperial Germany would see that he did—Germany would emerge
from the fracas strong and independent, with an almost unlimited
credit at the Morgan bank, while Great Britain would be humbled
into abject submission. It was, as Ballin himself thought, almost too
good to be true.

But Morgan had, in effect, presented the Germans with a devil's
bargain: in return for selling themselves and their fleet to him, he would
insure that they would win their race against the British. Such contests
meant nothing to him; if that was their price, he was more than willing to pay it. Moreover, the idea of nominal national autonomy was
mendacious at best: whatever control the German companies kept unto
themselves, they would be *allowed* to keep; they would still be owned
by the Morgan combine just as surely as if each ship bore his initials
on its masthead. But the Kaiser and his aides had invested so much in
their puerile race that they practically leapt at the chance to relinquish
the bulk of the German merchant fleet in return for the ephemeral
glory of besting the British. "The outcome of the proceedings," Ballin
records, "was that the Kaiser declared himself completely satisfied with

the proposals, commissioning me to look after the interests of North German Lloyd."

It was typical of the Kaiser to think nothing of entrusting the mission of convincing the directors of North German Lloyd to the man who was their archnemesis. The results were not favorable. In a meeting whose ironically stated purpose was to concoct "measures to protect German steamship lines from falling into American hands," Ballin pitched his case to the directors of Norddeutscher Lloyd. His argument was deceptively simple: the Morgan combine threatened to marginalize German interests in favor of British shipping, so therefore it was in everyone's interest to come to an understanding with Morgan. But Heinrich Wiegand, Ballin's opposite number at Lloyd, was far from convinced. While he admitted to some consternation about this new element of competition on the Atlantic, he simply did not share Ballin's dark view. Wiegand was, in 1901, a far more powerful man than Albert Ballin. It was Lloyd ships that had claimed the Blue Riband, introduced a plethora of new luxuries to sea travel, and held—except for the brief interregnum of 1899–1903—the title of world's largest. Wiegand thus regarded his alarmist opposite number with a certain amount of aristocratic disdain. Ballin retired, defeated.

Almost at once, the Kaiser intervened. He invited both men to a private dinner at which he heaped praise on Ballin and derided Wiegand as *ein eigensinniger Friese,* an obstinate Frisian. Wiegand bowed to the inevitable, and the final compromise between them was worked out over dessert. By February, 1902, a "treaty" had been prepared. An annual payment plan was devised, while pools of First and Second Class passengers were to be established. Steerage quotas remained unchanged, and still governed by the figures agreed upon by the North Atlantic Association in 1892. In sum, the treaty provided for a harmonious relationship between the German companies and I.M.M., determining how they would evenly divide their passengers, routes, and expenditures. Superficially, it seemed an enormous boon for Germany. But the fact remained that these German ships were now American owned, and—to underscore that point—Albert Ballin was given a one-million-dollar-a-year salary by J. P. Morgan to run the new trust. A further honor awaited him on his return to Berlin, where he was invested by the Kaiser with the Order of the Red Eagle, "second class with crown."

The German newspapers hailed the agreement as a triumph for Kaiser Wilhelm, for Albert Ballin, and for Germany. Yet the acclaim was not for their business sagacity, but rather for besting the British once again. The *National Zeitung* declared smugly that "the blow to England is all the greater since the German companies have been able to keep out of the trust and maintain their independence."

The paradox was sublime. J. P. Morgan, the man who had just absorbed the fleets of Hamburg-Amerika and Norddeutscher Lloyd into his own gargantuan trust, found himself hailed as a hero of the German people.

The Corsair and the Kings

In the midst of these tribulations, England prepared to crown a new monarch for the first time in more than sixty years. Morgan received his invitation to the coronation of Edward VII—scheduled for late June 1902—as no more than his due, then departed from England on his yacht *Corsair III* for an extended tour of Europe's "business opportunities": in reality, he would take a pleasure cruise, perhaps buying a few dozen new pieces for his unparalleled collection of antiquities and art along the way. He visited Paris, where he confronted fellow millionaire George Kessler with the extraordinary proposition that they corner the market in champagnes. Then he traveled on to Venice and the Adriatic. Each time the yacht dropped anchor and word of his arrival spread, messages would come by return carrier from counts, duchesses, and earls with unpronounceable titles suggesting centuries of nobility, offering their family treasures for sale. From the châteaus, palaces, and schlosses of the greatest families in Europe came a rich horde of booty, to be loaded into the *Corsair*'s hold like pirate gold from the Spanish Main. Indeed, in his more fanciful moments, J.P. imagined a kinship between himself and his seventeenth-century namesake, the great pirate captain Sir Henry Morgan. Each man had achieved in his lifetime that strange, paradoxical status: gentleman buccaneer. The later Morgan stretched the analogy still further, naming his yacht the *Corsair* after the Barbary corsairs who had been the scourge of Mediterranean trade and forming an exclusive club of robber barons that he lightheartedly termed the "Corsairs' Club." Yet despite Morgan's affectations, there were differences. Sir Henry's reward for thirty years' pillaging was respectability, a knighthood, and the governorship of Jamaica; for J.P. it was nothing less than control of the world's economies. The difference of scale was underlined each time he traveled abroad: whereas Captain Morgan had taken his loot by force, J. P. Morgan had it offered to him on a silver salver.

Morgan returned to England shortly before the coronation to find an invitation to dine with the uncrowned monarch. The dinner, hosted by the American ambassador, had three guests of honor: the King, the Queen, and Morgan. As if to underscore friendly relations across the Atlantic, Morgan was seated at the King's right. Edward—who, like all of England, knew all about Morgan's purchase of the mighty White Star Line—was especially warm. He also knew that Morgan intended to follow his attendance at the coronation with a visit to Kaiser Wilhelm in Germany, and even in the atmosphere of temporary *détente* between the two monarchs, Edward was worried. If the German firms reached an accommodation with Morgan while the British held out, England might find herself overwhelmed on the Atlantic. But if England capitulated to this American's demands, her dominion over merchant shipping would also be destroyed. So Edward, a master politician, flattered and feted his visitor in the hope of an agreement that would preserve for England her mercantile empire while allowing this Yankee usurper to leave satisfied.

But bad luck would undermine all his efforts, as the King was laid low by appendicitis only days after that convivial evening, on the very eve of his coronation. With the monarch hovering near death, plans for the coronation were stalled. Meanwhile, the Kaiser reiterated his invitation to Morgan to join him and the German fleet at Kiel. It was a classic piece of imperial tactlessness, and Morgan was caught in an uncomfortable position. If he accepted the Kaiser's summons, he would in effect be abandoning England and her ailing monarch at the worst possible time. But if he refused, the notoriously touchy Kaiser would certainly take umbrage, and friendly relations between them would be impossible. In the end it came down to a business decision: for his international marine combine to work, amicable relations with Germany were essential. With a heavy heart, J.P. packed up his tunic and sword and departed on the *Corsair* for Kiel.

The transition from one royal household to another was dramatic, as the *Corsair* left a somber England figuratively draping itself in black and arrived in a festive Germany gaily trimmed in ribbons and flags. The German Imperial Fleet had gathered in Kiel for the royal review, shamelessly aping the naval review at Spithead to the last particular but with even more pomp, more admirals, more brass bands. The Kaiser, dressed as always in navy braid, was in his element as his launch took him from one battleship to the next. All around him a constellation of smaller craft tooted whistles and hoisted flags. On shore, crowds gathered on the quay and waved merrily. Morgan's yacht arrived in the midst of a patriotic frenzy.

It did not take long for the message to reach His Imperial Majesty aboard the *Hohenzollern* that another yacht of equal pretensions had entered the bay. The Kaiser responded with customary élan, summoning his launch and setting off at once for the *Corsair*. His impetuousness was easy to understand, for he was almost childishly delighted. Morgan's presence at Kiel was a clear indication of where the great financier's favors lay, and he was one of very few men whose favor the Kaiser still sought. Wilhelm leapt up the bosun's ladder and stepped onto the *Corsair*'s deck with a wide smile. His staff followed him with difficulty, fanning themselves out behind the imperial presence like an honor guard. Morgan, not to be outdone, stood flanked by a "staff" of his own: thirteen men and eight ladies, including the famous actress Maxine Elliott.

The Kaiser could barely control his exuberance. After lunch the two men began pacing the yacht's deck, deep in conversation. Wilhelm, who seemed to require constant physical stimulus to think properly, moved briskly. But after only two circuits Morgan, who loathed exercise, was winded and gasping. "We will sit down," he murmured, and did so. The Kaiser's aides gasped themselves. His Imperial Majesty was not accustomed to being ordered. But for the sake of manners, and for the future of German shipping on the Atlantic, he sat down next to Morgan, and asked the magnate about his plans for creating an international combine on the ocean.

Morgan responded at length, and the two men discussed the future of their respective empires well into the evening. For the Kaiser the conversation must have had a ghostly quality. Not since the abrupt retirement of Chancellor von Bismarck had he been obliged to play the eager student to an elderly mentor. But it was a role that perversely suited him; when he wished, the Kaiser could be an excellent listener. To Morgan, the role of a pedagogue came naturally. With the quiet patience of an adult explaining the facts of life to a small child, he gave his views on the current state of things on the Atlantic. For anyone who knew him, it was a familiar refrain. Competition was wasteful, and unfettered competition was anarchy. Right now, he told Wilhelm, there are a score of companies competing for the same passengers on the Atlantic run— some from your country, some from Britain, and a few from Norway, Holland, France, and of course the United States. What he proposed was to replace senseless discord with international harmony. The Americans, British, and Germans would work together rather than against each other, and would all make a great deal of money.

The Kaiser listened, fascinated. First in his mind were the Norddeutscher Lloyd and Hamburg-Amerika lines, whose directors had initially viewed Morgan's approach with the sick sense of dread of field mice under the eye of a hawk. Even with Albert Ballin whispering excitedly in his ear, the Kaiser might still have had some reservations about ceding his beloved liners to this bulbous-nosed plutocrat. But he must also have thought of King Edward, the detested Uncle Bertie, now recovering from his recent illness. How terrified Bertie must be of the Yankee upstart!

The next morning, as Morgan and the Kaiser approached the shore in Morgan's launch, a diminutive figure with a top hat awaited them. It was Albert Ballin wearing a frock coat and introducing himself as Morgan's personal guide. Ballin greeted Morgan like an old friend, and the three unlikely allies set off for Berlin.

For two days, all Berlin opened its doors to Morgan. Flanked on one side by Albert Ballin and on the other by the Kaiser himself, he was the man of the hour. German newspapers had lauded him earlier that year as the savior of German shipping—paradoxical, given that he had in effect placed the German merchant fleet under foreign ownership. Invitations poured in from nobility, merchants, even the humble American expatriate community. He met with Dr. Wilhelm von Bode, the greatest living art expert, and agreed to take him on retainer to sniff out and authenticate any new collections for sale on the Continent. On the last night of Morgan's stay, Kaiser Wilhelm gave a private dinner in his honor, underlining the easy informality that had grown so quickly between the two men. Perhaps it was in this spirit that Wilhelm allowed his façade of assurance to slip, ever so slightly, as he shared his fears with Morgan about the rise of socialism. In conversational terms, this was almost like revealing the scar of a recent surgery. Socialist revolutionaries had claimed the lives of several European potentates, including the Russian Czar Alexander II in 1881. Socialism, the cancer of the monarchies, a destructive force aimed at their titles, their prerogatives, and their lives, terrified Kaiser Wilhelm II. But when he revealed this fear to Morgan, the differences between nobility of the blood and nobility of the billfold suddenly became plain. "I pay no attention to such theories," growled Morgan, the businessman.

Still, the Kaiser's efforts were an enormous success. A business arrangement had been reached and, more importantly, the seeds of a genuine friendship were sown. Morgan, who hardly ever granted interviews, talked with representatives of the American press on his return to England. "I have met the Kaiser," he announced, "and I like him."

Across the Channel, King Edward's condition steadily improved, and plans for the coronation were resumed. Morgan's son Jack had remained in England throughout his father's imperial sojourn, acting officially as President Roosevelt's attaché and unofficially as the House of Morgan's chief ambassador to the Court of St. James's. His special role was to assist in supplying Westminster Abbey with suitable furnishings for the coming festivities; a ceremonial task awarded him more in recognition of his father's stature than for any innate aesthetic abilities. Yet here the young Morgan was in a quandary: The house of Duveen, celebrated among the royals for its collection of *objets d'art,* had been asked to lend a portion of its regal trappings—tapestries, gilded thrones, and the like—to give the right touch of pomp to the affair. But unbeknown to the King, the fabulous Duveen collection was now the property of J. P. Morgan. The elder Duveen was forced to approach Jack and humbly request that he lend back a portion of the plunder, already bearing steamship tags for passage to America, so that His Majesty might not be crowned in an empty stall.

Morgan got the message on his yacht, and the old man must have found it particularly funny. *By all means,* he wired back gracefully, *let them use anything they wish. After all, we won't be leaving for another week, and they'll have plenty of time to take it down once the show is over.*

So it was that on August 8, 1902, J. P. Morgan stood respectfully in Westminster Abbey, looking on as King Edward VII was crowned monarch of England, Scotland, Wales and Northern Ireland, Emperor of India, Protector of the Commonwealth, and Defender of the Faith. Among the ornaments installed for the coronation was a magnificent tapestry, hung as a backdrop above the King. It had once belonged to Cardinal Mazarin and was nearly eight hundred years old, a gorgeous piece of Gothic weaving.

Less than two weeks later, on August 20, J. P. Morgan finally bade farewell to the Old World and began the voyage back to his fiefdom in the New. It was a triumphant procession, Caesar returning to Rome with a caravan of plunder in tow. Negotiations with the British and Germans had been outrageously successful, and the ship that bore him back to the United States was already his own. She was the White Star liner *Oceanic,* the largest vessel in the world. A similar arrangement had already been hammered out with the Germans, and even the venerable Cunard line had not yet refused him. Standing on the aft deck smoking his cigar, Morgan must have felt an almost Olympian serenity. The kings of Europe had recognized him as an equal; noble houses had prostrated themselves before him. Now he'd be master of the ocean itself. Six decks below his parlor suite, safely locked in the *Oceanic*'s hold, was a pirate's cave of treasures. All were crated and sorted, each bearing the shipping label of J. Pierpont Morgan, 219 Madison Avenue, New York, New York. Among them lay the Mazarin tapestry, neatly folded.

-4-

The Old Man
and the Sea

HOLED AWAY IN HIS H STREET HERMITAGE IN WASHINGTON, THE ACERBIC
Henry Adams surveyed the mounting unease across the Atlantic and
passed judgment: "London and Berlin," he wrote, "are standing in
perfectly abject terror, watching Pierpont Morgan's nose flaming over
the ocean waves, and approaching hourly nearer their bank vaults."

Adams was more right than he knew. The announcement of the
German agreement, hard on the heels of the White Star acquisition,
came as a stunning blow in the minds of the British public. Even as
the crown hovered over the head of King Edward VII, J. P. Morgan
seemed about to snatch the ermine robe from around his shoulders, box
it up with the orb and sceptre, and ship the whole business back to New

York in the hold of the *Oceanic*. In that summer of 1902 Morgan stood at the absolute apex of his power. A contemporary cartoon depicts him seated on a half-shell throne, resplendent in his pinstripe trousers and ascot, wearing a crown and holding a trident. He says to a discomfited Neptune, disappearing into the waves at his right, "You might as well slide off into the water, old chap. I'll boss the ocean from this on."

Street vendors in London sold official-looking documents for a shilling apiece; on close inspection they proved to be "License to Remain on Earth," signed J. Pierpont Morgan. Finley Peter Dunne, whose *Mr. Dooley* series typically made rustic jokes at the expense of Theodore Roosevelt (who, it must be admitted, loved them), turned his attention momentarily to another target:

> Pierpont Morgan calls in wan iv his office boys, the pris-
> idint iv a naytional bank, an' says he, "James," he says,
> "take some change out iv th' damper an' run out an' buy
> Europe f'r me," he says. "I intind to re-organize it an' put it
> on a paying basis," he says. "Call up the Czar an' th' Pope
> an' th' Sultan an' th' Impror Willum, an' tell thim we won't
> need their services afther nex' week."

It was not an implausible situation. While negotiations with HAPAG were still under way, J. P. Morgan made business history in another venue. In late 1902 he presented to the owners of the Jersey Central line a personal check for $23 million, the largest check ever drawn from a private account until that time. Consolidating his hold on White Star, he also investigated the possibility of financing the London subway system. The "Tube," as dear to Londoners as fish and chips, Harrod's, and the Kensington Gardens, nearly fell to American control until an ambitious group of British investors intervened. Faced with a pitched battle, Morgan lost interest.

This was just as well, for a greater battle loomed: Having wrapped the Americans, the Germans, and White Star into the voluminous folds of the I.M.M., Morgan was left with a single target—the Cunard Line. It would prove to be his most formidable. "A Cunard liner," said one English chronicler, "like an Armstrong gun, is a familiar object to the greater part of the civilized world." Cunard was unassailably, re-doubtably British. It may be wondered why a company founded by a Canadian and run by a board composed largely of Scotsmen should be judged a symbol of English supremacy, particularly since the White Star Line—British founded, British operated—never generated the same patriotic fervor. The answer lies in marketing. White Star promoted itself as a millionaire's line, offering a standard of luxury unsurpassed on the Atlantic, but luxury is not a national commodity. Cunard, on the other hand, marketed its ships as floating embassies of Empire. Though it could not hope to compete with P & O and Orient Lines in the routes it serviced, the image of a Cunard steamer—with its distinctive reddish boottop funnels—had already worked itself into the public consciousness as a symbol of England abroad. When Morgan made his intentions clear, Britons responded as though the Vikings had returned to pillage their shores.

Yet J. P. Morgan had every reason to anticipate success. I.M.M., which now comprised the White Star, American, Leyland, Red Star, American Transport, and International Navigation lines, controlled one-third of all transatlantic business. Morgan's 51 percent share of HAPAG and North German Lloyd gave him de facto control over an additional third. Thus, one man now held a controlling interest in the Atlantic itself, for the first and only time in recorded history. Cunard's ultimate submission seemed as inevitable as the tides.

Moreover, Morgan's first tentative discussions with the Cunard directors proved surprisingly benign. Far from being recalcitrant, they openly encouraged him to name his price. Morgan responded in typical fashion, offering them 80 percent above the value of their shares. But then the directors suddenly turned coy, and claimed it was not enough. Morgan must surely have blanched; it was likely he had never heard those words before in his life. He came back with fifteen dollars per share for 55 percent of all Cunard stock, a fabulous offer which would have netted a 120 percent profit for the shareholders. Still Cunard balked.

That's when politics came into play. Lord Inverclyde, the young man who represented Cunard at the Morgan negotiations, had conscientiously briefed the British government on every development. His tactics amounted to stalling for time, as he awaited the rescue that the Admiralty would surely provide. But no rescue came. The government said, astonishingly, that the decision whether or not to sell was Cunard's alone, and that no help could be expected from the Admiralty or its coffers. When Inverclyde returned to the bargaining table with Morgan, there was a new eagerness in his demeanor.

But while the British government might have been content to throw Cunard to the wolves, the British people were not. England was a nation of inveterate letter-writers, and the first manifestations of public displeasure appeared on editors' desks almost instantly. One waspishly pointed out that Americans were not, by nature, philanthropists, and that surely American control of British shipping would soon "close the door" to Britain on the Atlantic. The words of historian James Anthony Froude sounded the collective alarm: "Take away her merchant fleets," he wrote in dire tones, "take away the navy that guards them; her empire will come to an end; her colonies will fall off like leaves from a withered tree; and Britain will become once more an insignificant island in the North Sea."

Another embarrassment in late 1902 served to lend ironic counterpoise to the whole affair. The Cunarder *Etruria*, by then a floating relic of a past age, blew a propeller shaft in the middle of the Atlantic Ocean. On a newer ship this would scarcely cause a ripple in the passage; the remaining screws would compensate for one lost. But the *Etruria* was a single-screw ship. As she wallowed in the Atlantic, bleating across the wireless for help, her call was finally answered by a tiny tramp steamer, which turned out to be among the smallest and latest additions to the I.M.M. fleet. As Morgan's steamer towed the unfortunate ship into safe harbor in the Azores, the press had a field day. Cunard, mortified, found itself expressing gratitude to Morgan for his assistance even as it vigorously defended itself from his combine. Morgan, of course, was tremendously entertained.

Faced with Cunard's imminent obsolescence and decay, the government hastily reevaluated its position. Lord Selborne, First Lord of the Admiralty, took Inverclyde aside and made an appeal to his loyalty: "When such vast issues are at stake," rumbled Selborne, "a patriotic company is bound to keep its Government informed as you have hitherto done." Inverclyde, who had in fact ignored the government entirely since its negative response, answered that he and his stockholders were fed up with the government's inaction. "Frankly," he told the much older man, "I think the time has come when you should say what you intend to do with regard to the Cunard Company and not continue on the present indefinite course. If you do not intend to make any arrangement with us but prefer to work with somebody else I would much rather that you would say so and let us know where we are." Pausing for breath, Inverclyde then went for the jugular: "In any case," he said, "a time is coming when I must let my shareholders know what has been going on, so that they may judge for themselves whether their interests have been properly looked after, and moreover, the Directors of the Company cannot longer put off *certain arrangements* which they have had in view, but which latterly have been held in abeyance, to give you time to make up your mind whether to do anything or not." At the words "certain arrangements," Lord Selborne's flesh went cold.

"The Ocean Was Too Big for the Old Man"

J. P. Morgan sits on a dollar throne, wearing a crown even larger than Neptune's and smoking a cigar. At his feet, Kaiser Wilhelm assiduously blacks his boots. At his elbow, King Edward, dressed as a footman, holds a silver salver—he is clearly expecting a tip. The caption beneath reads:

> J. PIERPONT MORGAN
> Ruler of the Combined Continents
> And Consolidated Islands
> And the Profits Thereof

Such sentiments were, in 1902, almost universal. Even the conservative *Independent* magazine was driven to remark—not without a touch of shamefaced satisfaction—"Great is Mr. Morgan's power; greater in some respects even than that of President and Kings." As if in tacit support of this assertion, the Kaiser sent his younger brother Prince Heinrich of Prussia to New York in the spring of 1903, the first royal visit to the American continent since the Prince of Wales's grand tour forty years earlier. Ostensibly—and rather ironically—the occasion for the visit was the launching of a new *Meteor*, His Imperial Majesty's latest yacht. In fact, it was for the sole purpose of sounding out J. P. Morgan. Morgan, understanding this at once, did not disappoint. At a "Captains of Industry" dinner he introduced the Prince to some of the greatest financial figures of the age, and then sat down to a sumptuous repast. The Prince would later tell his brother that the lifestyle of an American plutocrat far outshone that of a mere Continental prince.

The Morgan combine was immensely powerful, but it was also terribly fragile. Like most dictatorships, its existence and livelihood were inextricably bound to the strong, resonant beating of a single heart. When Morgan faltered, the entire colossus of his financial empire shook with him. In 1903, it began to quake.

First there was the surprising resistance to the proposed Cunard merger. Though Inverclyde continued to exude oily cordiality, the forces arrayed behind him were becoming increasingly formidable and hostile. The Admiralty had finally reached the conclusion English newspapers had been screaming for months—if Britain's merchant fleet fell under American control, they asked themselves, to whom would its loyalties lie in time of war? This was no idle speculation; at the turn of the century, a nation's merchant fleet was the lifeline of its troops and the only means of conveying its armies to overseas theaters. War, moreover, was in this pre-1914 period very much confined to the colonial sphere, where the great powers played out their aggressions by proxy. Thus the logistics of any military undertaking required a fleet of merchant vessels to ferry troops to remote parts of the globe, then establish a secure supply line to maintain them. Given that the average speed of a passenger vessel was just over 19 knots, this necessitated a virtual relay race for ships passing between colony and home. In 1896, for example, the bulk of Britain's fleet had been mobilized to carry troops, ammunition, and supplies to the Transvaal, in present-day South Africa, where a group of Dutch settlers known as the Boers had—with the tacit support of Kaiser Wilhelm—declared themselves independent from the British Empire. If Morgan controlled the British merchant fleet, how could the British government force it into wartime service? Even more terrifying, what could prevent it from becoming an adjunct to the U.S. Navy? By 1903 tensions between the European nations had worsened. A British correspondent erred only in choosing the wrong hypothetical enemy when he asked: "Suppose that we are at war with France, and this 'British' (but really American) vessel is pursued by a French man-of-war; it is British blood and treasure which would have to defend it." He went on to recommend that the Com-

panies Act be amended to allow no more than a quarter of a steamship
company's shares to be held by a foreigner. "In this way," the correspondent ended triumphantly, "I imagine the Morganization of the
Atlantic would be nipped in the bud."

In point of fact, such a law already existed. British law declared that
no ship or any share of it could be owned by an alien. If some non-
Briton did purchase a vessel or a line, it would at once be seized by the
Crown—insuring, naturally, that the alien owner had been adequately
compensated. It sounded grand and magisterial, but in fact the law
was severely flawed, as by 1903 very few vessels of any size were owned
or purchased by individuals; they passed, instead, from one company to
another. Corporations were not, under the law, synonymous with private citizens. As such, while Morgan could not buy a ship from Ismay,
I.M.M. could certainly gain a controlling interest in White Star. Morgan shrewdly made sure that everything remained strictly aboveboard:
the White Star Line kept its British directors, its British registry, and
its coveted (though largely symbolic) contract to carry British mail.
White Star liners, including the *Titanic*, went to sea with the prefix
RMS which stood—as most *Titanic* enthusiasts already know—for
Royal Mail Steamer. Morgan, no fool, went out of his way to keep these
meaningless symbols intact. He sought to downplay I.M.M.'s American
character, eschewing the suggestion by Steele and other New York
shareholders that he give it "a name suggesting American control."
Morgan even went so far as to appoint J. Bruce Ismay chairman of
I.M.M. itself (a move bearing a striking similarity to Ballin's $1 mil-
lion patronage at HAPAG), insuring that the combine would have an
unmistakably British gloss. So successful was he, in fact, that when the
Titanic was lost a decade later, the blame centered largely on Ismay, and
not on the actual owner.

But the English public in 1903 was unimpressed by Morgan's con-
ciliatory gestures. A steady stream of virulent letters poured into newspaper offices throughout the country, and angry questions were asked
in Parliament. The pressure on the torpid Selborne and his Admiralty
grew intolerable. Eventually a canny individual named Sir Christopher Furness proposed a compromise: Cunard would, with the few
remaining un-Morganized British firms, form an *anti*-combine. They
would then be in direct competition with Morgan—and, by exten-

sion, with the Germans as well. White Star would be an aberration, and harmony would be restored.

The Admiralty seized on this proposal, and Lord Selborne hastened to press it with Inverclyde. The latter was immediately skeptical. The grand design had one fatal flaw; with White Star and Leyland lines under American control, there were not enough British firms left to fill a single day's shipping roster, much less form a viable alternative to Morgan. Inverclyde demanded instead that the Admiralty bail out Cunard or face the consequences. Having presented his ultimatum, he was fairly sure of the result. "Its hands and wrists fettered," one historian later wrote, "its beautiful white body tied to the tracks while the glinty-eyed locomotive from Wall Street came bearing down the line, Cunard cowered and blinked in the mock terror of those who know they are going to be snatched to safety."

Slowly, inevitably, public opinion trickled down through the wheels and cogs of the British government. Parliament grew more favorably disposed to saving Cunard, and even the Admiralty began to appreciate the value of keeping the British merchant marine under the crown's control. Joseph Chamberlain, who as Colonial Secretary had more to lose than anyone by Cunard's defection, argued passionately that the company's independence must be maintained through direct government subsidy, which, of course, was what Inverclyde had been waiting for all along. It was government subsidies that allowed the much smaller and far more vulnerable Compagnie Générale de Transatlantique (C.G.T., also called the French Line) to resist Morgan and the I.M.M. The idea of an autonomous French company sharing the sea with enslaved English firms was more than any right-thinking Englishman could bear. Public opinion hardened against J. P. Morgan, and with his unerring business instinct he began to sense that he would not ultimately succeed.

Yet the most telling blow to Morgan's aspirations came not from the British government, nor the Germans, but from the august gentleman at 1600 Pennsylvania Avenue. Whether or not President Roosevelt read the *Independent*, its message resonated throughout the United States: J. P. Morgan, a private citizen, was rapidly assuming the mantle of an American king. Roosevelt, who owed his presidency to the homicidal act of a disgruntled anarchist, felt he could brook no rivals.

With the next election only a year away, Roosevelt needed a cause. He found it in the vast, serpentine trusts that had by now extended their influence over virtually every form of industry and transportation in the United States. Patently unconstitutional, they had nevertheless been upheld by a deferential and rather elderly Supreme Court. Roosevelt, whose reformer's zeal was matched only by his love of self-promotion, fell on Northern Securities like St. George on a hapless, slumbering dragon.

Knowing that Morgan had allies even within his own Cabinet, Roosevelt moved with Florentine secrecy. He conferred with his loyal Attorney General, Philander Knox, and discussed the possibility of breaking Morgan's railroad trust under the long-standing—though rather obsolete—Sherman Antitrust Act. Such a coup would, if successful, represent a spectacular assertion of power by the executive branch, unprecedented since the days of Andrew Jackson, George Biddle, and the Bank of the United States. It would also curtail wanton and destructive capitalism, establish the government as a superior force to big business, and teach Morgan a lesson. But most of all, it would be enormously popular with voters. Thus, in one action, Roosevelt found a way to satisfy all the demons and the angels of his personality: his lusts for power and publicity; a pugnacious aggression toward rivals, real and imagined; showmanship; and the strange Calvinist morality that undergirded all these baser instincts.

Once he was sure of his ground, Roosevelt lost no time presenting his crusade to the American public. On February 19, 1902, Knox announced the immediate dissolution of the Northern Securities Trust "under the law." The reaction was galvanizing: While the market slumped alarmingly—the greatest shock since McKinley's assassination, the New York *Tribune* declared—popular sentiment was elated. "Our stormy petrel of a President," Henry Adams wrote gleefully, "without warning, has hit Pierpont Morgan, the whole railway interest, and the whole Wall Street connection, a tremendous whack square on the nose. The wicked don't want to quarrel with him, but they don't like being hit that way. . . . The Wall Street people are in an ulcerated state of inflammation."

At first, Morgan refused to believe he was in trouble. After his initial reaction—which was predictably explosive—he seemed to calm down considerably. This was just a ploy, he reasoned, a bargaining tool. In short, he believed, Roosevelt wanted something. All he had to do was find out what it was, give it to him, and make this whole silly business go away. Flanked by a loyal senator on one side and Republican Party boss Mark Hanna on the other, he went to see the President. He found Roosevelt and Knox seated together, almost conspiratorially.

Morgan, nostrils flaring, was the very picture of the indignant businessman. Why, he demanded, was he not notified in advance about this action? "That is just what we did not want to do," Roosevelt answered calmly. But still Morgan did not understand. His response was, in a single sentence, the entire age of the robber barons encapsulated: "If we have done anything wrong," said he, with heavy patience, "just send your man [the Attorney General] to my man [Morgan's lawyer, in effect his own "Attorney General"] and they can fix it up." To a businessman like Morgan, who "paid no attention" to political theories, this was an eminently reasonable request. He was dumbfounded when the President, sounding for all the world like a sanctimonious Boy Scout, answered smugly, "That can't be done." Knox added at once, "We don't want to fix it up, we want to stop it."

With that one sentence, Morgan was faced with the systematic ruin of his entire life's work. Choking out the words, but still with massive dignity, he asked, "Are you going to attack my other interests? The Steel Trust and the others?"

"Certainly not," said Roosevelt serenely, "unless we find out that in any case they have done something that we regard as wrong."

The battle lines were drawn. After Morgan left, Roosevelt turned to his ally with satisfaction. "That is a most illuminating illustration of the Wall Street point of view," he said, as though examining one of his stuffed specimens. "Mr. Morgan could not help but regard me as a big rival operator, who either intended to ruin all his interests or else could be induced to come to an agreement to ruin none." That was, in fact, precisely how Morgan did regard him. Raging in his hotel room, he dictated a personal denunciation of the President and his Attorney General in terms so inflammatory that, had it been published (as intended) in the morning papers, its like would not have been seen since the Alien and Sedition Acts. Fortunately for both Morgan and Roosevelt, a quick-thinking lawyer suppressed the state-

ment. If he had not, Morgan might have found himself branded an
anarchist.

The ensuing battle for Northern Securities, compared with that for
the Cunard Line, was rather sedate. A suit was filed in Buffalo, and
the lawyers took over. There is nothing like a legal case for turning the
most exciting events into a dreary tedium, and so it was here. The trial
was remarkable only for the brief appearance of J. P. Morgan *in person,*
who entered the witness stand grimly to defend his company, himself,
and his principles. In the same grave, patient, fatherly tones he had used
with the President and the Kaiser, he said much the same thing to a
puzzled panel of judges. He was not a monopolist. He was not interested in power for its own sake. There were no price-fixing agreements
with any lines within the Northern Securities Trust. My only goal, he
said for the umpteenth time, is business efficiency. Cool, collected,
dressed in the Wall Street uniform of black tailcoat and pinstripe
trousers, and clutching a gold-knobbed cane, he did not look like a
man fighting for his life.

Back in England, the inevitable had finally come to pass. The Cunard Line, with greatest regret, declined Morgan's generous offer. Lord
Inverclyde was triumphant. The line had just been advanced a government loan for £2,600,000 at an interest rate of just $2\frac{3}{4}$ percent, and was
granted an annual subsidy of £150,000. Cunard was happy to comply
with the only stipulations: they must remain a British company, in
fact and by law, and they must be willing to relinquish their vessels for
government use in time of war. Furthermore, as the astronomical sum
of the loan hinted, Cunard was expected to build more ships—not
just any ships, but the largest, fastest, and finest afloat—capable of swift
conversion to armed merchant cruisers should the need arise. England
had paid the ransom, and Cunard was now immune to foreign en-
croachment. But this would be a Pyrrhic victory indeed if she lagged
behind her German competitors. Thus the British government had, in
effect, invested Cunard with both money and the charge of besting
the Germans once and for all. Cunard was happy to comply.

"Things fall apart;" William Butler Yeats would write in his 1921
poem "The Second Coming," continuing "the centre cannot hold." For
no one in the winter and spring of 1903–1904 was Yeats's apocalyptic
vision more true than for J. P. Morgan. Cunard, infused with its new

subsidy, thwarted his plans for an Atlantic combine. Without it the central concept of universal harmony and accord on the Atlantic was doomed, and, as Yeats wrote next, "mere anarchy is loosed upon the world"—J. P. Morgan's world, at least. Stock in I.M.M. fell alarmingly, prompting Morgan to hold a rare press conference at which he announced that the public's lack of confidence was "not justified by the facts." But the facts justified themselves. News of I.M.M.'s decline sent a shock wave of panic through Wall Street, precipitating a brief financial crisis that came to be known as the "rich man's panic." A further blow was dealt in 1904 when the Supreme Court reversed its position in three preceding decisions and found for the government in the Northern Securities case.

Shortly thereafter, Morgan and Roosevelt found themselves dining under the same roof at the Gridiron Club. Roosevelt, as the evening's featured speaker, railed against the monopolistic practices of the trusts and their effects on American railroads. Immediate government intervention, he bellowed, was the only means of counteracting this menace. Roosevelt suddenly paused in mid-sentence, left the podium, and approached the table where Morgan was seated. The financier regarded the President with polite indifference. But then Roosevelt reached out a clenched fist and shook it under Morgan's face, threatening the great red proboscis that flushed angrily at this unparalleled impertinence. "And if you don't let us do this," Roosevelt shouted, still waving his fist under and around Morgan's purpled nose, "those who come after us will rise and bring you to ruin."

He did not have long to wait. An empire the size of Morgan's does not collapse all at once, and the great man would live another decade to see his company decline while its founder became increasingly obsessed with Egyptology, mysticism, and death. A comment by the liberal magazine *Judge* was cruel, but apt: "Mr. Morgan used to float better than he knew, and now he sinks better than he ever floated." I.M.M. was widely regarded as a fantastic failure. Every subsequent sale of assets, from 1906 to 1914, came at a thumping loss for the company. The agreement with HAPAG and North German Lloyd soon disintegrated, once Ballin and his associates smelled blood in the water. Morgan's shares were sold back to the original sellers, again at a loss, although I.M.M. itself would not be disbanded for another two decades. White Star continued to show modest profits, and the selection of J. Bruce Ismay as chairman proved surprisingly apt. It was Ismay who suggested, as a means of recouping the original investment, the construction of a trio of liners that would surpass anything Cunard or the Germans had yet introduced, and reestablish White Star (and I.M.M.) as the dominant force on the Atlantic. These ships were to be named the *Olympic*, *Gigantic*, and *Titanic*.

Such grand designs eddied around him, but J. P. Morgan cared little either way. With his empire beleaguered on all sides, he lapsed into a relative state of somnolence—he began to dally more and work less. Never again would he attempt to realize his dream of a "through bill of lading" from the Pacific to the Atlantic and beyond, nor would he again hope to exercise dictatorial control over the U.S. economy. Though still the most important and powerful private citizen of his age, he was relegated increasingly to an advisory role in American policy—a role his nemesis, Theodore Roosevelt, actively encouraged. Twice he would be called upon in times of national emergency, and twice he would rouse himself, play his part well, and relapse to slumber. A final picture shows him at the Pujo Committee hearings in 1912, where he was once again, in the last years of his life, commanded to defend his practices.

He sits upright in the hard, high-backed chair, seemingly alert and attentive. He wears the same frock coat and pinstripe trousers, clutches the same cane. But the head that once jerked imperiously now hangs over slumped shoulders, the hair grown white and thin. The eyes are lackluster, clouded. The mountainous nose that had characterized him most of his life seems to have lain siege to his entire face, its carbuncles drooping over his moustache almost to his upper lip. It is the face of a defeated man.

The engine of his destruction was, as early as 1904, painfully apparent. J. P. Morgan had taken on the American continent, and won. He had then taken on the Atlantic Ocean, and lost. The *Wall Street Journal* eulogized his efforts with customary pith. "The ocean," it said, "was too big for the old man."

Lusitania arriving in New York, 1907. Note the contrast between the liner's awesome size and modernity to the bucolic horse-drawn vehicles surrounding her.

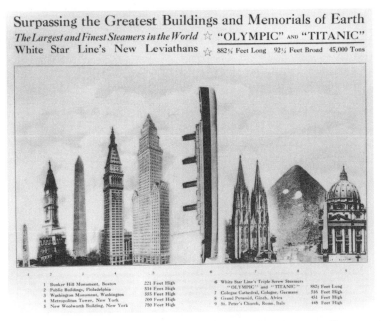

When size matters most: a publicity pamphlet depicting the White Star *Olympic* and *Titanic* alongside both ancient and modern marvels such as the Great Pyramid of Giza and the Woolworth Building of New York. Nearly every major passenger line used such comparisons to elucidate the almost unimaginable scale of their ships.

Imperial pretensions: the First
Class lounge of the *Kaiser
Wilhelm II.*
(DETROIT PUBLISHING COMPANY
PHOTOGRAPHIC COLLECTION—
LIBRARY OF CONGRESS)

Kaiser Wilhelm II of Germany
(c. 1913). Typical of his other
portraits, the Kaiser stands in
three-quarter profile, nearly
obscuring the withered left arm
that had once earned him the
derisive title "defective prince"
from his grandfather.
(LIBRARY OF CONGRESS)

"Part of the American business structure": J. P. Morgan in profile (c. 1907). (LIBRARY OF CONGRESS)

Charles Parsons's *Turbinia* cuts speedily across the *Campania*'s bow at the Naval Parade off Spithead, June 26, 1897. (PAINTING BY THE AUTHOR)

The First Class Palladian Lounge on the *Aquitania*. Debuting in 1914, her interiors were among the finest ever conceived. One year later, this magnificent room would be stripped of its furnishings and filled with hospital beds for wounded soldiers.

The *Aquitania,* "Ship Beautiful," being shined up in her graving dock (c. 1914).

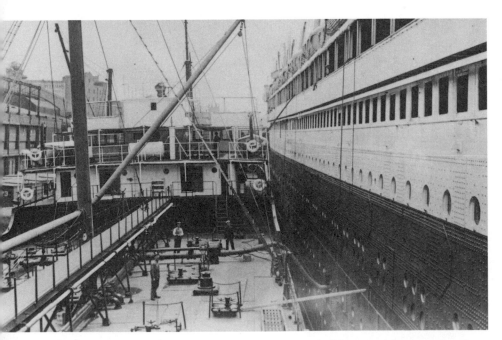

The *Olympic* in New York, readying to sail (c. 1914). This view along the starboard
flank suggests how her sister, the *Titanic,* might have appeared to those hoisted down
in lifeboats.

"Nothing short of a sea-going boast." The *Kaiser Wilhelm der Grosse* at Bremen, 1897.
(STEAMSHIP HISTORICAL SOCIETY OF AMERICA COLLECTIONS, UNIVERSITY OF BALTIMORE LIBRARY)

Liners as cruisers: the battle between the *Kaiser Wilhelm der Grosse* and HMS *Highflyer*,
August 26, 1915. (REPRODUCTION OF A PAINTING BY NORMAN WILKINSON, LIBRARY OF CONGRESS)

-5-

"A Mad Dash of Nelsonic Impertinence"

THE DEBACLE OF THE MORGAN COMBINE ENDED WITH CUNARD'S REFUSAL to join in 1903. Yet to understand what happened next, and why, we must go back in time to the singular events of June 26, 1897.

On that day, Queen Victoria had reigned over the British Empire for sixty years. In Hong Kong and Bombay, Ceylon and Rhodesia, Bali, Port George, Johannesburg, Hamilton, Moorea, Frederickstown, Dar-es-Salaam, and Blackpool, patriotic Britons raised their pints or glasses and said reverently, "The Queen, God bless her!" As night chased day, fireworks peppered the skies in a continuous arc of light that encircled the earth itself, each one beginning just as the last had ended. Never again would the English have so much to celebrate. Over one-quarter of the populated globe belonged to them, an empire far greater than Alexander, Caesar Augustus, or even Napoleon could have imagined. Britons could now, like Jules Verne's Phineas Fogg, circumnavigate the globe without ever leaving the comfort and security of their homeland; in the world's farthest reaches, they would still be greeted with the curiously clipped accents of English "colonials" and the reassuring sight of the Union Jack fluttering overhead. Moreover, just as Augustus had once commissioned statues to remind far-flung provinces of his symbolic presence, great bronze likenesses of Victoria Regina stood in almost every colonial capital, seated majestically outside courthouses in Zambia, constabularies in Kingston.

Though political pressures and gentleman capitalists might have provided the initial impetus, the miracle of empire was wrought largely by a single technological breakthrough: the reciprocating steam engine. It was steam that allowed the British to expand their dominions, ferrying the men and supplies needed to sustain them. Steam facilitated the exploration of rivers and made the distances between homeland and outpost finite and predictable, not subject to the vagaries of wind or current. For the first time, reliable schedules measuring the time between ports and trade routes could be established. Earlier, a merchant had taken an enormous gamble each time he sent a sailing packet to sea, not sure when, or whether, it would return. Now, thanks to engines, propellers, and iron hulls, the business of sea transport was rapidly becoming as regular and predictable as an inland railway. While the face of empire was indubitably that of Victoria herself, its heart beat with the clanking rhythm of pistons and shafts.

Thus when plans were made to celebrate the Queen's Diamond Jubilee at home, it was inevitable that the central role in the pageant would be given to the Royal Navy. Its ubiquitous presence across the globe was the glue that held her empire together. Other nations might vie for their "place in the sun"—Germany in particular—but ultimately it would be Britain's naval superiority that carried the day. The British had long understood a simple fact that escaped others: taken in whole, there was more water than land on this earth. Therefore, to control the land, one must first control the seas. Otherwise, colonies became unsustainable, cut off from their motherland, and reverted inevitably to their previous anarchical state. The fundamental wisdom of this policy had long eluded the Continent; Napoleon, though a tactical genius of the first order, failed to appreciate it, and thus ultimately lost his foothold in Europe. Only now, at the end of the nineteenth century, was Germany beginning to understand this truism; the visionary Admiral von Tirpitz was particularly vehement in advocating a renewal of sea power to the Kaiser. At the turn of the century, however, Britannia still ruled the waves, and the Royal Navy formed the sinews of her empire. Without it, said the London *Times*, the British dominions would be "merely a loose aggregate of States."

So it was that on a pleasant June day in 1897 some 165 British warships lay at their moorings in Spithead, a vast congregation of naval force that exceeded even the naval review held there eight years before. Twenty-one battleships, 42 cruisers, 30 destroyers, and 52 supply ships, merchant raiders, and other miscellaneous navy craft clogged the harbor, a seemingly invulnerable armada of turrets and steel. Just as before, hulls glistened with smart black paint and red boottops, white superstructures, and buff funnels. Signal flags danced merrily, spelling out birthday wishes to the Queen who, gazing at the spectacle through her spyglass from the Isle of Wight, couldn't decipher them. The 12,350-ton flagship *Renown* was there, fluttering the flag of her admiral as Commander of the Fleet. So too was the White Star Line *Teutonic*, trotted out once again as England's token merchant cruiser. Nearby was the *Campania*, the largest British ship on earth, holding up the honor of the Cunard Line. On this day, and surrounded by such awesome force, it mattered little that she was already running a distant second in size and speed to the magnificent *Kaiser Wilhelm der Grosse*. The most awesome aspect of the spectacle, in fact, was what was not there rather than what was: the flotilla of ships swaying at anchor was in fact only *half* the total fleet of the Royal Navy. The rest remained at their posts, guarding the dominions of the Empress of India from all would-be usurpers.

Then, at a signal given at precisely two o'clock, the royal procession began. The leading vessel was the lovely yacht *Victoria and Albert*. On her quarterdeck, in the uniform of a British admiral, was the Prince of Wales. Next to him, in equally ponderous finery, was Prince Heinrich of Prussia, brother to the Kaiser. As the only foreign royal invited to attend, he was not there by accident. Indeed, his presence served precisely the same purpose as the Kaiser's visit had in 1889; here, once again, Britain flexed her muscles to her close cousin and closest rival. Understanding his role perfectly, Prince Heinrich regarded the spectacle with polite detachment and feigned boredom. After the *Victoria and Albert* came the *Enchantress*, bearing the Lords of the Admiralty in full gold braid, with swords; then the *Wildfire*, her decks lined with colonial premiers; the *Danube*, where the entire House of Lords stood in baronial splendor; then finally the *Campania* herself, as the people's representative, bearing the House of Commons and an assortment of Tory journalists. Slowly, like a train of dowager duchesses, the procession picked its way through the stationary fleet. The warships' guns roared in salute as they passed. Seamen lining their rails doffed their caps and cheered in well-choreographed displays of affection. Navy bands played "God Save the Queen" over and over, until the tune became a harsh, throbbing irritant to the Prince of Wales and his assemblage. But still he held his cap aloft, acknowledging the salutes with graceful ease. A huge crowd of civilian craft gathered on the sidelines—fishing trawlers, yachts, excursion ferries, and daysailers—sounding their whistles, their passengers waving frantically.

Then all hell broke loose. From within the cluster of spectator craft there came a sudden va-*ROOM*, and a tiny sliver of steel hydroplaned across the water, almost totally obscured by the two flanks of white foam rising from its bow. It dodged nimbly around the stern of a French cruiser, then headed straight for the *Victoria and Albert*. For a moment it looked as though the craft was going to slice the royal yacht in two. It finally veered off just a point, overtaking the yacht and leaving her bobbing in the chop of its wake. A picket boat moved to intercept, but the strange little demon cut saucily around her, snapping off her ensign staff like a toreador's prize. The picket boat's commander was so demoralized that he hurriedly divested himself of his sword, preparing to swim for dear life. But the projectile had already moved on. "Here, there and everywhere the little craft flew through the water," one spectator recalled, looking like "a whale with a man on his back to steer." The vessel, whatever she was, was now moving at close to 35 knots—15 knots faster than any other ship on earth. A tiny launch was towed behind, whipping back and forth in its wake with frightening intensity. It seemed inevitable that the line pulling her would part. Then, just as the boat made a particularly sharp turn round the counter stern of a sleek French yacht, it did. The launch was flung with an awful thunk into the yacht's starboard flank causing an explosion of Gallic profanity. As the bizarre party-crasher passed into the sea lane and made a beeline through a gauntlet of lethargic navy craft, the men lining their decks in open-mouthed astonishment finally got a good look at her. She was perhaps a hundred feet long, but so narrow—only nine feet—as to look more like a torpedo than a surface craft. A little pilot-house was crowded onto her bow, where the single figure of a man could be seen at the helm. Her long stern fanned out in a low, graceful arc until it was scarcely inches above the waterline. A twenty-foot tongue of flame erupted from her stack, which, combined with the rude thrum of the engines, made it seem as though she was blowing a giant raspberry at the stodgy British fleet around her.

No one could get close enough to read the name stenciled on the boat's bows, nor could they catch a glimpse of it through their binoculars as she streaked past. But they would not have been much enlightened. She was the *Turbinia*, brainchild of one Charles Algernon Parsons, and her engine was unlike anything on earth: a steam turbine. At that moment, the fleet was staring full face at its own obsolescence. It was unimaginable that the future of Britain's maritime supremacy would soon owe itself more to this tiny, impertinent little vessel—and her bizarre machinery—than to all those great ponderous dinosaurs now assembled in mute outrage along her flanks. But it was so.

"If you believe in a principle," Charles Parsons once wrote, "never damage it with a poor impression. You must go the whole way." That was his motto, and he lived by it. The son of Lord Rosse, a noted astronomer, Parsons was raised in an Irish castle filled with telescopes, laboratories, and Royal Society fellows. The atmosphere of scientific inquiry and boundless possibility was infectious. Young Charlie would not eat unless he had a mechanical toy next to him; the earliest photograph of the child shows him proudly holding a crude paper helicopter. By the time Parsons reached maturity at Cambridge University, he was shy, rather bookish, and brilliant. More than anything, he was a tinkerer. While most of his fellows left the university and embarked at once on academic careers, Parsons apprenticed himself for three years at the Elswick Iron Works in Newcastle. Then he tried developing rocket engines for torpedoes. Finally, in the 1880s, he turned his attention to the most fundamental mechanical force of the nineteenth century, the steam engine.

To engineers in Parsons's day, the steam engine was the supreme achievement in machines. Its design had been gradually improved over the course of the last sixty years—oval boilers rather than square, four rather than two cylinders—but the basic principles remained entirely unchanged. Compressed steam drove a piston into a shaft, released steam brought it out again, and the process was repeated. Clanking, rattling, and often terrifyingly loud, this forward-backward movement lost a significant portion of its thrust through the inertia of repetition.

Yet there was an alternative, two thousand years older and potentially far more efficient. In 150 B.C. the Greek scientist Hero demonstrated a working model in which steam was passed through a series of blades, which turned in a windmill motion and drove a rudimentary shaft. The problem, however, was in harnessing enough compressed steam to drive the blades—called a turbine—fast enough and with sufficient force to achieve any sort of forward motion. Parsons understood engines the way equestrians understand horses, and he applied himself to the task. First he borrowed one of his wife's cotton reels and some cardboard, fashioning a crude model not much different from Hero's. But soon he had advanced to prototypes of his own. Perhaps remembering his childhood, he built his models as toys for his own children—including a steam-powered tricycle called "The Spider," which puttered about the room emitting sparks, leaving pools of oil and water, and occasionally setting off small fires on the carpet.

In 1884, Parsons had a breakthrough. By passing the steam through a series of baffles, each time turning larger blades at slower speeds, he effectively trebled the productive capacity of the vapor. He then lengthened the turbine shaft still farther, intent on extracting every last possible ounce of compression. Thus the so-called triple-expansion engine was born. Parsons's turbine revolved at an astounding 18,000 revolutions per minute, emitting a shrill whine that was utterly unlike the traditional clank and thump of a piston-driven motor. By 1892, Parsons had developed the first closed-system condensing turbine, meaning that the vapor, after it had passed through the turbine shaft, would be recycled through a condenser back to its liquefied form, and then back to the boiler again. Two years later, with a half dozen partners (including his older brother), Parsons launched the Marine Steam Turbine Company. His engines were already powering the electric lights of a skating pond in Gateshead, and might—with more refinements—have gone on to revolutionize electric generators across the world. But Parsons reverted to type; a born yachtsman, he instinctively saw engines as a motive rather than productive force. Thus he was concerned less with electric generation than with *speed*. The *Turbinia* was the catalyst by which the true power of the turbine engine would be suddenly and dramatically demonstrated to the world.

He constructed the craft in 1894, fitting her with a modified version of his turbine. The *Turbinia* was then let loose on the Tyne, a stoker frantically shoveling coal into her furnace as Parsons steered. She made 20 knots—respectable, but not earth-shaking. Parsons discovered that the problem was not the engines but the propellers; at that speed, they vaporized the water around them and lost thrust in the resulting vacuum. Fired by the zest of a difficult challenge, Parsons experimented with one combination after another: bigger screws, smaller screws, differently shaped screws, more shafts, fewer shafts, shafts in parallel, shafts angled apart. Finally he achieved the desired result with nine propeller shafts powered by no fewer than three turbine engines. The 100-foot hull was so full of machinery that there was barely room for Parsons and the stoker to operate her.

In 1897, Parsons was ready. The *Turbinia* ambled down the Tyne from Newcastle to East Anglia, then along to Portsmouth and finally to Spithead. At one-quarter speed, with her freeboard riding high out of the water and raising little chop, she looked like an eccentric sort of yacht; custom built, perhaps, for a rich idiot who fancied himself the captain of a destroyer. It was in this guise that she entered the teeming mass of spectator craft on Jubilee day. Then, at a signal from Parsons, she was released with a terrific burst of speed into the full and astonished sight of England's navy, its government, its press, and its Queen.

The reaction was, to put it mildly, mixed. It was "a mad dash of Nelsonic impertinence," the London *Times* sniffed, impressed in spite of itself. "At the cost of a deliberate disregard of authority, she contrived to give herself effective advertisement. Perhaps her lawlessness may be excused by the novelty of the invention." Perhaps it would be, but there was hell to pay first. The Admiralty was incensed, for it was *their* show that Parsons had spoiled. Worse, it was *their* ships that had been ridiculed. The *Daily Mail* put it bluntly: "If that shrimp of a turbinet comes to anything," it prophesied, "all these black and yellow leviathans are done for." That was precisely what the Admiralty least wanted to hear. Their naval display was meant to inspire confidence among Britons and strike terror into the hearts of all others; instead, the spectacle at Spithead made their ships look like slothful geriatrics. Parsons might well have found himself locked in the Tower for his "proper box of tricks," as one apoplectic admiral termed it, had it not been for two strokes of luck. First, with rare showmanship, Parsons had brought the *Turbinia* right alongside the *Teutonic* and offered the White Star Line's president, Thomas Ismay, and his son, Bruce, a ride. With some trepidation, they accepted. The *Turbinia* whizzed them about the bay, executed a few breakneck turns, then slid gracefully back up to the *Teutonic*'s side. Old Thomas Ismay, once he regained his senses, was delighted. A new future was opening up for him, of White Star liners streaking across the Atlantic faster than any competitor and using far less coal in the process.

The second circumstance was even more propitious. Just as the Admiralty was girding itself to give Parsons the full benefit of its outrage, a telegram arrived from Prince Heinrich. Now back on his own flagship, the *König Wilhelm*, he cabled to congratulate Parsons on his revolutionary invention—which he was sure would transform the future of maritime technology—and to ask if *Herr Doktor* would care to demonstrate his engine again, perhaps in Germany? It was enough to make even the most peevish navy man pause for thought.

The Admiralty officials were no strangers to the potential of turbine technology. Like everyone, they considered it "a wonderful piece of ingenuity but a practical impossibility," as Lord John Fisher later remembered. Parsons had proved them wrong and made them look like fools in the process. *Engineering* magazine summed up the matter succinctly: "He broke most of the accepted rules of the marine engineer, and traversed the lessons of half a century, and yet he produced a boat which was, and still is, the fastest in the world." Dearly as the Admiralty officials would have loved to kick him, the threat of German supremacy weighed first in their minds, so they sweet-talked him instead. The turbine engine was now "the most important topic of conversation in technical circles between the two Poles." It was imperative that it remain in English hands. Within months, Parsons found himself presented with the contracts for two torpedo boats, the *Cobra* and *Viper*. Long, lean destroyers, they came from a class of vessels that valued speed and agility above all. It was appropriate that they would be the first turbine-powered ships ever constructed. They put to sea with tremendous fanfare in 1900.

But the triumph was short-lived. The superstitious might point to the fact that the *Viper's* trials took place on Friday the 13th of July. One year later, she foundered on the rocks of Renouquet Island, off Alderney, England. The crew abandoned her quickly, and the thin-steeled ship collapsed upon herself, splitting open and disappearing beneath the surface. The accident was put down to faulty navigation. Six weeks later the *Cobra* ran into some dirty weather off the Lincolnshire coast and literally broke apart, drowning all but twelve of her crew. Many were Parsons's friends. It was patently obvious that the turbine engines were in no way responsible for either accident; the fault lay rather with the design of the ships: too long, too narrow, and too fragile. But there is no breed of man more superstitious than a seaman. Parsons went from prodigy to pariah in an instant. By 1902 the only vessel still powered by Parsons's turbines was the little *King Edward*, a 230-ton passenger ferry operating between Greenock and Campbelltown. It looked as though the turbine would be consigned, in spite of its merits, to the realm of lost inventions and failed dreams. And perhaps it would have, had not its fate suddenly been tied to the rising fortunes of the Cunard Line.

The Lion Rampant

Cunard emerged from the fracas of the Morgan merger stronger, fitter, and more adventurous than ever. Its wily president, young Lord Inverclyde, was the hero of the hour. His precious fleet was spared the humiliation of foreign ownership, and the company had netted a government loan of £2,600,000—with an additional subsidy of

£150,000 a year in the process. As White Star devolved into the play-thing of an American plutocrat, Cunard's Britishness seemed all the more solid. With a government contract to construct liners capable of swift annexation by the Royal Navy, the company now kicked over the faint traces of its Canadian origin and hoisted its standard, a ram-pant gold lion against a scarlet field, like the crest of a baronial clan.

"Ransomed and rehabilitated," was how one historian described the Cunard Line in 1903. Yet its rescue had some substantial strings attached. The first was the simplest: "No foreigner," the government agreement stipulated roundly, "shall be qualified to hold office as a director of the company or to be employed as one of the principal of-ficers in the company; and no shares of the company shall be held by, or in trust for, or be in any way under the control of any foreigner or foreign corporation, or any corporation under foreign control." The words "foreigner" and "foreign," repeated four times in a single sen-tence, were utterly superfluous. The contract could just as easily have read "No J. P. Morgan shall be qualified. . . ."

The second stipulation was trickier. Cunard had been bailed out on the promise that it would construct two new superliners—the largest and fastest in the world. The colossal loan was predicated on its use for their construction. It was the ultimatum of the *Kaiser Friedrich* all over again: build us the best, or else. Moreover, the government's mo-tives were somewhat murky. Certainly they wished to reclaim the speed record from Germany as a matter of national pride. Certainly, too, there was a national interest in possessing the largest and most luxuri-ous ship on the Atlantic. Yet symbolism could only go so far, and it would not go as far as £2,600,000. For that, there had to be more con-crete dividends. Thus Cunard was charged not only with constructing the finest ships ever seen, but also with designing them to be easily con-vertible to military use, though what that use would be was not entirely clear. The Boer War had demonstrated the necessity for troopships, but that did not seem to be what the Admiralty had in mind. Troopships do not need to be designed any differently from passenger liners, for the only change wrought in transition from one to the other is the cre-ation of more accommodation space. Even *Engineering* was puzzled. "These two ships," it wrote, "in addition to carrying the mails and maintaining the prestige of Britain—which we regard as a very important commercial asset—are to be at the service of the Government in the event of war. To some it may seem remarkable that such an agreement should be necessary to secure the services of such vessels in emergency, and we may even have the naval critic urging that our cruisers ought to be equal in speed for any duty that the proposed Cunarders may fulfill."

And there was the answer. The new Cunard ships were not meant to be for troops, but armed merchant cruisers. A cruiser's primary role was to outpace and overtake merchant shipping; like the raiders of old, it relied exclusively on its superior speed. Hence, in the rather tortured logic of the Admiralty, a liner that could outrun any other ship in the world was the greatest potential cruiser in existence. "In other words," said *Engineering*, answering its own question, "speed and weight of machinery are the main considerations in the merchant ship, whereas in the cruiser they are important, but probably equal only to gun-power and armour protection." Thus the most compelling aspect of the new Cunarders, from their sponsor's point of view, was neither size nor luxury nor even national prestige, but speed.

This was a serious problem. Marine architects could always draft bigger ships, and interior design firms were ever at hand to stuff more gilt and opulence into their lounges. But as a concept of engineering, the reciprocating steam engine had reached the limit of its possible refinement. Changing a valve here or a shaft there might wrench a fraction of a knot more, but all in all the engines in the *Kaiser Wilhelm II*, completed in 1903, represented a peak of mechanical perfection that was not likely to be surpassed. The Admiralty had, paradoxically, presented Cunard with the one demand they could not accommodate. The board went to one shipwright after another, explaining their needs and receiving the same reply: 23 knots was the fastest any engine known to man could be coaxed to run. The steam turbine was already so discredited that it never even occurred to them to consider it.

Charles Parsons had first approached the Cunard Line in December 1902, one year after the *Cobra* disaster. It was optimism on an unprecedented scale. Explaining the rudiments of the design to the line's superintendent engineer, a gruff Scotsman named James Bain, he found the man not entirely unsympathetic. Bain followed Parsons back to the Tyne, where he toured the Marine Steam Turbine plant. He even traveled on the little *King Edward*, ducking below to inspect the turbines first hand. Bain was sufficiently impressed to persuade the board to invite Parsons to their annual meeting. He came, presenting the board with an astonishing proposal: his engines, he said, could allow for the construction of a vessel 725 feet in length with 48,000 horsepower. It seemed like sheer fantasy. They declined his offer, for the present time. One year later, after the terms of the government loan were announced, Parsons tried again. This time Cunard did not waste any effort on pleasantries. "The Board does not see its way to adopt Turbine Machinery," Parsons was told.

But Lord Inverclyde was intrigued. He too had been present on that June day at Spithead, and had seen the little *Turbinia* streak through the waves. Though nearly everyone told him Parsons was a crank, he was not so sure. Fortunately, James Bain felt the same way. Now promoted to general superintendent of the line, he had been an enthusiastic convert to the turbine since he had seen its smooth, quiet operation on the *King Edward*. Another turbine vessel, the Channel ferry *Queen* of 1903, had exceeded her own projected speed by several knots. Bain, like Parsons a man who enjoyed seeing things for himself, booked passage on her. His report, sent back to Inverclyde and the board along with supporting letters from several engineers—including Parsons—positively glowed. Gradually, the ever-cautious Cunard Line was being cajoled into the new century, almost against its will. True to the Edwardian belief in clubs, experts, and shared responsibility, a commission was appointed to consider the possible applications of steam turbine technology; it consisted of four shipbuilders, two engineers, and a retired admiral. Within weeks, all were convinced. Steam turbines used less coal at greater speeds than reciprocating engines; moreover, their potential for acceleration and sustained speeds was exponentially greater than anything yet devised.

But in spite of this enthusiastic recommendation, the board was still undecided. Cunard Lines had been a public company since 1880, and accountability bred caution. What would the stockholders say if the line suddenly went against almost eighty years of tradition, placing its faith in whizzbang gadgetry that had never powered anything bigger than a vessel scarcely one-tenth the size of their ocean liners? And what if, God forbid, the engines failed? The Parsons turbine called for a leap of faith. With two disastrous accidents and relative obscurity on one side of the balance sheet, and the engineers' unalloyed zeal on the other, the directors were faced with a Catch 22: reject the turbines, equip the new ships with reciprocating engines, and thus fail the dictates of the Admiralty agreement; or stake the company's reputation, the government's money, and the future of British mercantile supremacy on an invention that could quite possibly turn out to be a dud.

With canny wariness that would have delighted old Sir Samuel Cunard himself, they finally reached a compromise. Two liners had been scheduled for construction since 1901. They were not, most emphatically, the wonder ships that the Admiralty was expecting. The *Carmania* and *Caronia* were, instead, eminently serviceable vessels following in the tradition and mold of the *Campania* and *Lucania* of 1893. At 19,524 tons they would be very slightly larger than the *Kaiser Wilhelm II*, but their service speed of 18 knots was nowhere near the *Wilhelm*'s record-breaking 23. Their keels had already been laid at the Scottish firm of John Brown & Co., Clydebank, in early 1903; they were due for completion in 1905. Staid, solid, and utterly unremarkable, they were the perfect guinea pigs to test Parsons's new designs. Once again, Cunard's predilection for sister ships paid off. The two ships would be exactly alike in every particular, save that the *Caronia* would be equipped with traditional reciprocating engines, while the *Carmania* would be the first British passenger liner to be driven by turbines. The two would then be placed on the same route, so that their respective speeds and coal consumptions could be assessed. If the turbine experiment proved successful, Cunard would be safe in equipping their projected superliners with them.

After one full season of serene operation, the *Carmania* averaged one full knot greater speeds at an identical consumption rate of coal. The board was finally convinced. In 1905, Parsons received the contract that would make him a legend: the two greatest ships of the new century would be equipped with turbine engines.

-6-

Song of the Machines

THE ADMIRALTY AND THE CUNARD LINE HAD ALWAYS NURSED VERY different concepts of the rivalry with Germany. As designs for the new Cunarders neared completion, these differences became increasingly marked. The Royal Navy cared little for symbolic victories or abstractions like the Blue Riband. It had spent more than two million pounds for a pair of armed merchant cruisers, and it expected to get its money's worth. The Lords of the Admiralty conceived the passenger liner race as an adjunct to their own naval race; a dash whose inevitable conclusion was war. Thus, Anglo-German competition on the Atlantic was merely the warm-up before the conflagration—a time, the Admiralty reasoned, when merchant vessels like the new Cunarders would abandon the pretense of luxury and reveal their true colors as vessels of the Royal Navy.

Cunard's perception of the race was drastically different. The Germans did not inaugurate competition on the Atlantic; it had existed since before the advent of steam-powered engines. Passenger firms throughout the nineteenth century had vied with one another for the fastest passage, the most luxurious appointments. But the race between them had never been more feverish than in the last two decades, when White Star and Inman—both British firms—were locked head to head in competition with their respective *Teutonic* and *City of New York*. As recently as August 1889, one week before the Kaiser's legendary visit to Spithead, the two ships crossed the Atlantic in a furious race that persisted for six full days, ending with a photo finish as they arrived in New York neck and neck; the *City of New York* arrived exactly nine minutes before her competitor, but lost on corrected time.

Thus the Germans, when they burst upon the scene with the *Kaiser Wilhelm der Grosse*, were perceived by the other shipping firms merely as new competitors in an old race. Unwelcome, perhaps, but—like the Kaiser at Cowes—still members of the same club. The distinction, in fact, was not in how the British perceived the Germans, but in how the Germans perceived themselves. From the outset, Germany embarked on its Atlantic adventure with an unsportsmanlike zeal that far exceeded the gentle rivalries of the British firms. Wilhelm's nation had something to prove. Nationalism was etched into every crevice of the *Kaiser Wilhelm der Grosse*, from the coats of arms displayed prominently in the First Class lounge to the portraits of Bismarck, Moltke, Wilhelm I, and other noble Prussians that gazed down disdainfully at diners in the saloon, as though chastising them for gluttony. While the British were not unmindful of this patriotic puffery, they disregarded it. If the Germans wanted to make their ships the floating embodiments of what they thought was the superior Teutonic culture, that was their business. British liners would continue to uphold the great maritime traditions of their nation more subtly.

Consequently, the Cunard Line conceived of its new superliners as challenges to German supremacy on the Atlantic, not Germany herself or, least of all, her navy. The purpose of the ships was, in their eyes, to restore the perception of British supremacy by creating vessels so obviously superior in every measurable capacity that the Germans would be incapable of exceeding them. Their wartime potential was not, at first, seen as detrimental to this goal. Possible conversion to an armed merchant cruiser was merely one more way in which the new Cunard Line vessels would dazzle the world with their innovation.

But then the reality of constructing a dual-purpose superliner began to intrude. The Admiralty's specifications were as exacting as they were implausible. All of the ships' officers and at least one-half of their crews were to be members of the Royal Navy or the Reserves, an incredible demand when one considers that one-half of any liner's crew must include hairdressers, lift operators, stewardesses, and pastry chefs. The new ships were to have a service speed of 25 knots, with longitudinal coal bunkers buried deep below the waterline, away from possible enemy bombardment. At the turn of the twentieth century submarine warfare was still as remote to naval engineers as aerial bombing; consequently, the hulls of the new ships were designed to resist surface shelling, not torpedoing. The ships were to incorporate into their design "pillars and supports" for the eventual placement of twelve six-inch guns; steel plating above the waterline was to be on a par with "armed cruisers of the County class," hence several inches thicker than the industry standard—particularly around sensitive areas of the ship such as the bridge. Extra plating and odd structural supports posed considerable logistical challenges to the designers, none of whom were naval architects. Even if they had been, the task before them was Herculean: build the largest, fastest, most luxurious ship in the world, then build the world's greatest cruiser, and incorporate them into the same hull. The Admiralty wasn't much help, either. Its imperious demands confounded engineers with blithe disregard for the laws of physics, as here:

> The ship must be steady as possible under varying conditions to which a ship of the high speed defined in the contract would be subjected in the North Atlantic Trade and the stability should be so arranged that, by the use of water ballast, the ship may have a positive metacentric height in the worst condition when fitted as an armed merchant cruiser.

Still, the architects of John Brown & Co. of Clydebank and Swan Hunter of Newcastle persevered. A pair of vessels emerged from the drawing boards incorporating dimensions and technology that boggled the Edwardian imagination. They would be 31,500 gross tons, more than half again larger than the 19,300 tons of their German rivals. The difference between them, some 12,200 tons, would have built the *Campania* over again. Their length would be 790 feet, exceeding the *Kaiser Wilhelm II* by a substantial 90 feet. They were, in fact, floating challenges to the conventional wisdom that ships exceeding 750 feet would break apart on the North Atlantic from sheer unwieldiness, and that tonnage greater than 25,000 would make them sink like stones from disproportionate displacement. Old hands on the Clyde and the Tyne muttered darkly as the leviathans took shape before them.

Although not mentioned, the ghost of the *Great Eastern* was in the back of everyone's mind. Built in 1858, she had been the last British vessel designed to be so big, fast, and splendid. At 693 feet long, with a then-unimaginable tonnage of 18,915 (her nearest competitor, the Cunard ship *Persia*, was 376 feet and 3,600 tons), she remained the greatest technological failure in English maritime history. Oversized, underpowered—despite *two* paddlewheels and a propeller—she wallowed in the Atlantic like a sick headache, throwing her terrified passengers from one end of the grand saloon to the other. Her transatlantic career lasted barely three years, all at a thumping loss for her owners, after which she was abruptly retired. Her example, said one naval engineer at the time, was instrumental "in demonstrating that there was a limit in steamships in the direction of size." British shipwrights had learned their lesson; it would be forty years before they attempted anything like her dimensions again. The first ships to do so, in fact, were the new Cunarders—as exponentially larger in their own day as the *Great Eastern* had been in hers. Thus the path of their construction was watched with a mixture of pride, awe, and—for many—anxiety. The empty shells taking shape simultaneously in Scotland and England were of such awesome size that spectators could only shake their heads in wonderment.

Admiralty stipulations were observed, after a fashion. "It was decided," *Engineering* later reported, "before construction was very far advanced, to enter upon a series of very careful tests in order to determine whether, and to what extent, increased strength could be imparted to the upper structure by the adoption of high-tensile steel. These tests . . . were watched with great interest by the officials of Lloyd's [the insurer], the Board of Trade, and the Admiralty." Indeed they were. With trenchant candor, *Engineering* went on to describe them: "The metal was subjected to tup—heavy metal weight—tests as well as other severe punishments, including the explosion of heavy charges of dynamite against the plates. . . ." Not to leave its readers in any doubt, the journal launched into an extended discussion of the processes by which steel is hardened against shell perforation, even including several photographs depicting iron and steel plates pockmarked with the dents of various caliber artillery. The net result, for the lay reader, was to reinforce the notion that these new Cunard behemoths were utterly impregnable and "practically unsinkable." Hence, in a stroke of marketing genius, their wartime capabilities became a splendid advertisement for their peacetime safety and invulnerability.

Once the details of construction were finally settled and the frames rose on their stocks, the final, inevitable problem arose of selecting names. Cunard, in customary fashion, produced a list of 461 names all ending in the obligatory *-ia*, from "Acarnania" to "Zenobia." But the number was deceptive, for most of the palatable choices—*Britannia*, for example—were already registered with other vessels. (There were no fewer than thirty-nine *Victoria*s, and it would not be until exactly one century later, in 2005, that the name was finally given to a Cunard ship.) In desperation, Cunard threw open their doors to suggestions. The British public responded with characteristic enthusiasm. One eager contributor offered "Cynuria" and "Cytheria," thus attempting to further the tradition of giving Cunard vessels names sounding vaguely mythic and remarkably like fatal diseases. Perhaps the most inspired suggestion came from the distant reaches of inland Canada; the Board of Trade of Saskatoon modestly suggested that "Saskatonia" would be "euphonious, catchy, and easily remembered." They were certainly right about the last. In the end, it was the classicist G. G. Ramsay of Glasgow University who furnished the answer. If Cunard was willing to switch from the names of eastern Roman provinces (*Etruria, Campania, Lucania*) to those of the west, they might consider naming their vessels *Mauretania* (Roman Morocco) and *Lusitania* (Roman Portugal). A little unorthodox, he admitted self-deprecatingly, but "perhaps these new monsters deserve an extra syllable."

Gradually the forms of the new liners took shape. In some ways they were not markedly different from their HAPAG and Lloyd competitors. Long and lean, they carried an extra tier of superstructure that gave them a greater vertical presence, without seeming top-heavy. A separate deckhouse at the stern housed Second Class, creating a fixture in Cunard profiles that would be repeated for the next two decades. The original builder's model displayed three raked funnels set wide apart on the top deck. Yet somewhere between design and execution, a fourth was added. Though functional (unlike those of the later *Olympic* and *Titanic*, which were dummies), it was added out of patriotism. The Germans had four; the British would not have any fewer, aesthetics be damned.

"Every Ship Has a Soul"

The *Lusitania* and *Mauretania* were launched from their respective berths three months apart, on June 7 and September 20, 1906. The morning of June 7 was bright and clear, a rarity for Scottish coastal summers. The Clydeside works had been transformed into a sort of midway, with platforms and balconies hastily erected around the looming black form of the *Lusitania*. In the carnival spirit that prevailed, machinery, derricks, and cranes became fascinating exhibits of technological wonder—it was almost as though the Crystal Palace had been moved to the Clyde. Some twenty thousand spectators—many of whom had come from England for the event—milled excitedly about. Ladies wore wide-brimmed hats and summer dresses that would befit a garden party; gentlemen wore toppers and morning coats. This spectacle of polite society seemed rather at odds with the honest grime and soot of the shipyard. On a high platform, separated from this genteel proletariat, were the builders, owners, designers, and an assortment of international dignitaries whose only purpose in attendance was to allow the newspapers to claim, as indeed the *Daily Mail* did, that "at no previous launch of a merchant ship had there been a gathering of so many people distinguished in the scientific and maritime world. They came from all parts of Britain and the colonies, while Naval and Mercantile Marine representatives from France, Germany, Italy, Japan, and Russia were also present."

Conspicuous among them, looking uncomfortable in top hat and frock coat, was Charles Parsons. This incongruous outfit matched his new station: he was now the Honorable Charles Parsons, KCB, and would soon attain the higher glory of knighthood. But next to him, in the most honored place of all, was a vacancy. George Arbuthnot Burns, second Lord Inverclyde, had died in October 1905 at the age of 44. The man who single-handedly saved the Cunard Line and facilitated the construction of these floating monsters lived long enough to see their keels laid, then succumbed to a long illness. His widow, Lady Inverclyde, was given the honor of christening the ship.

At precisely 12:30 P.M., Lady Inverclyde depressed a small electric button, and a magnum of beribboned wine arced down from the moulding loft. It smashed against the ship's hull with a satisfying burst, and Lady Inverclyde cried, "I christen thee *Lusitania!*" Then nothing happened.

"The most elaborate precautions have been made for the operation," said one newspaper, "That this was necessary may be gleaned from the fact that the launching weight of the leviathan was 16,000 tons—by far the heaviest weight ever carried on a cradle down the ways." As the electric button clanged and the ship sat still as stone, there was a collective intake of breath. At that moment, all the dread predictions surrounding the ship's size and construction rose in sharp relief in the minds of all present, from the owners to the throng below. The disappointment was almost audible. Then, finally, a distant creaking and thumping was heard, like branches in a high wind. The sound reverberated through the ship, rising in volume until it seemed as though a whole forest was being wrenched apart. The *Lusitania* began to move, almost imperceptibly at first, then with great and indecorous speed. It took just 28 seconds for the entire 787-foot hull to roar down the ways and into the Clyde. Amazingly, for some, she didn't sink. A cheer went up.

The time came for speeches. Sir Charles MacLaren, chairman of John Brown & Co., proposed a toast to "the *Lusitania* and her builders." Then, getting into the spirit of things, he went on to claim that the occasion was so momentous that not a single person present, even a potential rival (the German delegate bristled), could fail to be gratified by what they had just witnessed. Several looked as though they were trying their best, but MacLaren went on regardless: the ship in front of them was already the largest and longest the world had ever seen. Soon she would be the fastest and most luxurious as well. All the Isles had had a hand in building her, from Darlington to Wales, and even far-flung outposts in Asia and Africa. Her Britishness was more than confirmed, he went on, by the fact that she was, in reality, the latest addition to the reserve fleet of the Royal Navy—capable of swift conversion to become the most powerful cruiser in the world. Then, just as the Germans were recovering from this last blow, MacLaren drove the blade home. Britain was, he said, in every sense the mistress of the seas. She had always taken the lead in marine construction, both civilian and naval. It was intolerable, therefore, that the records for size and speed should belong to Germany. The *Lusitania* and her sister would, by their size, speed, and stature, restore maritime supremacy to England once and for all. Wild cheers erupted from the crowd.

Soon afterwards, it was the *Mauretania*'s turn. September in England was not what June in Scotland had been, and a persistent cold drizzle now accompanied the festivities. The Dowager Duchess of Roxburgh was on hand for the christening, as were most of the same dignitaries—including Parsons—and a host of builders from the Tyneside yard of Swan Hunter. In a way, this launching was bigger and more splendid than the *Lusitania*'s, for the *Mauretania* was an English ship, constructed in Newcastle, and far more accessible to the public than her sister had been. There was also more time for celebration. The vagaries of the tides postponed the launch until 4:30, by which time all the local businesses and factories had closed shop, allowing their workers to join the multitudes gathered around the great black hull. Thus it was a somewhat more democratic affair than the last had been, with flat-brimmed caps and overalls mingling with bowlers and pinstripes. One local newspaper described the scene:

> Gangs of workmen round the sides knocked the great dog-shores away one by one with huge battering rams fitted with handles, and the sound of their working "chanty" which they sang in chorus mingled with the incessant hammering that went on under the keel of the ship between the two ways where hundreds of carpenters who could not be seen were working by the light of torches.
> Ambulance men were posted all around the ship, and their presence gave a hint of the anxiety that lay behind the

ceremony that made this day a holiday for the northern
town.

This time the pause after the warning buzzer was even longer. A
tiny capstan turned by the Duchess's hand released the great steel trig-
gers holding the ship in place, but there was no answering creak from
the timbers beneath. The moment when a ship is cast free of her restraints and left to the mercy of gravity and inertia is tense for any
builder. Mr. Swan, of Swan Hunter, raised his hand nervously to the
engineers, signaling them to give the inert form a nudge. But before
they could comply a joyous rumbling was heard. The giant steel wall began to slide inexorably backward. The Duchess, caught unaware, barely
had time to cry out *"Mauretania!"* and fling the bottle—champagne
this time—at the rapidly receding bow. In 70 seconds, the *Mauretania*
was afloat.

For this event, the jocular Sir Charles MacLaren was replaced by
the staid and dignified Lord Tweedmouth, the Admiralty representative. Tweedmouth had been seen supervising the launch, examining the
stays, very much in control throughout. His presence, and his post of
honor, spoke volumes for the equivocal role of the ship before him.
After the Cunard director had his say—jovially reminding those assembled, to accompaniment of hearty laughter, that the turbine engines
still weren't paid for—Lord Tweedmouth took the podium. It was
evening now, and the speeches had grown more ponderous. It was true,
said his lordship, that as Admiralty representative he was in some ways
a partner in the enterprise of the *Mauretania*. But he hoped that he
would always remain a "silent partner," and that the dread possibilities
for which the *Mauretania* had been specially designed would never
come to pass. But if, by the grace of God, these magnificent vessels were
ever called to war, Lord Tweedmouth assured his audience, they would
be a credit to the fleet, to their builders, and to England herself. Their
greatness, he said, was not merely in their construction, but in their
symbolic alliance of navy and merchant marine. He had recently been
present at another great launching, that of His Majesty's Ship *Dreadnought*. He was reminded of that particularly today, because in his eyes
these two great vessels of English glory, naval and mercantile, stood
together in her defense and preservation. "Anything connected with the
sea must always be regarded with the greatest interest by the people of

this country," he concluded. "It is by the sea that we are united to our colonies and dependencies. It is by the sea that is brought the food to keep our people alive. It is by the sea that we have our greatest power of defense. Great companies like the Cunard deserve all the praise and all the encouragement that the population can give them."

If Lord Tweedmouth's speech represented the fullest articulation of the dual role of the superliners, it was also the last. Only when they stood in mute glory as great black shells, with their sinews thus exposed, could the *Mauretania* and *Lusitania* ever be mistaken for warships. Once the process of fitting began, as decks were added, paneling installed, and carpets laid, the structural supports and gun mounts were obscured behind an impenetrable veil of shoreside décor. After this camouflaging, the thought that the sister ships might be converted to naval vessels faded away to nothing, until it was merely an amusing architectural footnote to titillate shipping circles. Their proper role as transatlantic liners would commence with all the appropriate fanfare; their other, secondary, role would be forgotten—even, in 1914, by the Cunard Line itself. But the Admiralty remembered.

The intention of the ships' designers was, as it had been for the *Campania*, to remove as fully as possible any suggestion that their passengers were on board a vessel sailing through the middle of the ocean. On earlier liners, this was a difficult task: economies of size, the noise of the engines, and the persistent smell of the bilge made even the most valiant attempts at gilded luxury seem mocking, often hypocritical. In some senses they were. It was standard practice on most crack liners to lay down magnificent carpets and runners in port, dazzling shoreside visitors with their plush depths. Once at sea, however, the carpets disappeared; salt spray would have ruined them. Likewise, photographs depicting a liner's vast interior spaces were intentionally deceptive; a First Class lounge that seemed to rival Versailles in the company brochure often turned out to be depressingly undersized: a creaking, heaving stall where paneling squeaked and complained, tasseled lights jiggled alarmingly, and drinks slid off tables into their owners' laps.

Yet because the *Mauretania* and *Lusitania* were so much bigger than their rivals, passengers had far more breathing room. For the first time, a ship at sea could mirror in every respect the luxury, decoration,

and, most of all, spaciousness of a resort. Accordingly, Cunard broke
with the long tradition of hiring naval architects to fashion their ships'
interiors. Instead, they commissioned interior designers James Miller
and Harold Peto to create the public rooms of the new behemoths.
Neither man had ever worked with ships before.

Unlike the German liners, which shared the same designer and
thus bore the unmistakable mark of his style, the interior spaces of the
Lusitania and *Mauretania* were radically different from each other.
James Miller had been encouraged to tour the German ships prior to
his commission, mainly as a lesson in what *not* to do. They were, without exception, overblown, over-decorated, and dark. In the *Lusitania*,
Miller eschewed the traditional gentleman's club feel of most preceding liners in favor of light, airy spaces reminiscent of a seaside hotel.
Woodwork was painted sheer white, accentuated by gold filigree. Gutta
percha, the new rubberized material, a forerunner to linoleum, gleamed
from every floor. In the First Class dining saloon, Miller achieved a
masterpiece. Rising two decks, the entire room was a study in curves.
A central atrium, oval shaped, was capped by a magnificent oblong
dome, into which were set murals in oval frames; even the tables were
oval. Hammered bronze railings, gilt-capped columns, and Louis XVI
paneling—all white—completed the effect. The combination of high
ceilings, bright paneling, and soft contours was a psychological master-
stroke far ahead of its time.

Atlantic liners—and London pubs—had, until then, labored under
a décor that featured sharp angles, dark woods, and low overheads; in
either place, they did little to aid the appetite: passengers felt confined,
oppressed. Add the natural motions and sounds of a ship at sea, and the
total effect became intolerable. Not so very long before, when saloon
passengers were fed at long tables, the choicest spots had been at both
ends—to provide easy access to the lavatories or one's cabin in the likely
event of a hasty departure. Though Miller could not erase the motion
of a ship, he could and did provide an environment least likely to aid its
assault on the senses.

Perhaps because he had never been commissioned to design a ship,
Miller's final designs also carried a greater degree of luxury to the lower
decks. The traditional practice of steamship designers was to give full
vent to their artistic expressions in First Class, then hurriedly throw

together a Second Class out of the remaining space. The results were, without exception, unremarkable. The only concessions made to its bourgeois clientele were cabins (instead of open berths), a greater number of washrooms, and tablecloths in the dining room. Steerage was a cattle stable for humans. Metal bunks lined vast dormitory-like spaces, men and women were segregated, and meals were served from vast tureens by indifferent stewards.

James Miller's designs for the *Lusitania*, however, reflected a stylistic unity—what we might call today a "design concept"—throughout the ship. Second Class was housed in the stern, not a particularly choice location, as it was directly above the propellers and thus subjected to the worst vibration. Yet it was also self-contained, rising three decks just like First Class, with its own dining room, lounge, smoking room, and promenade deck. The lounge and smoking room were of similar design, rich wood panels capped by white-painted skylights. Bare wood floors were covered by decent carpeting, and the chairs—while not Louis XVI—looked comfortable. There was even a Second Class ladies' drawing room, almost indistinguishable in its design from that of First Class. Similarly, the dining room was in reality a scaled-down version of its First Class counterpart, with a somewhat smaller central atrium and dome and a little less filigree.

But the biggest surprise was Steerage. Now called "Third Class," a remarkable change in nomenclature in itself, it had an overall feeling of simplicity, dignity, and respectability. Third Class passengers were housed in cabins—spartan, to be sure, but with the added touches of white-painted paneling, a cut-glass decanter over the washstand, and company bedspreads bearing the Cunard lion. Incredibly, there were even columns in the Third Class dining room: not mere iron supports, but actual columns with Doric caps. There were chairs rather than benches at the tables, and wide alleyways for easy access and exit.

Harold Peto's creations on the *Mauretania* were no less remarkable, though radically different. His stipulation to his employers was simple and direct: if hired, he would design the vessel's public rooms in his own way, with no interference from the line or any of its members. This was a hard pill for the board to swallow. It had been the tradition at Cunard, as well as other lines, to allow boardmembers' wives the privilege of influencing the ships' interiors. As late as 1966, Lady Brocklebank barraged the *Queen Elizabeth 2* designers with "swatches of flowered chintz and dyed leatherette," before wiser heads prevailed. It was precisely in anticipation of a similar occurrence that Harold Peto dug in his heels. The results were staggering, and well worth the board's self-restraint. *Engineering* magazine abandoned its usual pith, adopting instead a rapturous verve as it hailed the grand saloon for providing "a wonderful impression of quiet grandeur, with its panels of beautifully grained mahogany, dully polished a rich brown, each lit by its surrounding moulding of gold, and relieved by slender pilasters of *fleur de pêche* marble of a lilac hue. . . ." and so on. In contrast to the *Lusitania*'s white majesty, Peto aimed for a more traditional concept of luxury—that of a gracious country manor. He was only partially successful: True country manors reflect the eras in which they were built, inside and out; but in this pre-Bauhaus era of the early twentieth century, designers looked backward rather than forward, and public rooms usually contained a pastiche of borrowed styles. Through their light touch and relative simplicity, the *Lusitania*'s interiors managed, more or less, to avoid this pitfall; the *Mauretania*'s did not. Georgian and Louis XVI influences rubbed shoulders with Renaissance, late Victorian, Adam, and even Tudor. Heavy draperies and chintz abounded. The total effect was, if not aesthetically proper, certainly impressive. There was a bright busyness and cheerfulness to the *Mauretania*, a sense of personality, which her sister quite lacked. Contrasted with the *Lusitania*'s almost antiseptic cleanliness and purity of line, the *Mauretania*'s public rooms had more color, more contrast, a little more sense of fun. Passengers felt it, even if they did not quite understand it. "There are several things about this great ship that are unique," wrote Theodore Dreiser. "It was a beautiful thing all told—its long cherry-wood paneled halls . . . its heavy porcelain baths, its dainty staterooms fitted with lamps. . . . And the bugler who bugled for dinner! That was a most musical sound he made, trilling the various quarters gaily, as much to say, 'This is a very joyous event, ladies and gentlemen; we are all happy; come, come; it is a delightful feast.' "

Different though they were in style, the *Mauretania* and *Lusitania* shared one thing in common. There were no portraits of King Edward VII or his family in either vessel to match those of Wilhelm aboard the *Kaiser Wilhelm der Grosse*; no Union Jacks, crossed swords, or any other such nonsense. Passengers aboard the *Mauretania* didn't need to be reminded that they were on a British ship.

The idea of an eighteenth-century château contained within an elongated steel hull seems now like an anachronism; propelling it through the elements at 25 knots seems even more ridiculous. The description in *Engineering* reflected this essential dichotomy, yet did nothing to reconcile it. This was scarcely surprising; mechanical wonders and retrospective trappings were still seen, even as late as 1907, as quite harmonious. Just fifty years before, in London's Great Exhibition of 1851, one of the most prized displays was an elaborately scrolled chair that had been fashioned, for the very first time, by machine. It was a pseudo-medieval monstrosity. The great scything blades of the device had been used to carve lions' heads, clawed feet, and gargoyles. Similarly, and in almost every respect, the *Lusitania* and *Mauretania* were the greatest machines yet devised. Even among their peers, both ships boasted significant engineering advances; their turbines were merely one invention among many. Both were unique, for example, in having the first truly unified electrical system at sea. Electricity steered the ship, operated the watertight doors, and even powered the mechanical potato peeler in the galley. Yet all these were advances, which, though perhaps known to some of the passengers, were not immediately obvious to them. They were concealed, along with the functional elements of the ship itself, behind the veneer of ageless gentility.

Only in one area did technology and luxury meet: the so-called conveniences. These were a list of mechanical objects that in some way aided or cosseted passengers—typically First Class passengers. Such items included the first hydraulically operated barber's chair on board the *Mauretania*, telephones in every First Class cabin on both ships, and the electric elevators. Cunard was particularly proud of the elevators, with their grinding machinery concealed in a latticework of aluminum and bronze detailing, complete with turret caps and heraldic crests at every corner. The finished product resembled a highly gilded birdcage for humans. A smartly attired boy would operate the lever, whisking passengers between stateroom and public room with unprecedented dispatch and style.

The *Mauretania* was ready for her trials in the fall of 1907. Few events in English maritime history have been awaited with more anticipation. The long, sleek ship with her four raked funnels, now painted in traditional Cunard colors of orange-red and black, moved gracefully down the Tyne on September 17 with a consort of tugs assisting her. Once on the open sea, Captain James Pritchard gave the order for full speed. For the first time, the telegraph on the bridge wired the command directly to its counterpart in the engine room, where Chief Engineer Alexander Duncan and his crewmates sprang to action at once. There was a shudder as the screws bit into the water, and a ferocious noise—not unlike the jet engines of some fifty years later— as the turbines accelerated to speeds faster than engines had ever known. Firemen doggedly stoked the ship's massive furnaces and the temperature in the boiler room soon exceeded 115 degrees. The ship began to pick up speed. The needle in the engine room crept past 16, 18, 20, 22, then arced slowly and steadily to 25, where it remained. It was a moment of triumph, for at that precise second the *Mauretania* was moving faster than any other ocean liner in history.

Then suddenly the warning buzzer on the ship's telegraph sounded, and the needle pointed to "All Stop." Duncan was confused. Was the *Mauretania* about to plow headlong into some obstacle? Thinking it might have been sent in error, he grasped the speaking tube and signaled for the captain. "Why are we stopping?" he asked. The captain's reply came back a moment later, "Because I am being shaken off my bridge."

It was true. Even at medium speeds, the *Mauretania* shivered painfully from end to end. Like the *Deutschland* before her, she had sacrificed too much for that extra knot of speed. The same problem beset the *Lusitania*, which had undergone her own trials in early June. Although they were the last word in marine technology, both ships contained serious structural flaws. And if the captain on his bridge could be discomfited by the vibration, the stern section must have been appalling. Both ships were quietly returned to their builders, where thirty tons of steel was added to brace their hulls. This helped, but only a little. "The result," said Superintendent Bain euphemistically, "is not all that might be desired." A later replacement of the three-bladed propellers with four-bladed ones did more than anything else to reduce vibration, but did not eliminate it. Throughout their careers, the

Cunard sisters would be remembered as fast, beautiful, and very shaky. In a perverse way, this seemed to add to their personality; the *Mauretania*'s captain once wrote that he felt his ship give "a shudder of delight." Even Franklin Roosevelt, who personally disliked both vessels, admitted that they were unique in their way. "Every ship has a soul," he said, "But the *Mauretania* had one you could talk to. At times she could be wayward and contrary as a thoroughbred. . . . At other times, she would do everything her Master wanted to do, with a right good will. As Captain Rostron once said to me, she had the manners and deportment of a great lady and behaved herself as such."

"There Are No Standards Whatsoever by Which to Judge Them"

The 1907 maiden voyage of the *Lusitania* brought some two hundred thousand spectators and well wishers to Liverpool, a record number for the coastal city. About twenty thousand had already visited her during open-house days the week before. The towering black-and-white riveted hull, with its four funnels soaring like the stacks of a giant factory, loomed over the docks in awesome solitude. One author described the scene as inherently strange: gathered around this 31,938-ton marvel of twentieth-century engineering was a huge collection of horse-drawn buggies, jitneys, hansom cabs, dog carts, and victorias—relics of a past age. The incongruity was not lost on spectators, either. "And so we come," said historian Keble Chatterton, observing the scene, "to those two leviathans which form, without exception, the most extraordinary, the most massive, the fastest, and the most luxurious ships that ever crossed the ocean." His enthusiasm, however, was tempered with some trepidation, and more than a little wistfulness:

> There are some characteristics of the *Mauretania* and *Lusitania*, with their lifts, their marbles, curtains, ceilings, trees, and other expressions of twentieth century luxury, which, while appreciated by the landsman and his wife, are nauseating to the man who loves the sea and its ships for their own sakes, and not for the chance of enjoying self indulgence in

some new form. But whichever way you regard them, from whatever standpoint you choose, there is nothing comparable to them, there are no standards whatsoever by which to judge them.

Even crusty old Rudyard Kipling was caught up in the awesomeness of it all. In his poem "The Song of the Machines," he wrote:

> You can start this very evening if you choose
> And take the Western Ocean in the stride
> Of thirty thousand horses and some screws
> The boat-express is waiting at your command!
> You will find the *Mauretania* at the quay,
> Till her captain turns the lever 'neath his hand,
> And the monstrous nine-decked city goes to sea.

Any talk of taking back the Blue Riband on the *Lusitania*'s maiden voyage was absolutely taboo, from the owners, to the builders, to even the British shipping journals. It was simply too risky. Maiden voyages were unpredictable; things inevitably went wrong, the ship needed time to settle into herself. The Cunard Line utterly disavowed any intention to break the *Kaiser Wilhelm II*'s record on her first voyage. The London agent, meeting with reporters, stressed the time-honored adage of the line: "safety above all." Yet it was the firm belief of nearly everyone that the "Lucy" would do so, all the same. Passengers embarked with a conspiratorial air, shaking hands with Captain James Watt and congratulating him for unspecified triumphs. As the *Lusitania* put out to sea, not a single person standing on the Liverpool docks doubted that in five days' time they would be reading of the fastest ever Atlantic crossing in their morning papers.

At first, the *Lusitania* exceeded expectations. Her daily run for September 9 was 556 miles, which she bettered the following day by an additional 19 miles. The weather was perfect. Each evening in the First Class Lounge her passengers gathered in the time-honored ritual of the ship's auction. The chief purser read the last day's run, the weather reports for the following day, and the average revolutions of the *Lusitania*'s engines. Passengers then bid on and purchased numbers representing predicted runs for the following day: 560 miles, 580 miles, and so on. So confident were they of their wondrous ship and her turbines that the most expensive number auctioned was inevitably that of High

Field, meaning that the ship would exceed all predicted distances. On September 11, she did. The *Lusitania*'s run for that day was an astonishing 593 miles, an average speed of 24.08 knots. She had traveled faster and farther in a single day than any ship in history. That night the bidding for High Field—greater than the highest estimate of daily miles logged—was as intense and exorbitant as for a Fabergé egg. But then misfortune struck. September 12 dawned gray and cold, with a thick fog blanketing the ship. There was a collective groan as passengers stared out their portholes at the empty white blankness and heard the long mournful bellow of the ship's foghorn. Some even tore up their auction numbers and tossed them over the side. Heeding Cunard's motto, Captain Watt reluctantly slowed the engines to three-quarterspeed. The *Lusitania* limped into New York on Friday the 13th, having completed the passage in 5 days, 54 minutes at an average speed of 23.01 knots. She missed beating the record by a scant half-hour.

The British journals responded to this news with a heroic display of stiff-upper-lip fortitude. "It is not right to compare her mean speed on her first voyage with the 23.15 knots of the record-breaking *Deutschland*," said *Marine Engineer*. "It were better to look at it in relation to the recent addition to the NDL fleet. Thus it will be seen," the journal went on, making the best of a bad situation, "that the *Kronprinzessin Cecilie* only attained a speed of 21.81 knots on her maiden trip and was thus beaten by the *Lusitania* by 1.25 knots. It would seem to all reasonable observers that the new ship has done quite as well as anyone had a right to expect and certainly as well it was advisable for her to do so." For those observers who might still remain unconvinced in response to all this spurious praise, *Marine Engineer* offered its own typically British homily: "Great speed on maiden voyages means constant trouble with machinery in later life."

This was all very well, but it was not what the British public or their government wanted to hear. They had, together, paid over two million pounds for these luxury liners, and they did not do so for the dubious distinction of having the second-fastest ships in the world. Denied any other outlet, the journals reverted to the ship's unparalleled luxury. "Of the hundreds of passengers who made a successful trip in her on this memorable maiden voyage," *Marine Engineer* went on, "how many could truthfully say that they had ever had so luxurious a time in their lives? Probably it would be found that passengers of every class, even the cheapest, were enjoying unaccustomed luxuries and comforts." Here was the first inkling that the standards of victory in the Atlantic race might be changing from speed to opulence—that change would come in earnest, and sooner than anyone yet imagined. But in 1907 the ultimate issue was still, as it had always been, speed. Having exhausted all else, the journal finally trotted out patriotism. "For the *Lusitania* is of British design and construction; she is owned and manned by our fellow countrymen. There has been much regret in many peoples' mind that for so long the palm of speed in the Atlantic, so long a British possession, has been enjoyed by vessels flying a foreign flag. But all that will be changed. . . . We may be sure that when she gets settled down and opportunity offers, the *Lusitania* will more than fulfill expectations and will prove as profitable to her owners as she is creditable to those who produced her." This was cold comfort indeed, for those same owners and builders were even now contemplating the wrath of all those who had invested so much in the *Lusitania*'s turbines.

Yet all this angst was for naught. On her second westbound crossing, clear weather and a light breeze gave free rein to the *Lusitania*'s engines, and they proved once and for all their superior design. From Daunts Rock in Queenstown, Ireland, to Sandy Hook outside New York Harbor, the *Lusitania* traversed the 2,780 miles in 4 days, 19 hours, 52 minutes, an average speed of 23.993 knots. When the victory of the ship became certain to her passengers, a nighttime concert was interrupted in favor of speechmaking. Several Americans rose and congratulated the captain on this immense achievement. "The lion," said one, "is again master of the ocean highway."

Germany handled this defeat with remarkable good grace. Though Albert Ballin stormed about his Hamburg office and denounced the government loan to build the *Lusitania* as shameless and unfair sponsorship (he himself had tried to secure a similar loan from the German government, and failed), it was not his ship that had been beaten. Instead, Norddeutscher Lloyd, whose record had been bested, deputized their New York manager Gustav Schwab to present the heartiest congratulations of the line to Cunard and to the *Lusitania*. Schwab handled the difficult task with aplomb. "The *Lusitania* is undoubtedly a wonderful steamer and she has made a splendid record," he told an assembly of New York journalists. "I am going today to congratulate Mr. Vernon Brown of the Cunard Company and, figuratively speaking, incidentally to hand him the Blue Riband of the Atlantic which the Norddeutscher Lloyd has held for several years. Of course," he went on, with dignified solemnity, "it is with regret that the Norddeutscher Lloyd parts with this ribbon which is the emblem of speed and superiority at sea, but in giving it up we have the consolation of knowing that there is only one steamer in the world which is faster than our *Kaiser Wilhelm II*. It is better to have held and lost the record than never to have held it at all."

A more realistic response than Schwab's paraphrasing of love and loss was that of the German engineers who swarmed aboard the vessel at her New York pier. They at once set up cameras and began taking photographs of the interiors, the passageways, and machinery. Imitation being the highest form of flattery, the ship's engineers and officers looked on indulgently. In fact, they were delighted. As Cunard's chairman later explained, "I believe our engineers are justified in their pride because we have the spectacle of our maritime rivals taking notes and photographs of interesting things and thus following all their derogatory opinions directed against the turbine engine."

The race for the Atlantic was once again being led by the British, and everyone eagerly awaited the next contender. The *Mauretania* was not ready for her maiden voyage until November 16, by which time the weather had chilled sharply. On the cold, wet day when she left her pier, some fifty thousand spectators (a sharp drop from the *Lusitania*, but still considerable given the conditions) saw her off. Certain subtle changes had been made to the ship's propulsion, which it was hoped would give her a slight lead over her sister. More rows of blades had been fitted to her turbines, and the diameter of her propellers was six inches greater. As if to underscore the latent power contained within her hull, the *Turbinia* was brought alongside for an historic photograph. The contrast between the two vessels was almost comical, like a circus freakshow in which Mrs. Tom Thumb is posed next to a gigantic Baby Huey. The whole of the *Turbinia*'s length scarcely covered the distance from the *Mauretania*'s mainmast to her bridge. Her funnel only barely cleared the liner's boottop, still well below its first row of portholes. The unspoken caption was immediately obvious: if the tiny little *Turbinia* with her homemade engines could still be the fastest vessel afloat, what on earth would the 43,000 horsepower, two-story high dynamos of the *Mauretania* achieve?

The *Mauretania* departed Liverpool for the first time with a British princess, an American multimillionaire named Drexel, and twelve tons of gold bullion valued at £2,750,000. "We'll lick the Lucy," said one of the stokers with grim certainty, "even if we bust the Mary to do it!" But once again the weather intervened. The first day of brilliant sunshine between Liverpool and Queenstown was followed by two days of fog and heavy seas. A crosswind battered the ship, driving mountainous waves over her forepeak and wrenching free one of her spare anchors. The liner was not at her best. One correspondent for the *London Times* later commented circumspectly, "As regards rolling also the *Mauretania* is extremely steady in quiet weather, but with a high sea she is capable of an immense but very slow roll—the sort of roll which sends palms in tubs clattering down the companionway, though it is too slow to compel any but the poorest sailors to follow them below."

The storm lifted, but any chance of capturing the Blue Riband was lost. Almost defiantly, the *Mauretania* logged 624 miles in a single day's run, beating the *Lusitania*'s record by six miles. Then a curtain of fog descended, and Captain Pritchard ordered the engines slowed. An angry delegation of Americans discussed the possibility of "compelling" the captain to increase speed, but fortunately nothing came of it. The *Mauretania* entered New York in 5 days, 5 hours, 10 minutes, an average speed of 22.21 knots. On her return voyage, however, she raced back in 4 days, 22 hours, 29 minutes, beating the *Lusitania* by a mere 24 minutes. It was a small margin, but still a victory. The *Mauretania* was now the fastest ship in the world.

In the months that followed, the *Lusitania* and *Mauretania* traded the speed record back and forth between them. Ultimately, however, the *Mauretania* proved faster by a significant margin. Her record run, achieved in 1909, would not be exceeded for an incredible twenty years. Her superior speed and the cozy luxury of her interiors would always make the *Mauretania* the favorite of the two sisters. Several authors have written of the maritime "canonization" of certain ships, which through their long careers transcended the mechanical and commercial aspects of their existence and became, in effect, living entities. The *Mauretania* was such a ship, and the *Lusitania* was not. Though the latter's career would be cut tragically short in 1915, passengers had already long preferred the other vessel. That is not to say that the *Lusitania* was not popular or successful; she was both. But the *Mauretania* was an extraordinarily well-built ship, perhaps the best example of marine construction in history. From 1909 to 1911, three years in which she saw some of the heaviest service of her career, she was never taken into dry dock. Minor repairs or alterations were made in the brief turnarounds at New York and Liverpool. Moreover, her engines were of such remarkable quality that as late as 1930, when she was twenty-three years old, she bettered her own best time in a valiant though unsuccessful attempt to take back the Blue Riband. Even when scrapped in the late 1930s, her engines were still capable of many years of further service.

Like the proud owners of a thoroughbred race horse, the Cunard Line constantly looked for new ways to demonstrate the *Mauretania*'s incredible speed. On August 30, 1909, she departed New York exactly twenty-four hours after the *Kaiser Wilhelm der Grosse*. Four days, 14 hours, 27 minutes later, she arrived in the Welsh port of Fishguard. The *Kaiser Wilhelm der Grosse* had reached Plymouth a scant four hours earlier. Signal guns saluted the British liner, and the normal customs routines were hastily completed. The *Mauretania*'s passengers reached London by train in time for dinner; the *Kaiser Wilhelm der Grosse*'s, having left New York a full day earlier, had arrived in time for lunch.

Cunard again created a stir when it announced in December of 1910 that the *Mauretania* would make the trip from Liverpool to New York and return in an unprecedented twelve days. German shipowners scoffed. Winter in the North Atlantic was feared as the most dangerous season of the year, with its notorious storms, gales, fogs, blizzards, and icebergs.

No ship had ever attempted a twelve-day round trip, and to do so in December would be the height of folly. The *Mauretania*'s Captain Turner, a nervous man in the best of circumstances, was nearly beside himself with anxiety. The first leg of the voyage was, as one reporter termed it, "eventful and tempestuous." Snowstorms buffeted the ship, sometimes as many as six in one day; the motion of the ship in heavy seas was such that "many ladies found it prudent to keep to their cabins for the greater part of the voyage." Still, despite everything, the *Mauretania* reached New York in respectable though not remarkable time. She entered the Hudson a "veritable Christmas ship," her decks coated with glittering ice and snow. After a breakneck pit stop in the Cunard dock, during which the *Mauretania* was loaded with food and coaled with lightning speed, she was ready to sail in less than twenty-four hours. A huge crowd gathered on the West Side pier to send her off. Turner gave the order for reverse, and the ship backed gently away. A flotilla of tugs turned her around, and the order was given "slow ahead." "Then with a gentle vibration from stem to stern the mighty engines began throbbing and the *Mauretania* leaped forward on the first stage of the long ocean flight," said the *Daily Telegraph* correspondent. "It was the noisiest send-off ever witnessed here. Thousands of people ashore cheered the Christmas vessel, and all the way down New York Bay, craft of all nations, with foghorns and steam sirens took part in speeding the departing liner."

It was a tremendous gamble for the Cunard Line. The firm, which prided itself on "safety above all," had sent out their finest vessel in the worst season of the year, into an Atlantic strewn with icebergs, to achieve a speed record that none before had attempted. In just a few years such reckless bravado would seem to challenge the fates themselves. But, in this instance, the luck of the line and its flagship held. Unseasonably good weather prevailed, and the *Mauretania* reached Fishguard, Wales, just before midnight on December 22. She had achieved the run in exactly twelve days.

The race for the Atlantic was reaching fever pitch. The *Lusitania* and *Mauretania* had wrested supremacy on the seas from the Germans so fully and completely that the *Kaiser Wilhelm der Grosse* and her progeny were swiftly being relegated—by the British, at least—to the status of a brief interregnum in the greater history of steamship travel. That history, it now seemed, would be forever written by the victorious British. Feats of technological triumph like the twelve-day Christmas run were met with an uncritical enthusiasm, everyone quite forgetting that the North Atlantic was not merely a great placid highway to be traversed at will. The warning of one editorial writer, written in 1890 before the race had truly begun, was now utterly forgotten: "Some of these days one of these record breakers will break a record he does not wish to break," he had predicted, "and then, too late, a howl will go up over the whole civilized world of the criminal folly of driving steamers at full speed through dense fogs and waters filled with icebergs."

Such sentiments seemed obsolete after the *Mauretania*'s triumph. Superior construction would carry the day no matter what hazards the ocean provided. But Keble Chatterton, for one, remained uneasy about the growing distance between ship and sea. "Cover them with tier upon tier of decks . . . " he wrote, "throw in a few electric cranes, a coal mine, several restaurants, the population of a large sized village . . . give them a length equal to that of the Houses of Parliament, a height greater than the buildings in Northumberland Avenue, disguise them in any way you please, and for all that these are *ships*, which have to obey the laws of Nature, of the Great Sea, just as the first sailing ship and the first Atlantic steamship had to show their submission."

Across the Atlantic, Lloyd manager Gustav Schwab also voiced his concern. Looking out his Manhattan window at the rows of gigantic liners tied to their piers, dwarfing the buildings and sheds around them, he felt he was looking at the final, finished product of the Industrial Revolution "There is a limit to all development," he said. "The limit for steamships has almost been reached."

He was wrong.

IN THE SMOKING ROOM OF A GREAT ATLANTIC LINER IN APRIL 1912, three men sat talking. It was nearly 11 P.M., and the cheerful, busy sounds of a ship in midocean had diminished, leaving only the muted hum of conversation and the dull throb of turbines. The smoking room, an elegant Jacobean creation of hardwoods and Moroccan leather chairs, was often compared in style and function to a superior London club. Now it resembled one more than ever: stewards busily emptying ashtrays, a lit fire burning merrily in the grate, several old men ensconced in their wing-back chairs in deep, well-fed somnolence. The discussion had gone on for some time, spanning the usual gamut of business, politics, and ailments. In America, former President Theodore Roosevelt had returned from relative obscurity—and

Africa—and was now embroiled in a spirited attempt to unseat his former friend and protégé and now bitter rival William Howard Taft in the forthcoming presidential election. In England, Prime Minister H. H. Asquith had just introduced the Irish Home Rule Bill to Parliament, where it was met with much consternation and dire warnings of revolution. Emmeline Pankhurst and her suffragette allies were busily chaining themselves to various London monuments, clamoring for the vote. It was a time of momentous political change, and the conversation in the smoking room that evening was significantly colored by the fact that many of the names on the First Class passenger list were responsible for those changes.

Perhaps inevitably, however, the talk wound its way back to transportation. For this was still a ship and, despite its pretensions, that elegant Mayfair club was now hurtling at more than 21 knots through a vast expanse of empty sea. One man at the table who was particularly well informed on the subject was Charles M. Hays, president of the Canadian Grand Trunk Railway. One of the forgotten heroes of monopolistic capitalism, Hays was deeply engaged in a battle of his own: breaking the Morgan stranglehold on East Coast railway service. In a bold sweep that would have impressed old J.P. himself—had he not been at the receiving end—Hays proposed to construct a combination sea-and-rail direct service between New York and Montreal. The overnight ferries of the Fall River Line would take patrons in silken splendor from New York to Massachusetts, where they would connect with Grand Trunk pullmans waiting at the pier. It was the first such proposal of its kind, a sort of "through bill of lading" for people instead of cargo, and would place Hays and his railway in direct competition with Morgan's formidable, but circuitous, New Haven Railway.

On this night, however, Hays waxed philosophic. His last few weeks had been spent traveling through Europe studying the hotel business with an eye to similar operations in North America. He had seen there firsthand the rising tide of competing nationalism, that toxic antipathy between England and Germany that still concealed itself within expressions of mutual accord, and he was currently seated within the latest and most grandiose manifestation of the rivalries. The liner that now bore Hays swiftly toward New York was the ultimate expression of seagoing luxury, a miracle of engineering and appointments.

Hays had just enjoyed a particularly fine Continental dinner served with meticulous perfection by the mostly French staff of the ship's à la carte restaurant; his wife was taking her ease in the elegantly appointed Louis XVI drawing room. A swimming pool, gymnasium, and Turkish bath were available, should either feel the desire to indulge. Two decks below, a First Class suite with brass beds, oriental rugs, and steam heat awaited them when they wished to retire. Yet Hays felt oddly discomfited. Leaning back in his chair and waving his cigar for emphasis, he addressed his tablemates with uncharacteristic intensity. "The White Star, the Cunard, and the Hamburg-Amerika lines," Hays told them, "are now devoting their attention to a struggle for supremacy in obtaining the most luxurious appointments for their ships. But—the time will soon come when the greatest and most appalling of all disasters at sea will be the result."

Three hours later the *Titanic*'s stern hung perpendicular above the surface, propellers glinting wet against the cloudless night. Among those still clinging futilely to its rails was Charles M. Hays.

-7-

Titans

THE BRIDGE WING OF A LINER JUTS OUT OVER THE SHIP'S FLANK, SEEMINGLY suspended in midair. Cantilevered above the sea, it is one of the highest and most secluded parts of the ship, and at night, it's ethereal. The ship disappears. The light from the portholes cannot reach the wing. The rumble of the turbines is drowned out by the rushing of wind. There is nothing to suggest that you are actually standing above 45,000 tons of moving steel or that 800 feet of lounges, cabins, dining rooms, and swimming baths trail behind. The stars seem not above but around, and unnaturally bright. The ceaseless, steady roar of the wind lifts the body and cushions it. The sea is a black void far, far below, as glinting rivulets of waves approach and disappear with incredible speed. At that moment, a captain once said, the world becomes perfect and serene. You are invincible, dominant, a master of the universe. You are flying.

Searching for a metaphor to describe the minds that conceived the *Titanic* and sent her charging full speed through an ice field in the dead of night, one is drawn back to that image. The *Titanic*'s master, Captain E. J. Smith, must have experienced it himself, gazing out over the horizon on that cold April evening. But so too did the *Titanic*'s builders, designers, owners, and passengers; that feeling is, in fact, a metaphor for the age. The Edwardian era produced a breed of men who believed that technology, ambition, and capital—in proper balance— could bend the world to suit their fancy. Nothing was impossible; everything was absolute. They met ravages of nature with the same benign tolerance and faint condescension that they would feel toward an unruly tribe of savages: interesting, but irrelevant. Natural law itself was but a challenge to human ingenuity; rivers existed for men to build bridges across them. In the *Titanic*, this attitude found its apogee. A steel ship, like an airplane, is a refutation of nature. Unlike its wooden forbears, it is not inherently buoyant. It floats instead by a strange mathematical jumble of displacement laws, volume, and marine physics. Common sense suggests that, as anything heavier than air should not be able to fly, anything heavier than water should sink. But by 1912, the Edwardians had not only forgotten the physical laws buttressing their creations, they had practically forgotten the creations themselves. Like the captain on his bridge wing, they soared above the earth in perfect serenity. Like him, they forgot that this flight was merely an illusion; they did not heed nor care about the balance of physics and machinery that sustained it. Worst of all, they did not realize how fragile that balance was.

The *Titanic* disaster has often been regarded as an act of retribution for the arrogance of man, either by a vengeful God or indifferent Nature. Fire-and-brimstone Christians claim her size and luxury were an affront to the Almighty, leading to the popular phrase, "Man proposes, but God disposes." For those of a more classical temperament, the *Titanic*'s alleged unsinkability was a challenge to the Fates. Some even believe the *Titanic* was cursed. Mrs. Henry Harris, a First Class passenger, was approached by a stranger on the boat deck who grabbed her arm—like Coleridge's wild-eyed Ancient Mariner—and told her that the ship suffered under bad omens. "Do you love your life?" the man asked her. "I love it," she answered. "Then get off this ship at Cherbourg," said the man.

All this is utter nonsense. The *Titanic* was neither the largest ship ever built nor even the largest of her age: the unfinished and unregistered German *Imperator* had her beat by almost 6,000 tons. She was no more an affront to God than her sister the *Olympic* would have been, and—if we're to equate gross tonnage with damnation—considerably less than Carnival Line's current 100,000-ton flagship *Fascination* or Cunard's 150,000-ton *Queen Mary 2*, which made her maiden transatlantic voyage in January 2004. The *Titanic* disaster was not a divine smiting; it was the inevitable result of twenty years' overextension past the technological and social limitations of the time. Nor was the *Titanic* a singular offender: her size and pretensions had already been surpassed, all great liners shared the fatal flaws in her construction, and the manner in which she was handled was standard practice among all company captains. What the *Titanic* did have, unquestionably, was the terrible luck of being in the wrong place at the wrong time when the overreaching confidence of the age reaped its gruesome harvest. Seen in its proper context, the *Titanic*'s fate was not an anachronism, but the product of a race between nations that had escalated wildly out of control.

Olympian Visions

By 1909, competition between the British and the Germans had produced a fleet of ocean liners whose size and power were vastly out of scale with the rest of society. Other means of transport grew slowly, haltingly; the Ford Model T of 1908 was still in production in 1920. Before the turn of the century, shipbuilding had proceeded apace. Since the advent of the first German wonder ships, however, their growth became exponential. Gross tonnage of a flagship doubled between 1897 and 1907; in the six years between the *Kronprinzessin Cecilie* (1906) and the *Imperator* (1912–1913), it tripled. The average length of a ship expanded from 400 to 900 feet. The docks of Liverpool, Hamburg, Southampton, and New York were repeatedly dredged to accommodate these new leviathans.

The two men most responsible for this explosion were the British White Star Line chairman J. Bruce Ismay and German Hamburg-Amerika Line chairman Albert Ballin. Even before Cunard's *Lusitania* and *Mauretania* made their first transatlantic crossings in 1907, Ismay had envisioned a *trio* of superliners to surpass them. The idea emerged at a dinner party hosted by Lord James Pirrie, the elderly and venerable partner of the Irish shipyard Harland & Wolff. Pirrie and Ismay were old friends, but unusual ones. Harland & Wolff had built every White Star liner since Thomas H. Ismay commissioned his company's first ship, the *Oceanic*, in 1870. It was Thomas who had toured the Kaiser around the White Star liner *Teutonic* twenty years earlier, igniting the race between them. It was Thomas as well who had single-handedly transformed White Star from a mediocre passenger-freight carrier into the second-largest steamship company of the age, Cunard's only serious rival in England. But Ismay senior retired in 1893, leaving the company to his son, Bruce, and died in 1899. One year later, in a move that would have made the old man apoplectic, J. P. Morgan purchased White Star. Yet even after selling out to Morgan, J. Bruce Ismay remained very much the image of the company president.

Tall, thin, and arrogant, with a full set of imperial mustaches and a Guardsman's posture, Ismay was a Hollywood producer's ideal of an English gentleman. But a sharper eye would note that the clothes were just a little too new, the manner a little too affected. Ismay lived under the curse that befalls countless first-born sons; he was not the man his father was. Worse yet, his deficiencies were well known. Thomas Ismay had a reputation for gruff integrity, great business acumen, and a singular lack of tact. His son, educated at Harrow and Oxford and a competent sportsman and man-about-town, was just a trifle effete. One story, oft repeated, was that when he returned from one of his six-month-long jaunts around the world, Ismay dropped by the White Star headquarters and left his coat and hat in his father's office. His father, knowing full well to whom the garments belonged, instructed a subordinate in a loud, clear voice to tell the new office boy to leave his damned coat someplace else.

In the years following the I.M.M. purchase, it seemed to Ismay as though he had merely moved from the shadow of one great man into that of another. Though Morgan was far too astute—and preoccupied—to meddle in the day-to-day business of steamship travel, his august presence hovered over White Star. Worse still, the company had suffered a sharp drop in fortunes since the death of the elder Ismay. Its last record-breaker had been the *Oceanic* of 1899, which had by now been so eclipsed by its Norddeutscher Lloyd competitors that it seemed, at the age of ten, almost decrepit. When Cunard released drawings of its stunning *Mauretania* and *Lusitania* in 1905, White Star had receded further into obsolescence. The company seemed doomed to go the way of Collins, Smith, Inman, and all others that had dared to challenge mighty Cunard.

Thus the man whose sleek white Mercedes now rolled into Lord Pirrie's driveway was proud, arrogant, perhaps a little stupid, and deeply worried. Lord Pirrie, in contrast, was a genial Irish gnome. Short and squat with a bristly white beard and a mischievous twinkle, he managed the massive building yards at Belfast with a fatherly discipline. Dinners such as this were invariably trials for Pirrie's guests, as his lordship suffered from the cold and ordered massive fires stoked in the dining room regardless of season. Then he would sit at one end of a huge table, swathed from head to foot in rugs. Lady Pirrie sat at the opposite end, flushed and fanning herself, complaining to all who would listen about the heat.

Pirrie and the elder Ismay had been great friends, and their friendship had cemented a unique business relationship, an arrangement that supplied a new White Star vessel from the Harland & Wolff yards almost annually. Thus, when young Bruce arrived at Pirrie's magnificent London home, the old man greeted him with fatherly affection. As no record was kept of this historic meeting, we can only speculate on its exact course. One rumor was that Ismay sketched the rough outline for three new liners on the back of a cocktail napkin. This is highly unlikely, as it is doubtful that Lord Pirrie would supply his guests with paper napkins. What is known, however, is that at some point during the evening Ismay and Pirrie resolved to build the three largest ships ever conceived to that time, inaugurating the first weekly service from New York to Southampton in Atlantic history. These ships would be nearly identical, differing only in slight decorative additions that could be amended during construction. They would surpass the *Lusitania* and *Mauretania*, making White Star preeminent on the Atlantic. Ismay justified them to Pirrie on strictly business grounds: the largest and most luxurious ships would, as a matter of course, garner the greatest share of passenger traffic. But old Pirrie was not fooled. Ismay, under his gentlemanly veneer, harbored a dark passion remarkably akin to that of Kaiser Wilhelm II, reflecting the same feelings of self-doubt, inferiority, and arrogance that drove the Emperor to greater and greater flights of maritime fancy. Just as the Kaiser's fleet would be his revenge on the English for Cowes, the White Star trio would be J. Bruce Ismay's revenge on a world that derided him for being his father's son, built on a scale that old Thomas Ismay could never have dreamed.

By the time Ismay's Mercedes rolled out of the drive, the plan was settled. Three ships would be built, two almost in tandem with a third to follow the next year. They would surpass the Cunarders in every respect save one, speed. Let the "Lucy" and the "Mary" break their backs streaking across the Atlantic, Ismay said carelessly. People didn't really care if they reached New York three hours earlier. What people wanted—at least, *rich* people—was to cross the Atlantic in a fashion as similar as possible to their home lives. That meant luxury and, as the Germans would phrase it, lebensraum. The defining characteristic of wealth on both sides of the Atlantic was personal space. Gilt alone was not enough. In Newport, Rhode Island, millionaires built summer "cottages" that more resembled New York's Grand Central Terminal than their shack-and-shingle namesakes. On the Atlantic, Ismay envisioned ships that carried their passengers in a comfort identical to that to which they were accustomed ashore. This meant bigger public rooms, added amenities like squash courts and swimming pools, and added tonnage in marble, gilt, and paneling. Overall, it meant ignoring the old seaman's adage that a ship exceeding 40,000 gross tons would overwhelm the delicate balance of displacement and buoyancy and sink like a stone. The plans, drawn up weeks later, called for three near-sister ships, each exceeding 45,000 tons. In a flight of metaphoric fancy, Ismay named them *Olympic*, *Titanic*, and *Gigantic*. The intention was obvious: Ismay wished to convey the awesome size and potency of his creations, a not-so-subtle snub to his nemeses in Hamburg, Bremen, and Liverpool.

Each of the names had mythological origins. *Olympic* was taken from the legendary Mount Olympus, from the summit of which Zeus and his entourage were said to view and rule all the earth. The name conjured up images of lofty and exclusive heights above lesser mortals.

Titanic came from the Titans, a mythical race of giants who challenged the gods to all-out war, and lost; the crash of their bodies into the earth created mountains and valleys. It suggested size, strength, and virility. About the last, *Gigantic*, there is some controversy. When she emerged in 1914, two years after the *Titanic* disaster, this third and largest liner carried the less pretentious name *Britannic*. It has been suggested by some that this was her intended name all along, although there is some reason to doubt that. The very purpose of giving ships such exaggerated titles would be lost if all three did not follow suit.

The construction of two 45,000-ton liners simultaneously in the same yard was a technological feat never before attempted. The most extraordinary thing about the *Olympic* and *Titanic*, indeed, was not their size, but rather the speed and manner in which they were built. Laid down in 1908, the *Olympic* sailed in early 1911. This in itself would not be remarkable were it not for the fact that her sister *Titanic* took shape right alongside her and was ready for delivery less than a year later. It was the first time any shipyard had attempted to build two sister ships at once, not to mention that these were the two largest ships ever ordered. The logistical challenge was enormous. Every order of steel plate was doubled, every piece of machinery, from winch caps to turbines, was made in duplicate. The *Olympic* and *Titanic* were almost identical, the two major differences being the enclosed promenade deck and Café Parisien—another White Star novelty—on the *Titanic*.

In 1908, the same year that *Olympic*'s keel was laid, the Ford Motor Company made history by introducing its mass-produced Model T. Not until the advent of the Liberty Ship more than thirty years later would this method be successfully adapted to shipbuilding. Harland & Wolff's double order of *Olympic* and *Titanic* deserves historical credit as the first attempt at applying assembly-line principles to ocean liner construction. It still remains the most ambitious endeavor of its kind; while sister ships are common, no other passenger line has since attempted to build them simultaneously at the same yard.

But this ambitious feat of engineering had its darker side. While shipbuilders Harland & Wolff in Belfast scrambled to complete their mammoth order, the rest of society lagged behind. The furious pace of shipbuilding set by J. Bruce Ismay overwhelmed the three entities most responsible for insuring the *Titanic's* safety: the captain who sailed her, the lawmakers and regulators who governed her, and the engineers who built her. First, captains such as the *Titanic's* E. J. Smith—most of whom had begun their careers on tea clippers—simply could not understand the size of their new ships. They handled them the same as ships half the size, with terrible results. And second, the laws governing lifesaving procedures and requirements were woefully outdated, written for ships carrying less than half the passenger and crew complement of the *Titanic.* Strange accidents in the early years of the *Olympic's* career, including the accidental ramming of the Royal Navy cruiser *Hawke,* sounded the warning. But in the *Titanic,* all these deficiencies coalesced.

"The Olympic Is a Marvel!"

The seeds of the *Titanic* disaster were sown almost exactly one year before, in May 1911. In that month occurred three important events in English history: George V was crowned King of England, the completed *Olympic* was handed over to her owners for sea trials, and—on the same day, May 31, 1911—the great glistening hull of the *Titanic* was launched from her Belfast yard. It was a red-letter day for the White Star Line and J. Bruce Ismay. The timing was anything but accidental; by delivering one sister and launching another, Ismay sent a smug message of victory to his rivals. It was all the more apparent from the manner of the launching. White Star traditionally eschewed grand affairs when launching their ships: unlike Cunard and the Germans, it refrained from the usual ceremonial champagne, brass bands, and speeches. When the *Olympic* had been launched seven months earlier, in October 1910, signal flags spelling "SUCCESS" were draped across her bows and a single rocket arched into the sky. It was a grim, cold day.

The *Titanic's* launching, in contrast, had the aura of a village fête, taking place under pleasant spring skies, with several grandstands erected to corral the multitudes. Specially chartered Belfast trolleys deposited an ever-increasing horde of day-trippers to view the spectacle. Members of the press were awarded a place of honor near the bow. Three rockets were fired. Under a giant marquee stood Lord and Lady

Pirrie, Mr. and Mrs. J. Bruce Ismay, the Lord Mayor of Belfast (with topper and chain of office), and J. Pierpont Morgan. Morgan had made a special crossing aboard the *Adriatic* to attend the launching. It was a brief bright moment in a dismal year. His interests were assailed on all sides by competitors and the U.S. government; the replacement of Theodore Roosevelt with fat and genial William Howard Taft had made precious little difference to him or his company. Even I.M.M., once lauded as the cornerstone of the Morgan empire, was failing. The firm had never quite recovered from its failure to purchase Cunard, and without its raison d'être—unfettered and uncontested control of the Atlantic seaway—puttered along sluggishly as a distant third behind Cunard and Norddeutscher Lloyd. But the White Star superships would, Morgan hoped, alter his fortunes for the better. Perhaps, after their success, I.M.M. might again be in a position to challenge the monolithic Cunard. Morgan stared benignly at the great black hull before him, in which so much of himself had been invested. He had already selected an A-deck suite, yet to be built, for his personal use.

Contrary to popular myth, there was no formal christening. At 12:13 the hull began to move, and a cheer went up. Seconds later the *Titanic* was afloat, straining against the long chains that tethered her to shore as tugs blew their whistles in salute. Three hours later Pirrie, Ismay, and Morgan boarded the *Olympic* and sailed for Liverpool to begin her trials.

The *Olympic*'s maiden voyage took place two weeks later. Morgan and Ismay were both passengers. It was late spring, and the weather for the crossing was ideal. The pleasant conditions attracted a select coterie of international luminaries, and representatives of both the English and American press were on hand to cable details of the trip to those less fortunate on the shore. Indeed, the maiden voyage progressed along much the same lines as the *Titanic*'s should have. In all the unremitting reams of literature devoted to the aborted first crossing of her sister, there's virtually no mention that nearly the same cast of characters had assembled on a near-identical ship ten months before, with all the attending hoopla in the newspapers. On board the *Olympic*, as on her sister, her designer Thomas Andrews used the maiden voyage to iron out the kinks common to all new ships, and the crew—many of whom would later serve on the *Titanic*—settled into the routine of running their new ship. E. J. Smith, the de facto commodore of the White Star fleet, transferred from the *Adriatic* to take command. A surviving photograph shows Smith and Lord Pirrie conferring under the shadow of the *Olympic*'s enormous funnels, the very image of two men in complete mastery of their surroundings. J. P. Morgan kept aloof, speaking only with Smith, Pirrie, and Ismay and sending and receiving cables through the ship's wireless. Ismay was less reclusive: Like Albert Ballin on his own ships, Ismay kept a diary on the *Olympic*'s maiden voyage, writing both from personal experience and from overheard conversations in the lounge (he was a shameless eavesdropper). Ismay's memoranda were a veritable catalog of woe: the beds were too springy; there were no cigar holders in the bathrooms (a revealing statement about Edwardian toilet habits); the best cabins lacked private promenades; the galley should have a potato peeler. Almost a year later, on another maiden voyage, this pettifogging intrusiveness would brand him a pariah. Allegations that he had acted as the *Titanic*'s "super-captain" hounded Ismay the rest of his life. But on the *Olympic*, J. Bruce Ismay stood at the very pinnacle of his power and prestige. It was quite possibly the greatest moment of his life. Despite his incessant fault-finding, Ismay cabled back exuberantly to his shareholders, "The *Olympic* is a marvel!"

Indeed she was. The *Olympic* was 882 feet long, 92 feet wide, with a gross tonnage of 45,324 tons. Her draft was 37 feet. She carried 2,764 passengers: 1,054 First Class, 510 Second Class, and 1,200 in Steerage. It was the first time a ship's First Class complement nearly equaled her Third Class. The *Lusitania*, in contrast, carried only 560 First compared to her 1,300 Steerage. The *Olympic* was indeed the clarion call of a new era and a new kind of liner: the "millionaires' ship." From then onward, the standard of excellence on the North Atlantic would shift from speed to luxury. That the *Mauretania* would hold her speed record for an incredible twenty-two years was as much a testament to these changing values as to her engines. Both British and German ships abandoned the restraints of taste and functionality in favor of sybaritic one-upmanship.

Yet, as with most statistics, the *Olympic*'s dimensions can only be fully appreciated in comparison with her peers. The greatest German liner of the time, the *Kaiser Wilhelm II* of 1903, had a gross tonnage of

19,361 and a length of 707 feet. The *Lusitania* and *Mauretania* shared a tonnage of roughly 32,000 and a length of 790 feet. By eschewing that extra knot of service speed that had won the *Mauretania* her record, White Star gained an additional 15,000 tons and an extra hundred feet of living space. Contrasts between *Olympic's* appointments and those of Cunard and German ships were inevitable—and welcomed. The lounges and dining rooms were vastly oversized outclassing the *Mauretania's* staid and sensible Adam paneling with a glittering explosion of Louis XVI décor. The *Olympic* and her sisters borrowed from HAPAG the idea of an extra tariff restaurant, which was termed the Grill Room. As in the Ritz-Carlton grill aboard the *Amerika*, White Star passengers were provided with an exclusive haven where private parties could be held without fear of interruption by vulgarians. It was perhaps for this reason that the regular First Class dining rooms aboard the *Olympic* and *Titanic* were less than inspired. Though White Star had learned from the *Lusitania's* stunning success and fitted out the room with the same white walls, trim, and curves, it was distressingly low-ceilinged. The one novelty, however, was the installation of green-leather dining chairs with high arms that sat loose on the carpeted floor; in all previous ships, including the Cunard sisters, the chairs had been bolted to the floor in a strange, rather archaic holdover from the mid-nineteenth century.

Two other architectural features distinguished the *Olympic* from her predecessors. The first became apparent once White Star released its advance photos of the ship as she was fitted out. In marked contrast to the profusion of ventilators, winches, davits, and lifeboats on the *Mauretania*, the boat deck of the new White Star ships provided a clear expanse of teak, rails, and sea. Where determined strollers were once forced to dodge through a veritable obstacle course of machinery, they now enjoyed a serenely unencumbered promenade. Lifesaving equipment was nestled discreetly, almost negligently, in the forward and aft portions of each ship. It was startling and, later, ominous.

The second was a newfound attention to a sound mind in a healthy body. Previously, British ships of the *Campania* variety assumed that their passengers would be engaged primarily in idling and, to recall Cunard's flowery prose, "dolce far niente." The Atlantic voyage was seen as an opportunity to catch up on one's reading, enjoy the salutary effects of sea air on the boat deck, play cards and gossip with one's shipmates, and—of course—eat. Hence, the days between Liverpool and New York were whiled away in a sort of languid boredom. The new Norddeutscher Lloyd liners had changed all that, introducing deck games, competitions, sporting events, and gymnasiums. Passengers were encouraged to moderate the idleness of sea travel with brief bursts of frenetic activity. The experiment was a resounding success. Consequently, when Ismay pondered what additional luxuries might set the *Olympic* and *Titanic* apart from their peers, he happened upon a unique combination of German sports and English idle relaxation, and the seagoing spa was born. It was not called that, naturally, but rather consisted of four separate elements located in different parts of the ship: the gymnasium, the squash courts, the swimming pool, and the Turkish bath.

Such titles sound grand while implying the notion of hard exercise, but that was not the case. Rather than providing a place for passengers to work off their Sunday dinners, as the German liners proposed to do, the amenities on board the White Star ships were designed instead to give the *illusion* of exercise, when in fact they required little more exertion from their patrons than the ship's writing room. The gymnasium was a case in point: Each of its machines was a product of the worst excesses of late-Victorian faddism, including muscle belts (which vibrate the abdomen in an unpleasant manner), electric camels and horses (precursors to those now found in Southwestern roadhouses), and so-called electric baths—a euphemistic term for sweatboxes. The gym instructor, T. W. McCawley, would eagerly demonstrate each device to visiting passengers, then they would be encouraged to mount the device and try it for themselves—still in their shirtsleeves or, in the case of lady passengers, dresses and petticoats. The efficacy of the machines was highly dubious, but the passenger left with a sense of accomplishment. The ship's gymnasium was, in fact, a sort of miniaturized midway, where spectators could goggle at and even take turns on the very latest technological wonders.

While one cannot doubt the healthful potential of the squash courts and swimming pool (though the pool, only fifteen feet long, was more accurately termed a "plunge bath" and not suited for anything more than splashing about), the infamous Turkish bath was quite possibly the most bizarre addition to any transatlantic liner. Ismay installed Turkish baths onboard the *Olympic* and *Titanic* to further cement the image of their unparalleled luxury. A Turkish bath conjured up images of the mysterious Orient, of robed pashas and fawning servants. To the Western mind, it was the epitome of decadent self-indulgence. Yet, simultaneously, it also seemed somehow sinister, a spiritual kin to the opium den. Forty years earlier Mark Twain had related his experiences in one such establishment, vividly describing the dirtiness of the chambers, the indifference of the servers, and the horrors of Turkish coffee. He concluded in an essay that the Bath was a "malignant swindle. The man who enjoys it is qualified to enjoy anything that is repulsive to sight or sense, and he that can invest it with a charm of poetry is able to do the same with anything else in the world that is tedious, and wretched, and dismal, and nasty."

Ismay wished to provide his patrons with an experience of the mystical East without all the irritating encumbrances of reality. The *Titanic*'s Turkish bath looked less like the genuine article and more like the set of a Rudolph Valentino movie. It was a sop to the most lavish of tastes, decorated in Moorish tiles and shaded lamps. Passengers reclined on chaise longues, ministered to by a staff of undoubted Caucasians in crisp uniforms. To further cater to Edwardian xenophobia, the Turkish bath aboard the *Titanic* was managed by Maude Slocum, a formidable woman who resembled an Irish nanny built along heroic lines. But even with these concessions, Ismay's experiment with Turkish self-indulgence was a failure. *Titanic* passenger Mrs. Frederick O. Spedden confided to her diary: "I took a Turkish bath this morning. It was my first and will be my last, I hope, for I never disliked anything so much in my life before, though I enjoyed the final plunge in the pool."

Scores of writers have eulogized the grandeur of the *Titanic*'s interior spaces, some even troubling themselves to point out that the *Olympic*'s were nearly identical. The consensus throughout is that these were the most glorious and luxurious rooms that ever put to sea. This is untrue. In reality, neither ship's interiors were revolutionary. They were certainly grand, more so than their English and German counterparts, but the uniqueness and luxury of the White Star ships had more to do with amenities than interior appointments. There were more open spaces, more distractions, more bizarre yet pampering novelties. The *Olympic*-class ships were, in fact, a unique blend of English aristocratic pretensions, German preoccupation with physical culture, and Gilded Age America's love of excess. In line with this policy, Ismay and his peers were willing to risk vulgarity—and the disdain of Mrs. Frederick O. Spedden—for the distinction of maintaining the only true "floating palaces" on the Atlantic.

As the *Olympic* ended her first season of transatlantic service and the *Titanic* reached the final stages of her fitting out, the race for the Atlantic seemed to have reached its height. The British now had the world's fastest and largest liners, while in Hamburg construction had begun on a vast supership that would, it was hoped, wrest all glory for herself. The advent of the *Titanic* was thus regarded by both parties as the latest, untried entrant in an ongoing steeplechase. Getting into the spirit of things, the London *Standard* treated the whole business like a jolly day at Ascot:

> To the battle of Transatlantic passenger service, the *Titanic* adds a new and important factor, of value to the aristocracy and the plutocracy attracted from East to West and West to East. With the *Mauretania* and *Lusitania* of Cunard, the *Olympic* and *Titanic* of the White Star, the *Imperator* and *Kronprinzessin Cecilie* of the Hamburg-America Line, in the fight during the coming season, there will be a scent of battle all the way from New York to the shores of this country—a contest of sea giants in which the *Titanic* will doubtless take high honors.

The *Southampton Times* was even more blunt. Ignoring with splendid disdain the unfinished hull rising in the stocks at Hamburg, it provided its own tally of the race results: "The ultimate object of the White Star Line," it crowed, "is to have a weekly service of mammoth steamers from Southampton, and apparently they are to be challenged at every step by the Germans. For once in a way, however, the Germans have been bested, and the White Star Line can themselves take the credit of having done something practical while the Germans were holding their hands. *The present score is two to nil.*"

-8-

A World's Fair Afloat

THE MORBID FASCINATION OF THE *TITANIC* DISASTER PERPETUATED THREE myths that persist to this day: (1) that the *Titanic* was the largest and most luxurious ship ever built; (2) that the *Titanic* was touted by her owners as unsinkable; and (3) that the *Titanic* was attempting to break a speed record for fastest Atlantic crossing, which would account for failing to slow down in the presence of icebergs. These can be disposed of briefly. First, the *Titanic*, at 46,329 tons, was exactly 29 tons heavier than her sister *Olympic*, a trivial discrepancy caused by the addition of glazing to the forward promenade deck. Her length and tonnage would be eclipsed as early as 1913 by the 52,117-ton, 919-foot HAPAG liner *Imperator*; size and gross tonnage would continue to expand throughout the century, culminating in Cunard's 2004 entry, the 150,000-ton *Queen Mary 2*. Second, the White Star Line never advertised their ship as unsinkable. They did, to be sure, stress the safety features of her bulkheads, watertight doors, and fire controls, but so did every major shipping firm for their latest flagship. And third, neither Ismay, Smith, nor anyone else had any intention of breaking the *Mauretania*'s record. The ship was not designed for it and, indeed, could not possibly have done so. Her engines were somewhat archaic even when constructed: two reciprocating steam engines driving the port and starboard screws while a single turbine propelled the center one. Together, these produced an eminently serviceable and quite uninspiring 21 knots—if pushed, she could briefly reach 23. Her course and speed on the night of April 14 were exactly identical to those of every other large passenger steamer on the Atlantic.

Where did these myths come from, and why have they survived so long? Part of the answer lies in the tone of *Titanic*'s popular eulogy: the greatest ship in the world, an affront to God, challenging the elements, meeting her cruel fate. This Old Testament approach has found great favor with lyricists and moviemakers, whose creative output ranges from lowbrow cinema melodrama to Thomas Hardy's ethereal "Convergence of the Twain," which reads in part:

> And as the smart ship grew,
> In stature, grace, and hue,
> In shadowy silent distance grew the Iceberg too. . . .
>
> Till the Spinner of the Years
> Said "Now!" And each one hears,
> And consummation comes, and jars two hemispheres.

Such evangelical sentiments may have appealed to chroniclers in 1912, but one is hard pressed to understand why they should still resonate today. The other, more subtle source of *Titanic* mythology was the hyperbole surrounding her construction—and thus, by one degree of separation, the Anglo-German liner race itself. England and Germany both trumpeted their ships, as is obvious from even the most cursory study of press coverage of the time. For most ships, including the *Kaiser Wilhelm der Grosse* and the *Mauretania*, the headlines flared briefly—beginning with the launch, continuing through the fitting-out, and culminating in the maiden voyage—then dissipated. Each new ship was hailed as the wonder of the age; her interior appointments were pronounced palatial; her engines, elevators, and other mechanical apparatuses were dissected ad nauseam by engineering journals and disseminated in layman's terms to a breathless public. Then the ship sailed, began her active life on the Atlantic, and the press moved on to other stories until the next challenger rose from the stocks.

The *Titanic* was advertised in exactly this manner. The brouhaha surrounding her construction was no greater than that for the *Lusitania* or the *Mauretania*. In fact, it might have been less so. The Cunard sisters were record-breakers, the first great ships built for England in almost a decade and the first to hold the Blue Riband in twenty years. The *Titanic*, in contrast, was a middle ship: slightly larger than her predecessor *Olympic*, and slightly smaller than her successor *Britannic*. Her interiors, with few exceptions, were replicated from the earlier liner, and would be again for the third and last. Thus, aside from being the largest ship in the world in 1912—an honor she would have lost before the year was out—the *Titanic* was unremarkable.

How then did she become synonymous with excess, vanity, and arrogance? It is because the patriotic, overblown press surrounding every new ship in this period was, in the *Titanic*'s case, shocked from its context—twenty years of competitive shipbuilding—and frozen in amber by the convulsion of horror and pity with which the Western world responded to her sinking. Outliving their contemporary context, both praise and blame became distorted beyond sense, and the tragic ship assumed an iconography of overweening pride and Divine retribution.

This warped mythology obscures other, more justified ways in which the *Titanic* was symbolic of her age. Two are of particular interest, for they go far toward defining the Edwardian Age itself. First, ships like the *Titanic* were microcosms of Edwardian class and social structures, recreating the tiered hierarchy that prevailed ashore. Second, perhaps even more important, they were floating world's fairs, representing the themes of mass culture, consumerism, technological fetishism, and phantasmagoria that some later historians would believe contributed to capitalism's persistent survival in the face of severe, widespread economic injustice.

In 1912 Karl Marx had been dead for almost thirty years, yet the promised day of revolution still had not come. Society was, if anything, even more rigidly stratified than it had been during his lifetime. The Industrial Revolution created a new class of market capitalists, the so-called robber barons whose small coterie controlled nearly all the major industries in the United States. They were men like John D. Rockefeller, Andrew Carnegie, and, of course, J. P. Morgan. As factories replaced farms and immigrants flooded into America to power them, a new labor force was created. The social distinctions between landed gentry and subsistence farmer were replaced by a new, even greater dichotomy: industrialist and factory worker. Even as a few self-made men became the heroes of the age—and of Horatio Alger novels—the concept of "wage slavery" was born. Port cities fed an endless supply of new laborers into the great factories of the Eastern Seaboard, grist to a mill. In his brutal exposé *The Jungle*, Upton Sinclair compared them to animals willingly approaching their own slaughter. Thus was the "wage slave," like Upton Sinclair's unfortunate Lithuanian family, consumed by the great industrial monolith that was now America. Big cities like New York and Chicago were refashioned to reflect this new reality: the distance from Manhattan brownstone to Brooklyn tenement was no longer measured in miles, but as separate and distinct universes. Between them—physically, economically, metaphorically—was the burgeoning middle class of shop owners, clerks, salesmen, academics, factory foremen, city workers, and the like. These three classes existed almost wholly apart from one another, taking their entertainments in different forms (the opera versus the music hall), eating in different establishments (Delmonico's versus the corner pub), and traveling to different places (Europe versus Coney Island). All in all, each class worked, shopped, lived, and died in distinct, isolated communities, with virtually no contact between them. Only in one place did they find themselves within close proximity: on board the Atlantic liners.

This is scarcely surprising. The liners might be billed as floating palaces, but in fact each ship was more accurately described as a floating city, populated by as diverse a group as any ashore sharing only one thing in common—the desire to cross the Atlantic. One's reasons determined one's station, and vice versa. The rich crossed for pleasure, business, or both. The middle class did the same, though with less capital to spend on the journey. The working class, however, crossed of necessity. The vast majority were immigrants, traveling to America in the hope of finding employment, security, and a new and better life for their families. They traveled, not in pairs, but in clans, with often as many as three generations undertaking the voyage. Some quite literally spent their last cent on the cost of the trip, placing all their hopes in the promise of a job waiting for them on shore. Hence Steerage travel was largely—indeed, almost exclusively—a one-way journey. Holds that were filled to capacity westbound were "empty as a school in summer" on the eastbound return.

To handle the vast discrepancies between their passengers, shipping firms developed intricate schemes to separate one class from another, thus in effect creating the illusion of three distinct ships within one hull. In the old days this was accomplished very easily by relegating Steerage to the lowest, most foul recesses of the ship; "steerage," in fact, comes from the area of the steering mechanism in the stern, where early immigrants were once berthed. Even after the business of immigrant transport had been cleaned up and sanitized, ships like the *Titanic* continued to house the immigrants in the lowest decks, near the cargo, machinery, and other spartan spaces of an Atlantic liner. Meanwhile a series of baffles, one-way doors, bulkheads, fences, and chains separated Steerage from the rest of the ship. The task was not overly difficult; on a ship of the *Titanic*'s size, there would be no fewer than six decks between the cramped compartments of Steerage and the deluxe suites of First Class—each deck acting as an effective buffer.

The barriers between Second and First were subtler but no less enforced. Cunard solved the problem by giving Second Class passengers their own "ship" at the very stern, physically separated and almost inaccessible from the rest of the liner. White Star was less draconian aboard the *Titanic* and *Olympic*, allowing Second Class to occupy almost the whole of E deck, while its public rooms were, like those aboard the *Lusitania*, located aft of First. White Star was also noticeably less class-conscious than its rival: it was a reluctantly tolerated game among the Second Class younger set on the *Titanic* to make dinner-jacketed forays to the First Class lounge and Café Parisien. No such indulgence was permitted for the Third Class, however.

With their serried decks, elaborate buffers, and extraordinary heterogeneity of passengers, the Atlantic liners became symbolic of class distinctions ashore. As they grew larger and larger, the distance between First Class and Steerage increased as well, physically and metaphorically. In the *Titanic*, they reached their apex. Descending deck by deck through the *Titanic* was akin to seeing the whole of Western society laid bare before one's eyes. First Class lolled about on the topmost decks, taking sun and leisure and enjoying three-hour meals; Second Class reposed, content and secure, in more modest quarters beneath; Third Class endured stark surroundings, the steady clank of machines, and close, cramped conditions; finally, in the very bowels of the ship, stokers stood stripped to the waist in hellish heat and sulfurous fumes, feeding the great black beast with coal. Filson Young, writing shortly before the *Titanic*'s maiden voyage, gave a distinctly Marxian interpretation of the ship and her denizens. "If, thinking of the *Titanic*," he wrote, "you could imagine her to be split in half from bow to stern so that you could look, as one looks at a hive, upon all her manifold life thus suddenly laid bare, you would find her a microcosm of civilized society." He went on:

> Upon the top are the rulers, surrounded by the rich and the luxurious, enjoying the best of everything; a little way below them their servants and parasites, ministering not so much to their necessities as their luxuries; lower down still, at the base and foundation of all, the fierce and terrible labor of the stokeholds, where the black slaves are shoveling as though for dear life, endlessly pouring coal into furnaces that devoured it and yet ever demanded a new supply— horrible labor, joyless life; and yet the labor that gives life and movement to the whole ship. Up above are the beautiful things, the pleasant things. Up above are the people who rest and enjoy; down below the people who sweat and suffer.

The rigidity of class distinctions took on a new and dreadful significance as the *Titanic* went down. A single, appalling statistic tells the whole story: despite the oft-quoted doctrine of "women and children first," a higher proportion of First Class men survived the

disaster than Third Class children. How could this happen? Some
authors suggest there was a deliberate conspiracy among the officers to
keep Third Class away from the boat deck, fearing that the upsurge of
humanity would create a panic. The evidence for this speculation lies in
the almost total failure of the *Titanic*'s crew to organize and transport
Third Class passengers from their quarters deep below up to the boats.
Indeed, even as the ship foundered, passageway gates remained locked,
and most Steerage passengers milled aimlessly about in the corridors—
some, horribly, believing that the ship had arrived in New York. There
they remained, most of them, until long after the boats had departed.

Yet the fate of the *Titanic*'s Third Class was worse than discrimination; rather, nobody seemed to have paid a thought to them at all.
True, several crew members attempted to organize parties of women
and children to take up to the top deck; their efforts were confounded
by the babble of conflicting languages and sheer number of passengers
they confronted. But these attempts were piecemeal at best, and there
was certainly no concerted effort to rescue the more than a thousand
people locked deep within the *Titanic*'s hull. Captain Smith's over-
emphasis on avoiding panic may be partly to blame: the fiction that
everything was perfectly all right persisted long past its usefulness, resulting in the deaths not only of Third Class but many among First and
Second Class who might otherwise have occupied the half-filled
lifeboats. This "business as usual" mentality might well have filtered
down to the crew as well, accounting for their overall reluctance to
lower the barriers between classes; one instructive example involves a
steward berating two Third Class passengers for knocking down a door,
and promising them they would pay for the damages when the ship
reached New York. Only at 1:30 in the morning, almost two hours after the collision, were the bronze gateways opened. By this time the forward funnel was nearly touching the surface of the sea. A torrent of
men and women rushed up the stairs, only to be confronted with a
labyrinth of First and Second Class passageways. They fanned out in all
directions, desperately seeking the boats. Two Finnish girls found
themselves instead in the deserted First Class dining saloon, now tilted
at a crazy angle. For a moment they stared, mesmerized, at the crisp
white tablecloths, plush chairs, and glittering silver. Then the dread
realization came upon them of where this pretty room was taking them,

and they renewed their search for the boat deck. Those who finally reached the top deck were lucky; almost as many remained far below in their Third Class quarters, awaiting instructions that would never come. They moved aimlessly back and forth through the broad thoroughfare between the men's and women's quarters—called "Scotland Row" by the crew after another long and infamous street—viewing with alarm the seawater that was already waist-deep in the forward lounge. When the lights flickered and pools of water crept slowly toward them, many fell to their knees and prayed.

The terrible casualty rate in Third Class should have brought the iniquities of class to the fore in the subsequent inquiries, yet—once again—they were overlooked. Neither the British nor American inquiries paid any attention to the discrepancies among those saved; only a handful of Third Class passengers were examined, compared with the scores of First and Second Class passengers who gave exhaustive testimony. In rendering their verdicts, both inquiries focused on the handling of the ship and the inadequacy of lifeboats; neither had anything but praise for the gallant crew's lifesaving efforts.

Nevertheless, the gross disparities between First and Third Class victims would eventually filter into the public consciousness. Until the *Titanic* aftermath, "women and children first" was a doctrine that had more often than not been honored in the breach. For example, on board the stricken *Republic* and *Florida*, two ships that collided in mid-Atlantic on January 23, 1909, emigrant passengers aboard the *Florida* watched with horror as First Class women and children from the *Republic* were taken aboard the rescue ship *Baltic*, followed by the First Class men. All the men, women, and children of Third Class on both damaged liners still remained. It was an outrage. "There are no classes here," one emigrant shouted, "we are all equal." The other Steerage passengers soon joined in the refrain. Yet the officers in charge remained unmoved. Later, while acknowledging the "disturbance," one blithely commented, "Discipline, however, was maintained, and the privilege of class upheld."

Though there was never a public outcry against this sort of discrimination aboard the *Titanic*, the ensuing requirement of "boats for all" made class distinctions during rescue largely obsolete. From then on, all passengers would find in their cabins a small notice indicating which boat was theirs and where it was located. When unrestricted immigration ended in the years following the First World War, Third Class was revamped to reflect new realities, and became "Tourist Third," a cheap and respectable way for university students and Middle American families to "do" Europe. Thus, the fate of *Titanic*'s Third Class represents a sort of summit for Edwardian class distinctions, when the socio-economic barriers between rich and poor were replaced with real ones of bronze and steel.

In its second symbolic incarnation, the *Titanic* serves as a monolithic icon of the Industrial Age, a floating amusement hall where technology, consumerism, and spectacle combined as never before. A coterie of Marxist scholars at the University of Frankfurt, writing in the mid-1930s, supplied a novel and compelling framework in which socio-technological marvels like the *Titanic* might best be understood. Walter Benjamin, Theodor Adorno, and their colleagues identified and interpreted the "modern" era: the industrialized Western world that emerged in the late nineteenth century and that still provides the matrix of cultural interaction, self identity, and social norms today. Taking as the crux of their critique the central theme of class struggle and inevitable revolution posited by Marx, scholars of the Frankfurt School questioned why, a century later, that revolution seemed perpetually postponed. Class disparities in the industrial world had grown ever wider, yet the working class remained basically content with their lot. Labor unions had not brought about revolution, but had—paradoxically—placated workers into a state of truculent acceptance. How could laborers have been so cruelly duped?, the professors asked.

Though each formulated his own answer, the common thread among them was the idea that capitalism, through its attendant instruments of mass production, mass consumption, and mass culture, had become self-perpetuating. Rather than being spurred toward inevitable revolution by adversity, the proletariat were dazzled by the false promises of democratic consumerism. Walter Benjamin, in particular, examined the strange and symbiotic relationship between mass culture and technology.

The Industrial Revolution, Benjamin argued, produced a culture that continually adapted to each successive technological innovation. Thus, just as steam travel transformed the way people moved from place to place, a thousand other inventions transformed how they ate, worked, dressed, interacted, and shopped—in short, these developments changed every aspect of daily life. As innovation and existence converged, a new technological fetishism emerged: Western society became fascinated by the new and unprecedented, and the working class was transfixed by an illusion of the "good life" provided them by the introduction of labor-saving devices and mechanical amusements in their daily lives.

Thus, according to Benjamin, technology and culture combined to produce a carnival-like "spectacle" that obscured the grim realities of life behind a façade of leisure, choice, and wonderment. Benjamin pointed to the Paris Arcades project of the 1880s as the paradigm for this dazzling deception. He might just as well have looked at London's Great Exhibition of 1852 or the Chicago World's Fair of 1893. In each case, technology had been enshrined, wedded to an unbounded optimism and faith in the future that characterize every attempt to create a "perfect world." At the Chicago World's Fair, technological wonders were showcased in a Romanesque plaza complete with fountains, mirror pools, and buildings that could have been lifted intact from the lithographs of Pompeii. This seeming contradiction aptly reflected its age: at the turn of the century, technological progress remained profoundly interwoven with the neoclassical humanist tradition of reclaiming ancient glories. A "model" city was one that combined the innovations of the modern with the spectacle of the ancient; thus, Benjamin's concept of the "phantasmagoria" or illusions was born. In an age when the commodity was swiftly becoming the *highest point* of society, the consumerist phantasmagoria was the center at which technological innovation, commodity culture, progressive optimism, capitalism, and spectacle coalesced.

Later authors have extended Benjamin's analysis to examine such other mass culture "dreamworlds" as amusement parks and railway depots. Yet none has identified the most telling of all: the Atlantic liners. Nowhere else do the separate strands of technology, commodity, and spectacle interweave so tellingly. In the hyperbole surrounding the *Titanic*'s construction, the slavish attention given to her interior appointments, and the exhaustive technical discussions of her machinery, the elements of technological fetishism and spectacle are on clear display. Again, perhaps the easiest way to understand the *Titanic* and ships like her is to envision them as giant floating world's fairs. The two share many commonalities. To begin with, both are ephemeral: the vaulted structures of the Chicago World's Fair were not built to survive much longer than the fair itself; the magnificent interiors of the great ocean liners lasted only as long as the active service life of the ships, and were then—like the fair—dismantled. This fleeting, quicksilver nature has profound effects on how both were perceived: the fair and the liner were momentary spectacles, products of their time but embodying the promise of future glory. A liner that survives into the next generation soon appears obsolete and dowdy, just as the technological wonders of earlier fairs seem hopelessly dated to those who come afterward.

The *Titanic* and her peers also carried with them the same contradictions of technological progress and architectural regression that characterized the fairs of that era. William Francis Gibbs, designer of the SS *United States*, summed it up best. When asked to define the term "superliner," Gibbs responded: "A superliner is the equivalent of a large cantilever bridge covered with steel plates, containing a power plant that could light any of our larger cities, with a first-class luxury hotel on top." In the ocean liners, then, technology and spectacle appeared hand-in-glove, even more so than at the fairs. The fair was constructed *around* its mechanical wonders, with classical architecture providing the backdrop to displays of machinery, but in an ocean liner, technology and architecture were fully integrated; thus the spectacle of eighteenth-century luxury was contained *within* the machine itself. The liner became both the spectacle and its backdrop, both the showcase and the machine. At the turn of the century, the Atlantic liner was thus the greatest single embodiment of technological innovation; hence it was with some accuracy, and no irony, that newspapers termed the *Titanic* "the seventh wonder of the world."

Finally, both a world's fair and *Titanic* shared that element of experience as a commodity that is the backbone of Benjamin's argument. For both, the key to admission was a ticket. At the fair, the entrance ticket entitled its holder to experience all the delights of a perfect world: to be entertained, educated, and bedazzled. For that brief moment, the spectator was removed from the humdrum of ordinary life and transported to a world in which all was bright and beautiful, a place of perfect optimism and certain faith in a future Eden. Similarly, though a steamship ticket entitled its holder to nothing more than passage from one city to another, by the early twentieth century it came to represent a great deal more. As ships became floating wonderlands, Atlantic travel became a sort of five-day world's fair; in other words, the *ship* became a destination in and of itself, not merely a means of conveyance. W. T. Stead, noted journalist and ill-fated passenger on the *Titanic*, described the ship as a "monstrous floating Babylon," and so it was. The experience of an Atlantic voyage at this time was utterly unique.

For the price of admission, the passenger was removed from the reality of everyday existence and placed within a cosseted and quite unworldly atmosphere. Neither in one country nor another, neither on land nor in the air, the six-day voyage was akin to being suspended in a netherworld—familiar yet somehow unreal—where all the distractions of normal life were replaced with forced inactivity, self-indulgence, and sloth. In this, the *Titanic* and her confreres were only the beginning. The concept of the ship as alternate universe had become so deeply entrenched that the idea of cruising emerged later; ships now drop anchor in ports only as a distraction from the "experience" of the cruise itself, and some never touch port at all. In 1912, at the earliest stage of this process, the maiden voyage of the *Titanic* was already correctly understood not as a mere means of transit from Southampton to New York but a ticketed admission to a unique, technologically astounding, and quite pleasurable spectacle.

Understanding the *Titanic*'s technological and consumerist symbolism also helps us understand both the circumstances of her construction and the outcry after her loss. As already mentioned, the owners and designers of the *Titanic* were blinded by their optimism and unalloyed faith in technology. They, no less than the gawking multitudes at a world's fair, remained in awe of their creations and could not conceive of any mishap that could humble them. The phantasmagoria of the *Titanic*, if you can call it that, was a spectacle of luxury and progress; the illusion of the floating palace could not allow for any catastrophes—the sea itself, with all its dangers, was an intrusive and unwelcome element in the *Titanic* experience. Since any mishap would shatter the illusion that the owners and builders had so carefully constructed, it was quite literally unthinkable that any such disaster could occur. Like the best salesmen, they had been convinced by their own words: J. Bruce Ismay and Captain Edward J. Smith were as blithe as anyone on board in believing that nothing could harm the *Titanic*.

This fatal complacency helped lull passengers into a false sense of security even after the collision. Nothing could be wrong with the ship: the band still played, the lights still glowed, the sea still seemed far and remote from the windows of the smoking room. The spectacle, in other words, persisted. Only when this fragile world began to break apart did anyone appreciate the true nature of their peril, and by then it was too late.

As the full reality of the disaster gradually settled on both sides of the Atlantic, the most common reaction—besides shock—was a firm renunciation of pre-existing faith in technological progress. It was for this reason that would-be prophets began to speak of the *Titanic*'s loss as a divine retribution. In one sense, it was. The minds that had conceived and propelled the *Titanic* had fallen victim to the false promises of the world's fair; they had, in messianic terms, made graven images out of Technology and Progress. The retribution was thus not the work of God, but of man. As one minister pithily termed it, "That iceberg had a right to be where it was, but that ship had no right to be where it was. . . ."

Some would later claim that the Edwardian Age ended when the *Titanic* went down. This is only partially true. Much of the mores, customs, social structures, and political realities that defined that era would persist past 1912—though not for very long, as they would all come to a crashing halt with the outbreak of the First World War. Yet it could be said that one defining element of Edwardianism did indeed end with the *Titanic*. That was the resolute faith in technological prowess, the naïve optimism that had conceived both the world's fairs and the great liners. Though the lavish scale and mechanical wizardry of the ships would not decline (indeed, with the ongoing Anglo-German competition, it intensified), their creations would never again be imbued with such serene complacency. "All the people on board existed under a false sense of security," wrote Joseph Conrad. "And the fact which seems undoubted, that some of them actually were reluctant to enter the boats, when told to do so, shows the strength of that falsehood. These people seemed to imagine it an optional matter." Yet this was, said Conrad, inevitable, when such persons were sealed within a "technical farce" like the *Titanic*, "a sort of marine Ritz . . . sent adrift with its casual population upon the sea, without enough boats, without enough seamen (but with a Parisian café, and four hundreds of poor devils as waiters). . . ."

It was left to Henry Adams, who had just a few years before lampooned J. P. Morgan's Atlantic ambitions, to supply the last word. He was, he admitted, shaken to the very core. A remarkably transatlantic man who despite his oft-proclaimed anglophobia spent much of the year being hosted by British friends, he had been planning yet another trip to England—on the *Titanic*'s first eastbound crossing—when the terrible news reached him. At once, his world collapsed. Adams's hand shook terribly as he wrote a friend: "The foundering of the *Titanic* . . . strikes at confidence in our mechanical success. By my blessed Virgin, it is awful! This *Titanic* blow shatters one's nerves. We can't grapple it . . . I've shifted my passage to the *Olympic* on May 4 . . . but my nerves are now so shaken that no ship seems safe, and if I am wrecked I might as well go under." In fact, he never made the journey at all. Ten days after the *Titanic* went down, Adams suffered a massive stroke. His doctor credited the sinking as the contributing cause.

"J. Brute Ismay" and the End of I.M.M.

The *Titanic* sank on April 15, 1912, and with her went many of the hopes, ambitions, and certainties of the age, and none more than those of J. Bruce Ismay. When the *Titanic*'s stern stood on its end and began its final plunge, he looked away. Taken aboard the rescue ship *Carpathia* wet and shivering and suffering from shock, he muttered over and over, as if it were his mea culpa, "I'm Ismay, I'm Ismay. . . ." He declined all offers of food or drink, snapping at the kindly doctor, "If you leave me alone, I'll be much happier here." Eventually Ismay allowed himself to be taken to the doctor's surgery, where he was soon joined by the *Carpathia*'s captain. "Don't you think, sir," the captain said, "that you had better send a message to New York, telling them about the accident?" Ismay nodded and scrawled on a piece of paper: "*Deeply regret advise you* Titanic *sank this morning after collision iceberg, resulting serious loss of life. Full particulars later."* Ismay looked up at the captain and said, in a strangely lost voice, "Do you think that is all I can tell them?"

His horrors were only beginning. The fact that the company president had escaped the *Titanic* with his life made him accountable, in the eyes of the public, for all the lives lost instead of his own. The instinctive reaction to a disaster of this magnitude was to find someone upon whom to pin the blame, and poor, proud, arrogant Ismay was a perfect scapegoat. In him, all the misplaced confidence and errant pride of the Anglo-German liner race was embodied. The press pilloried him, depicting him cowering in a lifeboat dressed in women's clothing over the caption "J. *Brute* Ismay." Mrs. J. J. "Molly" Brown—the plain-spoken Colorado millionairess whose actions in Boat 6 earned her the nickname "Unsinkable Molly Brown"—told Ismay to his face that in her hometown he would be "strung up on the nearest pine tree." Even the *New York Times*, abandoning its usual gray circumspection, remarked on the singularity of his survival. At the American inquiry, Ismay was subjected to several grueling days of testimony whose only purpose seemed to be to demonstrate that he was not only responsible for the disaster, but deliberately caused it.

His imperious manner made everything worse. On the *Titanic*'s maiden voyage Ismay acted much as he had aboard the *Olympic* the year before: making notes, conferring with the crew, being very much in the middle of things. At Queenstown he dictated to Chief Engineer Bell the speeds he wanted at various points in the voyage. On the day of the sinking Captain Smith had handed him an ice warning from the *Baltic*, and Ismay waved it around the Palm Court for several hours before finally giving it back. Even after the collision, he could not relinquish his image of himself as the *Titanic*'s chief proprietor. As Fifth Officer Lowe prepared to undertake the delicate business of lowering Boat 3, Ismay leaned over the railing, waved his arms in a circular motion, and shouted, "Lower away! Lower away!" The Fifth Officer turned on him ferociously. "If you'll get the hell out of the way," he bellowed, "I'll be able to do something. You want me to lower away quickly? You'll have me drown the whole lot of them!" Ismay, abashed, stalked away silently.

The British inquiry after the disaster exonerated Ismay completely. It was pointed out that the changes of speed he suggested actually *lengthened* the voyage, anticipating an arrival on Wednesday morning instead of Tuesday night. Moreover, despite his behavior, Ismay's actions in no way influenced the captain's decision to enter the ice field at full speed. His outburst at Boat 3 was put down to understandable hysteria, and evidence was given that he entered Boat C with several other men after a last call for women and children had produced none. His only crime was that he survived, but that was enough. The press reacted to the inquiry's pronouncement as though it had never been made. Just after the inquiry announced its verdict, one journal responded savagely by depicting him as "the boy on the burning deck," saluting under a Union Jack in mock, ironic heroism.

Laying aside caustic journalism, the *Titanic*, in all her vaunted size and doomed luxury, was largely the brainchild of J. Bruce Ismay. Despite his protestations at the inquiry, Ismay vetoed the proposal for extra lifeboats. But if Ismay deserves any blame for the *Titanic* disaster, it must be equally shared by his nemesis, Albert Ballin. Both men were committed to seeing their ships triumph, and it was the race between them that condemned the *Titanic*. Indeed, Ismay and Ballin were kindred spirits, ignited by the same desires and pursuing the same course. Both were witty, arrogant, and determined; respected rather than liked. Both had an obsessive love of their ships and shared a proprietary interest in them. Both were perfectionists. And most importantly, both served masters greater than themselves; masters whose ambitions were, if possible, even larger than their own. For Ballin, it was Kaiser Wilhelm; for Ismay, J. P. Morgan. Even their respective fates were intertwined, and thus cursed, by the ships they created. After the *Titanic* disaster and its horrible repercussions, J. Bruce Ismay retreated into seclusion and retirement. He saw few friends, wanted no reminders of his past life. He lived out the remainder of his days as a walking ghost, the spectral afterimage of a man who should have died on board the *Titanic* in April 1912. As it was, he would live another three decades. Ballin's fate was even less kind, though more dramatic: he would survive only until 1918, when a very different sort of nemesis finally caught up with him.

The last casualty of the *Titanic* was her owner, J. Pierpont Morgan. I.M.M. had been in a sort of limbo since the failed Cunard takeover in 1903. The stock declined rapidly, recouped somewhat, then resumed a slow downward spiral that stretched out over a decade. By 1910 only the strength of Morgan's name—and his limitless capital—kept the enterprise afloat. The *Olympic* and *Titanic* were to be his salvation. Their size and magnificence would garner the lion's share of passenger traffic, eclipsing both the Germans and the insular Cunard Line in one masterful stroke. The introduction of the third sister ship, *Britannic*, would drive the last nail into Cunard's coffin. After a long and arduous campaign, I.M.M. would emerge victorious, and J. P. Morgan would finally realize his long-cherished dream of Atlantic hegemony. In the First Class stairwell of each ship stood a clock, recessed into the wall just above the landing, which framed Morgan's struggle in allegorical terms. On either side of the clock stood two Hellenic figures in long robes, clutching laurels; they represented, according to the shipbuilder's journal, Honor and Glory crowning Time. The symbolism was not hard to interpret. Morgan had been content, as ever, to wait on events. But now the time was his, and honor and glory would surely follow in the wake of his wondrous new ships.

Morgan had, in fact, intended to make the maiden crossing on the *Titanic*, just as he had aboard the *Olympic*. He chose his personal suite, A39, which included a drawing room, two bedrooms, and a private veranda. Then, at the very last moment, ill health forced him to cancel his passage and seek a cure at Aix, in the south of France. His suite was given to Emil Brandeis, of department store fame, who did not survive. Lord Pirrie had also canceled passage, under doctor's orders that the disruption of the sea voyage would surely kill him—as, indeed, it probably would have.

The telegram reached Morgan at Aix, in the evening of April 15. Ismay's terse communication with White Star had been relayed, in absolute secrecy, to both the New York and Southampton offices. Morgan, typically, knew most of the details before anyone else. Yet even he could not comprehend what was to follow. Morgan collapsed into shock as the reports came over the wire, each more horrific than the next. He had lost friends, John Jacob Astor and Harry Widener. He had lost business acquaintances as well. A significant portion of New York and Philadelphia aristocracy was suddenly torn out of existence, leaving behind a gaping hole in Morgan's social circle.

But most of all, I.M.M. was ruined. The White Star Line would never recover from the *Titanic*, nor would it ever again introduce a ship of her size and stature on the Atlantic run. The *Britannic* was seized by the Royal Navy for troop duties before she was completed; the White Star flagship of the 1920s would, in fact, be German-built. In 1930, long after I.M.M. disintegrated and White Star returned to British hands, the company tried one last time to build a challenger. She would be the largest and fastest ship in the world and was given the fortuitous name *Oceanic*—in honor of the last White Star liner that had enjoyed success untainted by tragedy. The keel plates were laid and construction begun when the line's ailing fortunes finally overtook it, and it was absorbed into the Cunard monolith. The lovely *Oceanic* was a casualty of the deal; her plates were broken down, refashioned, and used to build the next great Cunard ship, the *Queen Mary*.

J. P. Morgan did not live to see this final humiliation. The *Titanic* broke his spirit once and for all. He became, like Ismay, a recluse. His travels now took him farther afield than Europe, and he spent his last days dwelling on his own mortality. He began designing a mausoleum, a vast pyramid that would preserve his body and protect it from the ravages of time. The project was never begun. In 1913, after catching a slight chill while touring through Italy, Morgan declined rapidly and died in his sleep. War broke out the next year, and the total failure of Morgan's grand design was at last complete.

The *Titanic* represented the apex of British maritime supremacy on the Atlantic, and her fall from grace was thus England's as well. Though the *Olympic*, *Mauretania*, and *Lusitania* continued on, they never fully escaped the long shadow of the disaster. The irony was not lost on observers. Suddenly, at the very moment of her crowning triumph, when the greatest ships on Earth were all British-built, England had abandoned the field to her German challengers.

Germany was ready.

-9-

Talons
of the Eagle

THE MAY 23, 1912, LAUNCH OF THE NEW HAMBURG-AMERIKA SUPERLINER
Imperator was a refutation of the value of omens. When the *Titanic*
had thundered down the ways at Belfast on a beautiful spring day one
year earlier everything went smoothly. When the *Imperator* followed,
just weeks after her competitor had disappeared into the North Atlantic,
everything went wrong. But while the *Titanic* had a shorter career than
the life span of the average housefly, the *Imperator* sailed for thirty years.

Though beset by almost comical misfortune, the launch did not
fail for lack of planning. Anticipating the official birth of his beloved
progeny, HAPAG chairman Albert Ballin outdid himself in every respect. A twenty-foot-high platform erected on stilts was surmounted by

a spired cupola whose roof was just level with the curve of the *Imperator*'s stem. Garlands wreathed the whole structure, the perimeter fences of the Hamburg yard, and the prow of the ship itself; compared with the restrained celebrations at Harland & Wolff, the *Imperator*'s launch fell somewhere between a national holiday, a naval parade, and a day at Coney Island. Thousands crowded around the hull while marching bands serenaded them with patriotic airs. Whereas King George had confined himself to a congratulatory telegram to the *Titanic*'s owners, the Kaiser insisted not only on attending but on performing the christening himself.

It was a decidely masculine occasion. The Germans, unlike the British, did not refer to their ships as "she." They were always "he" or, if too small for male nomenclature, "it," and the *Imperator*, towering above the spectators with splendid hauteur, was indubitably male. The ship shared more than the Kaiser's imperial title; there was something of his arrogance, even his virility, as well. While the British traditionally appoint a "godmother" to christen their ships, investing the ritual with feminine blessings, the Germans saw it more as a fond father sending his son out into the world.

The Kaiser arrived dressed as an admiral. With measured strides and a stern, paternal scowl, he inspected the ship from stem to stern. The performance was somewhat farcical, though, since actually viewing the hull required him to tilt his head back to an undignified angle—and probably remove his visored admiral's cap as well. But on the inspection went, with entourage in tow, until the Kaiser reached the steps of the platform. A line of guards clicked their heels and presented their sabers in salute. Wilhelm mounted the first set of stairs, where a crowded platform of dignitaries awaited him. He shook hands punctiliously with each one, turned on his heel, and was presented with more guards, more salutes, and more stairs. He mounted the second set. There, in the ultimate chamber, was Albert Ballin. The HAPAG chairman was dressed in his best: three-piece suit, gold watch chain and fob, enormous silk topper. Standing next to—and well beneath—the regal and uniformed Kaiser, the finery only made his deficiencies more glaring.

It was then, at that climactic moment, that the whole show began to fall apart. A piece of planking, dislodged from the forepeak, thundered down past the platform. The Kaiser leaped backward as the lethal edge passed within inches. There was a collective gasp, and for a moment it appeared he had been hit. But Wilhelm, though shaken, was unharmed, and he stepped forward again to do his duty. He pressed a trigger and a bottle of wine sailed down from above, shattering against the *Imperator*'s bow. She began to move. A great cheer went up as the whole 919 feet slid effortlessly down the ways and into the Elbe. To prevent her wayward hull from skidding unchecked across the river and into the opposite bank, the port anchor was released. The chain roared out of its hawsehole, then disappeared. In the haste to launch, someone had forgotten to secure the chain to the ship. Several tons of anchor now lay uselessly at the bottom of the Elbe, and the *Imperator*'s stern continued its backward track, now aimed directly at the newly completed Kaiser Wilhelm Quay, teeming with spectators. For a few seconds it seemed as though one Kaiser would demolish the other, and crowds on the quay saw the awful specter of the ship's mammoth stern bearing down on them like a vengeful giant. But the inertia finally expended itself, and the *Imperator* halted just three hundred feet short of disaster. Immensely relieved, her builders towed her to an adjacent yard to begin the year-long process of fitting out.

The Peculiar Genius of Albert Ballin

The timing of the *Imperator*'s launch, just weeks after the *Titanic*'s disastrous maiden voyage, was no accident. In the endless reams of literature devoted to the building of the *Olympic* and *Titanic*, the most important question has never been asked: *Why?* Why did White Star and J. Bruce Ismay feel compelled to build their superliners in pairs? Why the tremendous hurry to put them into service?

The answer was Albert Ballin. To understand the course of the Atlantic race in the last years preceding the outbreak of war, it is necessary to understand first that it was largely the brainchild of this one extraordinary man. Kaiser Wilhelm may be credited for having inspired the race in 1889, and Norddeutscher Lloyd for having given it shape in the early years of the twentieth century, but only Ballin conceived of the competition as anything other than a magnified yacht race. For him, it was a symbolic struggle of empires. Ships became floating monuments of their nation's greatness, its technological prowess, its culture. The stakes of the Anglo-German race for the Atlantic were for more than the fastest or largest ship, but the symbolic strength of England and Germany themselves. To some extent, this patriotic metamorphosis was already in the works when Ballin arrived on the scene, as subtly suggested by the heraldic interiors of the *Kaiser Wilhelm der Grosse* and her sisters. Yet Ballin, a humane and introspective man, went further: the race between the liners, he believed, would replace that between the navies. England and Germany would remain amicable competitors for the Atlantic, besting one another in marble and gilt, not armor and guns. Ballin, an ardent anglophile, could thus declare in 1915 with absolute sincerity: "I am the only German who can say with truth that he has been fighting English supremacy in the shipping world during the last thirty years." He went even further: "During this long period I have, if I am allowed to make use of so bold a comparison, conquered one British trench after another." Yet his peaceful understanding of Anglo-German rivalry, which drove Ballin to aspire to greater heights than any other shipping magnate in history, would in the end destroy him.

Even before becoming the Kaiser's conduit for German supremacy on the Atlantic, Albert Ballin had revolutionized the shipping world. Born into a middle-class Jewish family in Hamburg, young Albert began his career as an emigration agent on the docks. It was a grueling business. Hamburg and Bremen were thriving centers for Eastern European emigration to the United States, and passenger firms competed fiercely for customers. Ballin routed most of his passengers through England (standard practice at the time), and onto ships of the fledgling American Line of Philadelphia. In the lean years of the 1870s, it seemed as though his family-owned company would soon founder. Then, in the early 1880s, business began to pick up. The floodgates of Eastern Europe were opening, and a veritable torrent of emigrants sought passage to America. It was then that Ballin was struck by inspiration. Transferring employment to the tiny Carr Line, he persuaded its directors to enter into a potentially ruinous fare war with the mighty Hamburg-Amerika Line. Carr, with its few ill-serviced ships, nevertheless began picking off the cream of the emigrant trade, in much the same way as deregulation would later give rise to a host of small, no-frills airlines. In less than a year, the Carr Line and Albert Ballin were a serious thorn in HAPAG's side. Rather than continue to buck this little challenger, HAPAG solved the problem by purchasing the Carr Line itself and appointing feisty Ballin as its new passenger services director.

In his first year, Ballin convinced HAPAG to order two twin-screw ships to run in direct competition with the much larger North German Lloyd Line. The *Columbia* and *Augusta Viktoria* were unremarkable in every way, but they were by far the largest vessels yet commissioned by HAPAG. Ballin kept costs to a minimum by encouraging multiple bids from competing shipyards (quite different from the British approach, which stressed long-standing relationships between owner and builder). As a result, the *Augusta Viktoria* was constructed on site in Germany, while the *Columbia* was built in Scotland.

In 1899 Albert Ballin became managing director of the Hamburg-Amerika Line, a post equal to the one his rival, J. Bruce Ismay, acquired at White Star the same year. The two men, who would later share much the same drive and destiny, were otherwise markedly different. Whereas Ismay was an entitled aesthete from a moneyed family and inherited his place from a domineering father, Ballin was scrappy and unquestionably bourgeois, having fashioned his own career from the dockside muck of Hamburg. He was also, as one acquaintance put it, "somewhat less than handsome." His small stature was made worse by a pair of stumpy legs and a cylindrical belly that he concealed within immaculately tailored suits. He did his best to hide a protuberant upper lip underneath a large moustache modeled after the Kaiser's, but the result was rather mousy. His face, always animated with emotion, seemed "formed of rubber, so that it had almost a comical effect." But patronizing descriptions of Ballin's appearance by his contemporaries (and there were many) must be tempered by the fact that his favored place in the Kaiser's entourage aroused considerable resentment. Unlike Benjamin Disraeli and others, Albert Ballin never sought to deny or conceal his Jewishness. Despite the overwhelming anti-Semitism of the Prussian court, he remained "the genial Jew," ever courteous and respectful in the face of naked prejudice and hostility. It says much that he was able to foster and maintain a relationship with the Kaiser all the same, all the more so since most of Wilhelm's other friends and family, including the Kaiserin, openly despised him.

The first of Ballin's revolutionary reforms was perhaps the most inevitable. As an emigration agent he had seen firsthand the appalling conditions in which emigrants were ferried to the New World. Posters and notices throughout Eastern Europe brought hopeful travelers in droves to the German ports, where they were confronted at once by squalor and corruption. Consigned to filthy tenement housing, lured by false promises into investing in cheap passage on nonexistent liners, many were robbed of their money so quickly that they never left port at all. They remained, existing on welfare and public charity, until large sections of the city itself were transformed into sprawling slums. As the slums increased, the problem deepened. Worse still, ships continued to depart the German ports erratically, leaving after their scheduled date or often not leaving at all—the whole city was bedlam. Even as late as 1890, charlatans continued to waylay would-be emigrants, posing as representatives of shipping companies and guiding their unfortunate victims to overpriced lodging—even exchanging their currency for counterfeit American dollars.

Once Ballin had the position and capital necessary, he set about transforming this predatory system. The problem as he saw it was that anarchy bred inefficiency. There was a virtually unlimited supply of potential customers, and the German ports, Hamburg and Bremen, were the most logical destinations. They were the closest harbors to Eastern Europe, easiest to reach by rail or roadway. Yet the wasteful competitiveness and complete disorder in both had, in effect, created a roadblock to emigration. Ideally, the emigrant's sojourn at his point of departure should be as brief as possible, allowing another emigrant to take his place, and so on. The important thing was to keep the people moving and prevent them from being sidetracked or, worse, robbed.

What Ballin did was to create a city within a city, a virtual emigrant town, serviced directly by the railroads and opening right onto the HAPAG docks at Hamburg. This *Auswandererhallen*, conceived by Ballin shortly after he came to HAPAG in 1891, was finally completed in 1904. A colossal structure reminiscent of a cross between an amusement park and a factory, it contained within four high walls a delousing facility, baggage shed, barber shop, numerous hotels, food and dry-goods stores, a beer garden, music hall, two chapels, and a synagogue. This bustling little community of transients was bisected by tree-lined streets and serenaded with regular outdoor concerts by the ships' bands. Seemingly serene and pleasant, it was nevertheless operated with machine-like efficiency. Scarcely a moment of the visitor's experience, from arrival to embarkation, was unaccounted for. One entered through a high archway crowned with an enormous and somehow sinister clock tower. Almost immediately, the emigrant and his family were herded into the delousing facility, where they were stripped naked and scrubbed with a foul green soap smelling of kerosene. Their belongings were subjected to a blast of purifying steam under pressure, leaving garments damp and wrinkled but clean. A huge staff of barbers was on hand to shave the heads of "questionable" emigrants—as many as forty heads an hour on a good day, they boasted. Once released onto the "clean" side, the emigrants' experience improved markedly. Having been treated like prisoners, they were now greeted as customers. One deutschmark a day bought room, board, baths (communal, of course, but spotlessly clean), and any necessary medical care. The vast majority of HAPAG's emigrants were housed within three dormitory-like structures, segregated by males, females, and families. As an added kindness, and good business, indigents who could only afford the price of their ticket were allowed to stay for free—better that than releasing them into the stinking mire of the city around them. At the opposite end of the spectrum, passengers who could afford an additional surcharge could choose to stay at the Hotel Sud or the Hotel Nord — French names denoting greater luxury, which in this case meant a maximum of four beds per room. The emigrant and his family enjoyed a single evening sampling the delights of the *Auswandererhallen* and were up bright and early to catch their ship the following day. A final round of medical inspection awaited them on the pier, and they were off.

Ballin's sweeping reforms extended to the ships as well. The *Mauretania* and *Lusitania* had introduced a new standard of luxury for Steerage, but in many ways they were merely improving on Ballin's reforms. HAPAG was primarily an emigrant carrier, earning the bulk of its profit from the hoards that crowded the lower decks of its ships. Before Ballin, the line was content to transport them as cheaply and indifferently as possible. Emigrants carried their own linens, often their own food. There was little or no segregation of the sexes, and voyeuristic crewmen roamed the women's areas at will.

Almost as soon as he became general manager, Ballin turned his attention to the fetid squalor of Steerage aboard his ships. His first forays into the dark recesses were disappointing, even revolting. He returned to Hamburg with a notebook full of revisions, ranging from new paint schemes to completely redesigned interior spaces. Soon the entire HAPAG fleet saw their lower decks revamped, as cramped and dirty Steerage areas were scrubbed clean, straw mattresses replaced with real bedding, and laundries installed to prevent the spread of vermin. New HAPAG ships also reflected this enlightened policy, offering cheerful, though spartan, emigrant quarters. Where once the denizens of Steerage had been left largely to fend for themselves, doctors, stewardesses, and translators were now employed to assist them.

Ballin's impulses, though commendable, were not merely altruistic. First, a reputation for the best and cleanest ships gave HAPAG a crucial edge over its competition, both German and international. Second, and far more important, the introduction of cleanliness and efficiency to the emigrant trade facilitated a far greater number of passengers. The dockside medical inspections, after all, were only the first of several that prospective emigrants were forced to endure. The second was on board when the ship was anchored in quarantine, just short of its New York pier. The third, final one, occurred on Ellis Island in New York harbor or, outside New York, in similar immigrant processing centers. If at any time the immigrant failed inspection, he and his family were returned to their point of departure at the line's expense. Thus it was sound business to keep the emigrants fed, clean, and healthy.

Ballin's policies soon made HAPAG the largest emigrant carrier in the world. The efficiency of his operations also meant that a record number of passengers were transported every year, and the numbers only went up as the fleet expanded. Thus, in a way, Albert Ballin may be partially credited for facilitating the great exodus to the United States at and after the turn of the century. Before his reforms, emigration was a haphazard, disorganized, and dirty business. Afterward, it became as punctual, ordered, and sterile as a well-oiled machine. Smaller lines withered and died in competition with the mighty

HAPAG and Norddeutscher Lloyd; those large enough to compete shamelessly copied Ballin's innovations aboard their own ships. As the business expanded, many of the lines, and especially Hamburg-Amerika, commissioned newer and bigger ships to handle the overflow. It was then that Albert Ballin began to nurture another, greater dream. As emigrants were the bread and butter of every line, HAPAG was wealthy indeed, but it still remained a distant second in luxury and prestige to the older, more venerable Norddeutscher Lloyd. It was Lloyd that had mounted the challenge to the British fleet, while Hamburg-Amerika continued its more modest service with smaller, less pretentious ships.

The *Deutschland* of 1900 changed all that. With this, its first superliner, HAPAG became a serious competitor. Despite its mechanical flaws, the *Deutschland* was—if only for a short time—the biggest and fastest and thus the reigning queen of the Atlantic. Yet when the *Deutschland* nearly shook herself to pieces to claim the ephemeral Blue Riband, Ballin shrewdly realized (like Ismay) that the future of the Atlantic rivalry lay not with speed, but luxury. His next ship, the *Amerika* of 1905, reflected this shift of priorities. At 17.5 knots, her service speed was that of an intermediate liner, but her interiors were like nothing ever seen. With canny foresight, Ballin had engaged an architect named Charles Mewès to design the public spaces of his new flagship. Mewès, a dumpy little man with thick spectacles and a goatee, had just completed two new hotels, the Paris Ritz and London Ritz. He was the most recognized, revered, and expensive interior designer on earth. His artistic partnership with Cesar Ritz would, ultimately, transform the concept of a hotel from the oversized hostelries of the nineteenth century to the glittering, vaulted, self-contained cities of today. In 1905 he was at the height of his powers, moving from one dazzling commission to the next. He looked on the *Amerika* project as an interesting challenge—how would one erect a first-class hotel within a great steel tub?

The finished product was almost a carbon copy of the Ritz hotels, complete with period rooms, potted palms, mullioned windows, and high coffered ceilings, all put to sea. The idea was to make the transition from shoreside hotel to seagoing liner as seamless as possible, establishing an architectural unity between ship and shore that would disguise the fact that these magnificent interiors were, in fact, mobile.

Ballin, with Mewès's consent, even took the idea one step further. He approached Cesar Ritz with a remarkable proposal: the first extra tariff restaurant on the Atlantic. Ritz responded enthusiastically. The new restaurant would be entirely separate from the main dining room, complete with its own kitchen. The chefs, waiting staff, and maitre d' would all be recruited by Ritz himself, under the supervision of a manager employed not by Hamburg-Amerika but by the Ritz hotels. It would offer a menu of almost impossible sumptuousness and, most of all, privacy. In recognizing that seclusion was itself a luxury, Ballin was, again, far ahead of his time. Rather than being subjected to the fishbowl of public scrutiny in an enormous ship's dining room, Ballin's most famous and notorious passengers were offered a place to congregate in glorious isolation. There they could host private parties, dine à deux with women who were not their wives, or simply enjoy a quiet meal superbly presented and as far removed from the old-fashioned ship's tureen as possible.

The *Amerika* was an unalloyed triumph. Her First Class spaces were hailed as the finest ever seen, and her Steerage carried a record number of emigrants in sterilized comfort. Most of all, she proved Ballin right: for all the talk about the Blue Riband, passengers still flocked to a ship that boasted the finest quarters at sea. Her technological advances—including the first elevator, which preceded those on the *Lusitania* and *Mauretania* by two years—made her a wonder, and her stunning success inspired Albert Ballin to dream on an even bigger scale. He was already conjuring up newer, bigger ships even as the *Lusitania* and *Mauretania* streaked across the Atlantic and into international fame. The two new Cunard superliners merely acted as a catalyst. Before, Albert Ballin was a successful businessman trying to maximize his profits. But now Ballin's vision was hitched to quite another sort of ambition, the ferocious pride and jealousy of Kaiser Wilhelm II.

Wilhelm had taken an active interest in both German lines as early as 1875, even before becoming Emperor. He enjoyed playfully setting one line against the other, wavering in his sponsorship and praise between them like favorite children. Occasionally he lent his imperial influence to broker a deal or end a stalemate, as he had with the Morgan combine in 1902. Yet while he remained officially impartial in his favors, the Kaiser soon took a strong liking to the diminutive HAPAG chairman, which warmed into friendship. They had been briefly introduced on board the *Augusta Viktoria* in 1891, when the Kaiser and Kaiserin (for whom the ship was named) inspected her at her berth in Hamburg. Wilhelm was charmed by the dapper HAPAG chairman, although Empress Augusta loathed him on sight. Shortly thereafter the two men would meet again, this time at a conference in Berlin concerning the upcoming festivities at Kiel.

Ballin and the Kaiser could scarcely have been more different, yet they shared two crucial similarities: a love of the sea and a passionate desire to best England. The Kaiser found Ballin an agreeable listener and a lively talker; Ballin, in turn, was entranced by Wilhelm's eager, almost boyish exuberance. When Ballin approached the Kaiser with his proposal for a trio of ships in 1909, Wilhelm seized upon it enthusiastically. As plans for the liners were drawn, memoranda containing unsolicited advice, structural suggestions, and even interior designs rained on the Hamburg office, all bearing the imperial crest. Such meddling occasionally went too far and more than counterbalanced the benefits of royal favor. One HAPAG director even declared that "Ballin's friendship with the Kaiser hurt more than it helped the Hamburg-Amerika Line," a statement that, though untrue, is nevertheless revealing.

As their friendship deepened, Wilhelm became the standard-bearer of HAPAG: He christened their ships, attended their annual dinners, even forgave the public relations department for claiming that the silver service aboard the *Amerika* was his personal set—simply because he had once touched it. Finding Ballin and his Hamburg entourage a pleasant contrast to the stuffy circle of Prussians at court, the Kaiser invented more reasons to visit his house in the Feldbrunnenstrasse— so often that an English newspaper termed it "Little Potsdam," after the Kaiser's official palace. Though Wilhelm came often, he came unaccompanied: Kaiserin Augusta Viktoria, despite Ballin's naming a ship in her honor, remained huffily in Berlin. Her husband didn't care, nor did he object when Ballin presented him around Hamburg drawing rooms and public receptions like the prize at a village fête. It was all good fun. For the Kaiser, despite his limitations of character, could be a generous and solicitous friend. When Ballin suffered an attack of neuralgia, Wilhelm at once recommended doctors and even proposed sending a court official to assist Ballin until he recovered.

Though the Kaiser himself remained sanguine about his friendship with Ballin, others were quick to draw more ominous conclusions. For many, it seemed as if Ballin—a bourgeois Jew and therefore immediately suspect in those prewar times—was leading the All Highest around by the nose. Thus the imperial title "Seine Majestat" was reworded, by jealous courtiers, to read "Siegfried Meyer." One newspaper even went so far as to say that Albert Ballin was "now the autocrat of Germany, in spite of the monarchy, the constitution, and the law. In this country today, one really obeys Ballin more than all legal factors. This is so because Herr Ballin dares to play the role of a Russian viceroy in Germany."

Ballin himself began to fancy that he alone had the Kaiser's ear. And as long as their interests remained in lockstep, there was no reason for him to believe otherwise. With enormous capital and imperial will, they were allowed to realize the scope of their ambition; together, their unique partnership would produce liners that exceeded even the bounds of fantasy and humbled the British. The first of these was the *Imperator*.

"Mein Feld Ist die Welt"

The one-two punch of the British *Lusitania* and *Mauretania* had dealt a stinging blow to the Kaiser's dreams of Teutonic supremacy on the Atlantic. With the triumphant Cunarders seizing headlines across England and the Continent, the still-mighty *Kaiser Wilhelm II* and *Kronprinz Wilhelm* suddenly seemed very much yesterday's news. Their raison d'être was gone. Built as fast, sleek greyhounds, they could not compete with the *Lusitania*'s luxury or the *Mauretania*'s turbines. Moreover, a spate of building between 1897 and 1906 had produced no fewer than five major German passenger liners (not counting the unfortunate *Kaiser Friedrich*); HAPAG and Norddeutcher Lloyd were surfeited. The last German four-stacker, the *Kronprinzessin Cecilie* of 1906, looked obsolete even when she was new. Her First Class saloon, complete with winged cherubim and Grecian bas-relief, was distressingly mid-Victorian and out of date.

By 1909, with the news of the *Olympic*'s construction, the Germans were getting desperate and felt they had to do something for national prestige. It was then that Ballin presented his plan to the Kaiser: a trio of German ships, one per year from 1912 to 1914, beginning at 50,000 tons, with each one successively larger. Unlike the cookie-cutter White Star ships, the German liners would each be unique: an evolution, not a reproduction. The first of these was tentatively named *Europa*, and Ballin proposed to further frustrate the White Star Line by ordering it from the same shipyard, Harland & Wolff. This would have been a master stroke, for it would inevitably have slowed down construction on the *Olympic* and *Titanic*. Ultimately however, patriotism, pressure from the Kaiser, and a new government mail contract forced Ballin to turn instead to the German shipyard Vulcan Werke. The first keel plates for this 52,117-ton "colossus of the Atlantic" were laid on June 18, 1910.

From that moment, the race was on. There was no question that the *Olympic*, with almost two years' head start, would be ready before her German competitor. The challenge was to complete *both* liners before Hamburg could catch up. Ballin's superliner, originally titled *Europa* but now dubbed *Imperator* in deference to the Kaiser's active interest (and, of course, his ego), was taking shape with lightning speed. Spring of 1912 was the pivotal moment. With the *Olympic* in service and the *Titanic* and *Imperator* both on the stocks, the race reached a fever pitch. But on April 15, 1912, as the Hamburg workers were frantically scrambling to complete last-minute alterations to the *Imperator's* hull, it suddenly seemed as though she had won by default. Her rival lay at the bottom of the Atlantic, and the blind worship of size and grandeur that had motivated both vessels was subsumed by a black pall of remorse. Far from being elated, Ballin and his company were horrified. Certain that the press would be more skeptical than ever about her size and luxury, HAPAG carefully monitored their release of the ship's statistics. In fact, the *Imperator* was considerably bigger and faster than the *Titanic*: 52,000 tons to 46,000; 919 feet to 882; 23-knot service speed to 21 knots. The most impressive difference was her passenger complement: 4,594 in First, Second, and Third Class, as compared with the *Titanic's* 2,603. Once calculated to impress, HAPAG now regarded these dimensions with the self-critical eye of a portly woman examining herself in the mirror.

With the launching behind them, Ballin and his associates began fitting out the *Imperator* in earnest. Conceived with the sole intention of surpassing the *Titanic*, she was now being made ready for a different world. White Star's dreams of a superliner trio were gone; it would be another two years before the third and final triplet, the *Britannic*, appeared. Until then the *Olympic* sailed alone, the similarities to her lost sister making her seem like Banquo's ghost. But the Germans had learned from their rivals' mistakes, and plans were hastily redrawn to give the *Imperator* enough boats for *more* than her actual capacity of passengers and crew. There were no fewer than eighty-two boats and two motorized launches altogether, an incredible number when one considers that the *Titanic*, only 36 feet shorter, had only sixteen boats and two collapsibles. But Ballin did not stop there: The whole fitting-out process ground to a halt as the *Imperator*'s hull was lined with an inner skin that acted like a ship within a ship. To test the soundness of their work, Vulcan called in the Hamburg Fire Department and ordered them to fill the gap with water from the pumps. The firemen complied with gusto, the seams held, and Vulcan Werke announced to a delighted Ballin that the ship was iceberg-proof.

German anticipation of the *Imperator*'s debut grew steadily. Overcoming initial squeamishness after the *Titanic* disaster, they came to regard her as their Kaiser did: a floating monument to the nation's prowess. In fact, the Germans were consistently more inclined to see their ships as symbols of national unity than the British, who regarded them primarily as a commercial reaffirmation of England's maritime dominance. This is reflected most poignantly in the names each country gave their crack liners. While *Olympic* carried intimations of size and *Mauretania* of far-flung empire, the Germans chose names with heavily political symbolism: *Kaiser Wilhelm der Grosse, Kaiser Wilhelm II, Kaiser Friedrich, Kronprinzessin Cecilie, Prinzessin Augusta Viktoria, Imperator, Bismarck*, and, of course, *Vaterland*. The reasons for this are twofold. First, the race between the British and the Germans was far more personal for the latter. Beyond maintaining an active interest, Kaiser Wilhelm was personally involved in the conception, construction, launching, and operation of his ships. Given this sponsorship, it was natural that some should bear his name.

The second and more important cause was the issue of statehood. England's history was ancient and sublime, replete with victories, dynasties, and glory. The history of the united imperial Germany was younger than the Kaiser himself. The nation, like Wilhelm, was brash, arrogant, and eager to take on its elders. The German navy's feverish construction program was one such challenge, aimed at the very center of the British psyche: dominance of the seas. Ballin's wonder ships *Imperator* and *Vaterland* could either be seen as an adjunct or a separate, alternative challenge. While it is unclear which interpretation Wilhelm favored, Ballin clearly believed the latter, and as the *Imperator* took shape he would increasingly press this view with the Kaiser.

Plans for the *Imperator*'s interiors were drawn well before the *Titanic* disaster, and it showed. Every line and cornice seemed designed to do the White Star liners one better. This was evidenced by the choice of style: Louis XVI, the same period that graced the lounges and dining rooms of the *Olympic*. But if the *Olympic*'s public spaces suggested an elegant country house in Aix, the *Imperator*'s were nothing less than a chateau. Once again, Ballin had commissioned Charles Mewès to give shape to his ship's interiors. The stunning period rooms Mewès designed reflected two predominant influences: eighteenth-century France and Kaiser Wilhelm II. From the former came the style, from the latter the scale. The Kaiser made frequent visits to Mewès's cluttered office, favoring the architect with his suggestions for everything from ceiling height to chair covers. He even offered Mewès the coveted job of enlarging Strasbourg's main boulevard. Mewès, an Alsatian, declined frostily. Yet the relationship between the two was quite friendly on other matters. That the Kaiser deigned to suggest rather than direct says much for Mewès's diplomacy. And, as John Maxtone-Graham has written, it is a testament to Mewès's genius that he was able to balance the dictates of taste with the Kaiser's Wagnerian visions.

The rooms that finally emerged from this strange alliance were among the most beautiful ever built on a liner. Mewès's creations had an equilibrium that no other German liners before or since have enjoyed. He accomplished this by ignoring the tastes of his employers as much as possible. The Germans, left alone, produced gathering areas that reflected either the overstuffed, antlered kitsch of a Bavarian hunting lodge or the stark, somber grandeur of a municipal train station. Accordingly, one caustic Englishman dismissed the *Imperator*'s First Class lounge as a place of "gloomy Teutonic majesty." This was nothing but sour grapes. While the *Imperator* was designed as a floating symbol of Germany itself, her interiors were anything but German. Mewès's elegant designs had actual kinship with quite a different source: the Ritz hotels. When drafting rooms for the *Imperator*, he drew heavily from his past hotel designs. His English partner Arthur Davis summed up this design philosophy: "[T]he people who use these ships are not pirates, they do not dance hornpipes; they are mostly seasick American ladies, and the one thing they want to forget when they are on the vessel is that they are on a ship at all. . . . If we could get ships to look inside like ships, and get people to enjoy the sea, it would be a very good thing; but all we can do, as things are, is to give them gigantic floating hotels."

The *Imperator*'s main lounge, a two-story creation of straight-backed chairs, tasteful paneling, and chintz, carried off the illusion with aplomb. It was the spiritual twin of the grand foyer at the London Ritz. Adjoining it was a palm court complete with wicker, tile, and live palms—the very image of the English veranda. Thus, in one of the most bizarre circumstances of the Anglo-German race, the ship that was meant to embody German culture seemed designed exclusively for an English clientele. The traveling Englishman aboard the *Imperator* might even have experienced a sense of déjà vu: her lounges were those of the London Ritz, her furnishings matched those of the royal castle at Balmoral, Scotland, and her swimming pool was an exact copy of the Royal Automobile Club's. But Germans seeking refuge in familiar surroundings were forced to retreat to the Smoking Room. There they found the only unabashedly Teutonic room on the ship: antlers, half-timbers, fireplace, and all.

If the *Imperator*'s interiors failed to convey that indescribable Germanic aura, the rest of the ship more than made up for them. As the upper decks took shape and the funnels were lowered into place, a profile appeared that was at the same time powerful, masculine, and surpassingly ugly. The *Imperator* would never have the yacht-like grace of the *Augusta Viktoria* or the clean, low-slung lines of the *Olympic*. She was, instead, a study in vertical geometry. Her sharp prow formed an exact 90-degree angle with the hull, and her five decks of superstructure were stacked like layers of a birthday cake without the slightest regard for grace over function. The necessity for accommodating eighty-two lifeboats meant obscuring almost every available stretch of deck with boats and davits, extending even to the shelter deck in the stern. An abnormally long bow was punctuated by an isolated, white well deck, further adding to the *Imperator*'s workmanlike appearance. Capping the whole business was a trio of monstrous funnels, the tallest ever fitted to a ship. Their sheer size accomplished the impossible: they made the rest of the ship look smaller. The single and overriding intention of the *Imperator*'s design seemed to be to stun the observer into inarticulate awe, and in this, she succeeded.

As the *Imperator* neared completion, it looked as though her supremacy on the Atlantic would pass unchallenged. The Kaiser was overjoyed. The *Imperator* was weeks away from her sea trials and work had already begun on the second of the HAPAG trio, the even larger *Vaterland*. And vast, ungainly thing that she was, there was no denying that the *Imperator* had the makings of a champion. While the British press had already exhausted their superlatives in the rapid succession of new Cunard and White Star ships, the Germans hadn't had anything to crow about since 1906. Moreover, the modesty brought by the *Titanic* disaster to the editorial style of British journals like the *Shipbuilder* had no counterpart in Germany. It was not *their* ship that had sunk. The press went into enthusiastic raptures about everything from the *Imperator*'s lounge ("the largest unsupported room on the Atlantic!") to the searchlight mounted conspicuously on her foremast—perfect, or so the company said, for spotting icebergs. Though never explicit, the ghost of the *Titanic* was everywhere, most particularly in HAPAG's repeated emphasis on the ship's improved safety and lifesaving apparatuses. While one cannot imagine that Ballin or the Kaiser were pleased by the tragedy (Germany had lost her share of citizens on her as well, and the Kaiser's telegram to London was appropriately morose), there was nevertheless a certain quiet satisfaction in these comparisons. The *Imperator* seemed poised to enter a race in which she was not only without peer, but without competition.

Then came the awful news that the Cunard Line, humbled by the size and grandeur of the *Olympic*, had begun construction on a new liner. That alone was not cause for comment: they held a steady contract with the John Brown shipyard, which delivered a new intermediate-class 20,000-ton liner for the company almost every year. But when in 1913 Cunard released the projected statistics on its latest ship, Hamburg convulsed. Though considerably smaller in gross tonnage, she was to be 910 feet long, one foot longer than the *Imperator*. The margin was so narrow it had to be deliberate. Once again, the British were thumbing their collective nose at the latest German leviathan—even before she had sailed. And not only at the ship, but at the man whose title she bore as well. It was intolerable.

The crowning symbol of the race between the British and the Germans was delivered to a Hamburg pier on its own flatcar in 1913, in a wooden crate postmarked from Berlin. The louvered sides were carefully removed, and loading cranes arched gently downward to lift the crate's contents for all to see.

It was an eagle, a monstrous, gilded, gimlet-eyed eagle with straining neck, outstretched wings, and talons over a foot long. In its steely grasp was a miniature globe with the inscription *Mein Feld Ist die Welt*, "My Scope Is the World." Never had the HAPAG motto seemed so ominous, the word "scope" seeming to be synonymous with "clutch." Perched daintily on the creature's head was yet another reminder of the one man most responsible for it all: a tiny imperial crown, looking rather like a beanie. As this avian monstrosity rose over the heads of the assembled Vulcan workers, making a long arc toward the ship's bow, its purpose became clear. The *Imperator*, the greatest, most technologically advanced ship in the world, was to have a figurehead. Those honest Hamburg shipwrights must have shaken their heads in disbelief. Figureheads had graced the sharply curved bows of eighteenth-century sailing vessels, where they served as mascot and talisman against the caprices of a cruel sea. But they hadn't appeared on transatlantic liners since Brunel's *Great Britain* in 1839. Even then it had looked a little silly, as it would on any screw-driven iron ship. Set against the stark lines and mechanical functionality of the *Imperator*, it was worse than silly—it was bizarre.

Even the German press wasn't sure quite what to make of it. Hideous and oversized, the beast hindered visibility for the docking pilot and had as much aesthetic appeal as a gargoyle. Anxious to ascribe a technological rationale to this medieval aberration, German papers announced smugly that it was in fact an ingenious device for iceberg detection. The globe, they said, was hollow, and had a tiny opening in the front through which a seaman would scan the horizon for danger. This was utterly false. The eagle had only one purpose: its nine-foot length gave the *Imperator* that extra edge over her unfinished British rival. The *Imperator* was duly registered at 919 feet, and Ballin and the Kaiser sighed with relief. They evidently thought it inconceivable that the British would employ a similar ruse to lengthen their own ship (a bust of Nelson, perhaps?), and they were right. Cunard Line, horrified, conceded the point.

It would soon be moot, anyway. The maiden voyage of the *Imperator* was a fitting counterpart to the *Titanic*'s in that it demonstrated almost as pointedly how far the race for supremacy had overreached contemporary engineering. At least the *Titanic* had made it out to sea before her defects caught up with her. For poor, bumbling *Imperator*, they surfaced even before her trials, beginning with the bathroom fixtures. "Particular attention," one HAPAG brochure noted, "is called to the almost total elimination in the first cabin of the folding wash stand. In its place is a commodious marble wash stand with running hot and cold water." The key word was marble. Marble was everywhere: in the bathrooms, on the floors of almost every First Class public room, lining the Pompeian Bath, even forming the impressive bust of the Kaiser himself in the main lounge. A ship not quite 40 feet longer than the *Olympic* was half again as heavy and carried over twice as many passengers. Determination to surpass the *Olympic* and *Titanic* in every way had produced a vessel weighed down by her own luxury. Her sea trials confirmed that the *Imperator* was dangerously top-heavy. Laden with so much gilt, marble, and machinery, she was what captains call a "tender" ship. In a flat calm, she listed. In even moderately heavy seas, she rolled like a drunkard. It was a disaster for Ballin and the Kaiser, one even worse than the *Kaiser Friedrich* had been, for they couldn't very well hand the *Imperator* back to her builders with polite regret. Both men—and Germany herself—were committed to the new liner, and the dangers of advance press, the same mistake that had destroyed J. Bruce Ismay, came home to Albert Ballin. But it was too late. The cabins had been booked, the date set, the press alerted. The *Imperator* had to sail.

More than thirty-one hundred passengers booked the *Imperator*'s maiden voyage: a record number and astonishing considering that the *Titanic's* had been just one year before. It was a burst of German enthusiasm. But two mishaps intervened. First, as the newly finished ship began steaming down the Elbe, her 30-foot draft betrayed her and she ran hopelessly aground. A day was lost as tugs dragged her from the muck. Then, as the *Imperator* was being fitted to sail, a flash fire ignited and killed five workmen. It was the first of many mishaps that would plague the ship over her long career. There was considerable damage to her interiors. It was a terrible omen and, worse yet, it meant postponing the maiden voyage. Ballin suppressed the story at once. A carefully scripted release put the blame on weather conditions and inadequate docking facilities, as crewmen frantically expunged the charred wreckage inside. The bodies were buried with the absolute minimum of publicity, at the company's expense.

But no amount of subterfuge could conceal the *Imperator* herself. The ship departed for America in early June, with Albert Ballin aboard. She rolled all the way there. Halfway across, Ballin sent a congratulatory telegram to the Kaiser; it was Wilhelm's twenty-fifth year on the throne. The occasion was appropriately timed: the ship that shared his title was passing over the grave of her rival, while the Kaiser's imperious gaze captured passengers from a portrait on the ship's main stairway and a bust in the First Class lounge. The Kaiser cabled back congratulations on a prosperous voyage. This, as it turned out, was premature. New Yorkers, denied the pleasure of a maiden arrival in 1912, turned out in force to greet the *Imperator*. Fire boats and pleasure craft saluted her with whistles, and the *Imperator* answered with lively signal flags and a deep blast from her own horn. Then, as she passed the Statue of Liberty, something seemed to go horribly wrong. The ship lurched heavily to starboard, her towering funnels exaggerating the list. A crowd of passengers had flocked to the starboard side to see Lady Liberty and this, combined with a nearly empty fuel bunker (coal acted as ballast) was just too much. The *Imperator* listed all the way into her dock at Hoboken. Local harbor pilots quickly dubbed her the "Limperator." The ship finished out her first season, wobbling back and forth across the Atlantic. In the deepest recesses of the liner were a series of ballast tanks, the curious brainchild of Dr. Framm of Hamburg. The tanks lay next to one another, connected by pipes. As the ship rolled, water would be forced from one tank to another to counteract the instability. It was a clever idea, and a dismal failure. The *Imperator* rolled worse than any ship on the Atlantic, terrifying passengers, crew, and captain alike. Then, after just two more voyages, came the ultimate humiliation: a trip back to the Vulcan yard. There workers truncated her enormous funnels by nine feet, removed her grill room, and poured several tons of cement into her hull as ballast. The marble fittings, however, remained intact.

The *Imperator* returned to service in early spring of 1914, leaner and sleeker. She became and remained an immensely popular ship. The shortened funnels suited her blunt profile better, and the eagle figure-head was mercifully obliterated by a freak wave soon thereafter; its tat-tered remains were removed but, naturally enough, the registered length was not adjusted. Yet despite these alterations, the *Imperator* never quite overcame the image of a blundering Brunhild. She would always seem just a little too big, too clumsy, too pretentiously vulgar. The Englishman who disparaged her First Class lounge found an un-usual ally in one of her captains. "She was a ship of gloomy paneled majesty," he wrote, "hard to handle, clumsy and Teutonic, a creation of industry without pretensions to beauty."

Be that as it may, the *Imperator* and her German sisters, by their sheer size, helped transform emigration patterns to the United States. In spite of the reams of literature devoted to their lounges, gymnasiums, and other accoutrements, it was in this role that the liners had the most lasting and profound effect. Ships built after 1900 could carry double, sometimes even triple, the number of Steerage passengers com-pared with those built before 1890. In 1907, the debut year of the *Mauretania* and *Lusitania*, over one million emigrants were ferried across the Atlantic from European ports. Between them, HAPAG and North German Lloyd carried the lion's share, and with the introduction of the *Imperator*, the numbers jumped substantially. In 1913, the last uninterrupted year of emigration to the United States, the two lines carried, respectively, 138,830 and 164,533 Steerage passengers to New York alone. Cunard, in contrast, carried only 84,762. Together, the great liners brought 1,414,000 new citizens to America in 1913; by the early 1920s, despite the disruption of the war, some thirty million persons had crossed in Steerage, changing forever the face of America. Here was yet another unintended consequence of Anglo-German rivalry on the Atlantic: by building ships exponentially larger than one another, all of which owed their livelihoods to the precious emigrant trade, Hamburg-Amerika, Norddeutscher Lloyd, White Star, and Cunard fashioned the means by which the narrow, perilous trail between the Old and New Worlds was widened into an express thoroughfare, opening the United States to a new generation of Americans.

-10-

"The Struggle for the Sea"

KAISER WILHELM MIGHT HAVE IMAGINED HIMSELF THE PEACETIME commodore of a vast fleet of ocean liners. But this image competed with another, just as potent: Supreme Admiral and Commander of the Imperial Navy. For over a decade these two roles battled against each other within the Kaiser's psyche. By 1913, it looked as though the latter was winning.

The Anglo-German naval race had been fomenting on both sides of the Channel for almost a decade. The similarities were startling:

just as the Kaiser's obsession with ocean liners began with a visit to English waters, his determination to best the Royal Navy was ignited by yet another naval parade at Spithead, this one in 1907. The newly completed *Dreadnought* class of battleships was the most significant advance in marine weaponry since the conversion from wooden ships to iron. Capable of withstanding an incredible battering, mounting far more armaments than their predecessors, and able to fire shells farther than the eye could see, they were technological marvels. British newspapers covering the review abandoned themselves to bold type and fevered punctuation: "A NAVAL SENSATION!"; "FLEET ASTOUNDED!" The German response was less enthusiastic. Grand Admiral Tirpitz had been pressuring the Kaiser for years to turn his attention to the deficiencies of the Imperial Navy; after the dreadnoughts appeared, his voice was finally heard. By January 1910 the British had four in service, three ready for trials, and six more laid down. That same month, in an extraordinary burst of energy, the Germans matched them with four dreadnoughts ready for trials and nine laid down. Just a few months earlier, British Foreign Secretary Sir Edward Grey had informed his colleagues: "The great nations of Europe are raising enormous revenues to kill one another."

Yet it need not have been so. The naval race that drove the two nations closer to war began as its commercial parallel did: more in a spirit of friendly competition than belligerence. The week before the review at Spithead in 1907, Rear Admiral Sir Percy Scott signaled one of his captains: "Paintwork appears to be more in demand than gunnery, so you had better come in, in time to make yourself look pretty by the 8th inst." The Kaiser himself was as reluctant to commit his beautiful new ships to war as he had been eager to build them. In this, he differed sharply with his aging advisor, Admiral Tirpitz, who was like the devil on one of the Kaiser's shoulders, while Ballin was the angel on the other. As Ballin advocated peace, Tirpitz whispered war. Both men guided their building programs with feverish intensity, and both were driven by a competitive spirit to humble the British lion. But there the similarities ended. Tirpitz, in his sixties, was hankering for one shot at glory before retirement. He constantly pressured the Kaiser to build bigger and deadlier warships with an eye toward the ultimate clash with the English dreadnoughts. The Kaiser agreed enthusiastically to the construction but balked at their use. Tirpitz found himself relegated to a desk job as Secretary of State of the Imperial Navy, with his chief duties being administration and supply. The admirals reported directly to the Kaiser himself, who added to his bulging list of titles Grand Admiral of the Imperial Navy. "I need no chief," he declared roundly. "I can do this for myself."

But events conspired against this attitude. The building of a massive peacetime fleet creates its own momentum, pressuring its creators into using it before it becomes obsolete, nothing more than a waste of money. Many of the Kaiser's top advisors—Tirpitz among them—said it was ludicrous to build a huge fleet simply to bring it out for naval parades. At first the Kaiser held fast: "For the present," he said, "I have ordered a defensive attitude on the part of the High Seas Fleet." As the Balkan situation worsened and tensions with England became rife, however, his resolve weakened. By 1913, Germany had a naval fleet to match anything the British could throw at her, and the Kaiser was predisposed to use it.

Caught in the middle was Albert Ballin. Initially he regarded the enlarging of the German fleet as positive, a friendly race to match his own. For the first decade of Tirpitz's tenure as Grand Admiral, the two sea potentates enjoyed a cordial, even warm, accord. Ballin sent frequent memoranda to Tirpitz's office; in 1898, when both men were relatively new to their posts, Ballin even employed HAPAG as a go-between for the establishment of a German naval base on the Virgin Islands. Flattered by the Admiral's continued interest, Albert Ballin came to view the relationship between merchant and naval fleets as fundamentally symbiotic. When Tirpitz introduced his plans for an entirely new fleet of dreadnoughts, Ballin was among his strongest advocates. "Without the support of a strong fleet, whose iron core can only be made of battleships," he wrote in 1900, "Germany has no real power against the tiniest exotic state which permits might to go before right and which, in possession of a few modern armored ships, can sneer at obsolete, impotent cruisers. Behind every German [merchant] vessel abroad must stand a German battleship!"

Such sentiments were short lived. As Tirpitz's campaign began in earnest, it became increasingly obvious that he did not intend his marvelous new warships to be used only as guard dogs for the Hamburg-

Amerika Line. Moreover, Tirpitz and Ballin had a starkly different conception of the "enemy." For Ballin, the threat came from imperial outposts, as Germany sought to claim her place in the sun. This was logical for a man who spent a good part of every day studying the departure sheets for ships bound for Africa, Asia, and the islands. But Tirpitz saw the enemy much closer to home: across the Channel, where Admiral "Jackie" Fisher was pursuing a naval rearmament policy disturbingly similar to his own. Germany's dash to build its navy was provoking a rift in Anglo-German relations, deliberately widened by Admiral Tirpitz. From the start, he regarded a conflict between German and English fleets, and thus all-out war between the two nations, as inevitable. Ballin found his stubbornness inexplicable. "At any time," he wrote later, "he [Tirpitz] could have negotiated with England as one power to another. But he did not wish to negotiate. He wanted no settlement, he wanted only to build ships. He put obstacles in the way of every understanding with England. . . . "

In 1909, Ballin wrote to his journalist friend Maximilian Harden: "Our relations to England are causing me great concern." Knowing that Harden had the Kaiser's ear on some matters, he went on: "Please use your maximum influence for support of an agreement on the question of naval construction. It is a necessity for both nations, and this necessity should offer to practical men the basis for a fair compromise." Ballin also used his own influence where he felt he could. He buttonholed the Kaiser at Kiel in June of that year, at a moment when Wilhelm was certain to be in high spirits, and offered his services to negotiate with the British via English diplomat and banker Sir Ernest Cassel. It was a role to which Ballin was particularly suited, that of mediator, and one in which he increasingly found himself. Whether acting as a buffer between the Kaiser and J. P. Morgan, Tirpitz and the colonies, or Germany and Britain, Ballin trusted his own self-deprecating charm and profound reasonableness to carry the day.

With the tacit support of Kaiser Wilhelm, Ballin began secret negotiations with representatives of the British Admiralty, starting in 1909 and continuing until the outbreak of war in 1914. His first foray into diplomacy was a proposed meeting between Admiral Tirpitz and Admiral Fisher. The suggestion was not as outlandish as it sounded; the two men had enormous respect for one another and were, in fact, quite friendly. But Ballin's proposal was ill-timed. Three weeks earlier, on board the *Hohenzollern*, Kaiser Wilhelm had accepted the resignation of his acid-tongued, sycophantic chancellor, Prince Bernhard von Bulöw. The man chosen by the Emperor to take his place was spare, scholarly, diffident Theobald von Bethmann-Holweg. It was a thankless task, and Bethmann felt the scorn of his colleagues keenly. Von Bulöw, though a poor administrator, had enjoyed remarkable leverage in his office; it was for that reason, among others, that the Kaiser forced his dismissal. Bethmann felt threatened on every side by his predecessor's allies. Then, not yet a month into his term as chancellor, he received word that Albert Ballin, a civilian with no official status in the government, had taken it upon himself to assume the mantle of ambassador-without-portfolio to England. Bethmann's response was acerbic. "I respectfully protest," he told the Kaiser. "I consider as my particular province and the principal object of all my efforts, the establishment of confidential and really friendly relations with England. . . . It is my special field and I cannot allow it to be encroached upon." After his stormy departure, Wilhelm turned to Ballin, who had been in the room throughout, and said apologetically, "Your proposal won't work. You see how vexed he was. I cannot afford a Chancellor crisis just a few weeks after appointing him." Still, he encouraged Ballin to continue seeking back-channel communications with England—often in direct contravention of Bethmann's official work.

Thus, ironically, at the very time in which he was constructing the vessels that would wrest supremacy from his British competitors, Albert Ballin was quietly brokering deals to keep the race amicable. He found many of the British sympathetic. Ballin may not have had a very prepossessing appearance, but he radiated integrity and purpose. Politicians, diplomats, and even admirals listened to his impassioned pleas for peace with grave interest. One of his earliest converts was, in fact, First Lord of the Admiralty Winston Churchill. Churchill, like Ballin a nationalist of the first order, nevertheless shared his conviction that the only result of unrestricted naval rearmament was certain conflagration. In March of 1912, as the *Imperator* rose in her stocks and the *Titanic* began her sea trials, Albert Ballin met quietly with Churchill, statesman and pacifist Richard Haldane, and German Ambassador Metternich. Churchill and Haldane informed him that the Cabinet and King George V were very much in favor of reaching an agreement on naval rearmament. Indeed, English politicians courted the little man like anxious suitors: he was obliged, by the pressing need to return to Berlin, to decline dinner invitations from both Sir Edward Grey and Prime Minister H. H. Asquith. Ballin returned to Berlin elated. At 11:00 A.M., March 17, he burst into the Kaiser's private office crying exuberantly, "Your Majesty, I bring the alliance with England!" He then went on to praise the British cabinet to the skies and castigate the German navy—Tirpitz in particular—as warmongers. For that brief moment, it seemed as though the crisis was resolved. Then a telegram arrived from Metternich later that same day, stating that he had just met with the British and on no account were they disposed toward settlement. The Englishmen's seeming cordiality had been at best a trial balloon, at worst outright duplicity. "Now at least we know where we stand," said Admiral Müller grimly. Albert Ballin, still flushed with self-satisfaction, looked like a total ass.

But the situation was still not completely lost. In April 1912, just as the *Titanic* was preparing to sail, Churchill proposed a "Naval Holiday," a moratorium during which both England and Germany would suspend the construction of new battleships. The predecessor of such détente concepts as the SALT treaties, it received much enthusiastic support in both countries, but the Kaiser refused. Ballin told British diplomat Sir Edward Cassel that the "frankness and honesty" of Churchill's letter "flustered . . . the leading parties of Germany, and caused a torrent of [comment] in the Press." Ballin then took the extraordinary step of communicating with Churchill directly, advising him to come to Berlin, where he might "have some useful conversation with Admiral Tirpitz." If not useful, it would certainly have been interesting, but it was not to be. Churchill declined the invitation with regret, writing Ballin that

> all that could be said on our part would be that till Germany dropped the naval challenge her policy would be continually viewed here with deepening suspicion and apprehension; but that any slackening on her part would produce an immediate détente, with much good will from England. Failing that I see little prospect but politeness and preparation.

Discouraged but not defeated, Ballin continued to press his case with the Kaiser. His reputation as a pacifist had become so widely known that when Churchill again tried to sell the Kaiser on a ship-building suspension in October 1913, he used Ballin as a go-between. But once again his overtures were rebuffed. Wilhelm never even bothered to respond. On taking his leave from Ballin, whom he visited shortly thereafter, Churchill implored him "with tears in his eyes" not to let the Kaiser drag Germany into war. Ballin said he would do all he could, but secretly he was becoming despondent.

In yet another ironic twist, the pacifist Ballin found himself pilloried by the German press as leading his country to war. It was the "autocracy" charge all over again, fueled by public anti-Semitism and the desire to shift the blame for Germany's diplomatic failures away from the Kaiser and his advisers toward other, more sinister, sources. Ballin, a Jew, a capitalist, and a close friend of the Kaiser who had neither title nor position in government, was a perfect scapegoat. One particularly poisonous attack took the form of an allegorical novel entitled *The Struggle for the Sea*, by Walter Freyer. In it, the Machiavellian intrigues of one Moritz Bebacher, shipping magnate and "Napoleon of the Sea," pit Germany and England against one another in an irrevocable slide toward war. The book, utterly mediocre as a work of fiction, was remarkable only for its date of publication—May 1914—and its author. Freyer was in fact the former president of the ship officers' union, an old foe of Ballin's. Ballin sued for libel—and won—but his friends still began jokingly to call him "Moritz." More serious damage, however, had been done to his reputation. Another critic, journalist Georg Schröder, published an inflammatory article arguing that Ballin's feverish desire to build more and bigger ships had antagonized the British into a war footing: "Germany has made an enemy of the whole world through HAPAG," he declared, "that is, through Ballin." This criticism was echoed by several on HAPAG's board, who felt that the liner race only exacerbated existing tensions that the naval race had engendered.

And indeed it did seem at times as though Ballin was pursuing his dream for Atlantic supremacy beyond the bounds of common sense, even sanity. A consummate perfectionist and chronic worrier, he seemed driven not only to build the largest and most luxurious liners, but to create—in every possible way—the *ne plus ultra* experience of ocean liner travel. Just as J. Bruce Ismay kept a diary of imperfections on the *Olympic's* maiden voyage, so too did Ballin, in his frequent trips across the Atlantic, fill notebooks with *"Obligatorische."* Nothing escaped his critical eye, and the memoranda he sent back to his office in Hamburg were astonishing in the sheer breadth of seemingly trivial concerns they addressed. Towels were too small; soup got cold en route from the kitchens to the promenade deck; there was not enough trunk space in the cabins; the wine cellar was inadequate; the pillows were too hard. Sometimes even aesthetic matters occupied him: why, he noted, don't we put the HAPAG crest on the playing cards in the First Class Smoking Room? Such suggestions were sent back to Hamburg with absolute dispatch, where they were treated with canonical reverence by Ballin's subordinates.

Thus Ismay's incessant nattering about coathooks and cigar holders was matched, even exceeded, by Ballin's rants on the subject of pressed table napkins. Indeed, to understand the passion that drove Albert Ballin, one must also understand J. Bruce Ismay, and vice versa. They cannot be viewed separately any more than two horses racing head-to-head. Both men saw the race for the Atlantic as a search for complete perfection. If Ballin shared with the Kaiser the scope of his dreams for German supremacy, he also shared with Ismay a burning desire to possess the biggest, the grandest, the best. Both men, Ismay and Wilhelm, stoked the fires of Albert Ballin's ambition.

Yet Ballin's obsession was beginning to create a dangerous backlash. As new and greater liners took shape in the Hamburg yards, Ballin was forced to answer allegations that his life's work was hindering Anglo-German diplomacy. It was suggested, unfairly, that he was putting his own financial interests above his patriotism. Ballin, cut to the quick, responded angrily that the economic rivalry between HAPAG and White Star, and therefore between Germany and Britain, was of necessity peaceful. What would be the result if war came? Both businesses would be subsumed by the conflict at terrible loss of revenue; both would see their ships seized as cruisers, perhaps even sent to the bottom by enemy fire. Once again, Ballin defended his building projects as the best insurance of continued peace and mutual prosperity, even as the second of his great liners took shape in 1913.

"Now We Have the Result of Our Lack of Courage!"

The penultimate HAPAG superliner, following in the same patriotic vein of nomenclature, was to be called the *Vaterland*, "Fatherland." In many ways she was the slightly bigger twin of the *Imperator:* they had the same profile, much the same interior appointments, and many of the same defects. The *Imperator's* majestic Pompeian Bath was replicated, this time without the viewing gallery. Once again, the German press had a plethora of incredible statistics to ponder; the *Vaterland* would carry 3,909 passengers, ministered to by 1,234 crew, and her provisions for each voyage included 13,800 table napkins, 45,000 pounds of fresh meat, 100,000 pounds of potatoes, 17,500 bottles of wine, champagne, and brandy, 10,000 pounds of sugar and treacle, and—this being a German ship—28,000 liters of beer. Five books of specifications roughly two hundred pages each covered everything from the ship's turbines to the clock in the officers' lounge. Ballin supervised the construction with even more interest than usual. The race against the British was as intense as ever, but with an added dimension. Ballin hoped desperately that the *Vaterland's* palatial splendor would turn the Kaiser's eye away from weapons of war. She was more than a symbol of the competition between the British and the Germans; in 1913, her unfinished bulk was a promise of years of continued harmony.

Across the Channel, Cunard's new flagship *Aquitania* seemed to project the same peaceful symbolism. As the ships were built for decades of service on a placid ocean between peaceful continents, it was unthinkable that either one would ever find her career hijacked by the insanity of war. The *Aquitania* was unquestionably the product of a gentler, more sportsmanlike contest. She relinquished willingly the distinctions of speed and size: the former to the still-unconquered *Mauretania* and the latter to the *Imperator* and *Vaterland*. Cunard had taken a long, hard look at the *Imperator's* stodgy bulk and decided that such aesthetic ravages weren't worth enduring simply for the title of "world's largest." The *Aquitania* was, instead, the "Ship Beautiful." She owed much of her overall look to the graceful *Mauretania* and *Lusitania*, sharing with them a dignified, well-balanced hull, evenly proportioned superstructure, and four funnels. Inside, her interiors eschewed the drama of scale for an almost cozy, reassuring luxury. Her First Class spaces were vaguely reminiscent of the *Imperator*'s, with good reason: they were the work of Arthur Davis, Mewès's partner. An earlier agreement prohibited Mewès himself from designing anything but German ships, but no such agreement extended to Davis. A product of the same school of Beaux-Arts, he conceived designs for the *Aquitania* that ran the gamut from Carolean to Adam, Louis XIV to Christopher Wren. They were the artistic equivalent of Mewès's earlier work on the *Imperator*, but lacked—fortunately—the taint of vaulted excess brought by the Kaiser's interference. The *Aquitania* conveyed an aura of intense wealth checked by the restraints of good taste, a mute, aristocratic rebuke to the *Imperator*'s vulgarity. Her luxury suites were named after great artists: Rembrandt, Reynolds, Holbein, Gainsborough, Van Dyck, and a copy of the artist's most celebrated work hung in each room.

The *Aquitania* radiated a sense of Britishness throughout. Designers boasted that the forests of England and the Empire had been scoured to supply her magnificent paneling, while her lounges were copied from the drawing rooms of great English estates. The Garden Lounge was intended to remind passengers of an English garden, even to the point of obscuring the deckhouse wall with props designed to resemble rock and trellises. This pervasive English influence was found even in the lights in the First Class writing room, which were, according to Cunard, "made in the same way as the lead lights which were originally made by the Brothers Adam to be placed over the front door of many London houses in the neighborhood of Portman Square." The whole ship, in fact, was a floating museum of British history, and passengers were encouraged to revel in the glories of the empire, "from the far-off days when that goodlie ship the *Great Harry* was one of the world's wonders down to the end of Europe's struggles for supremacy with Napoleon."

One historian describes the *Aquitania* as Cunard's *Olympic*-class ship, and he's right. While restrained in comparison with the German leviathans, her interiors lacked the austere grace of the *Mauretania*'s. She was, in fact, a product of the same quest for resplendence that had fired the imaginations of Ismay and Ballin several years before. As if determined to best both with the same stroke, she had *both* a Pompeian and a Turkish Bath. "They are as comfortable as can be," the company enthused. "The bather can perspire as happily and healthfully in one as the other, the attendant of either will liberate him spotlessly clean; the cooling room, where coffee and cigars will be enjoyed, will enable him to regain an agreeable temperature and catch no cold afterwards, and he will return to the company of his fellows immaculate physically and charmingly placid."

The race between the *Aquitania* and *Vaterland* had reached a fever pitch by the spring of 1914. Both ships were nearly ready; it came down to a matter of days between them. In the end, the *Vaterland* won. Steaming down the Elbe for the first time in May 1914, she was—as one historian termed her—"an over-decorated hostelry in the disguise of an ocean liner." But she was also magnificent. On the morning of her maiden voyage her captain, Commodore Hans Ruser, said airily: "I will just point the *Vaterland* towards America and let the ocean blow by." As she passed the British ship *St. Louis* off the Isle of Wight on May 14, that ship's first officer remarked to his captain how proud the *Vaterland*'s master must be. "Let him try to get up the English Channel some dirty night when he doesn't know where he is," growled old Captain Jimmy Jamison, "and he won't feel so damned proud."

They were prophetic words. At first, it seemed as though the *Vaterland*'s maiden voyage would pass without any of the incidents marring her sister's one year before. Everything worked smoothly, and Ballin was delighted to hear from her master that the *Vaterland* was stable as a rock. From midocean, *New York Times* publisher Adolph Ochs, traveling in First Class, cabled Ballin ecstatically: "The most sanguine expectations of the passengers have been fully realized. The *Vaterland* is a veritable palace afloat and its colossal proportions, ample accommodations and superb comforts are only surpassed by the sense of safety and security that in every direction impress the intelligent observer."

As she approached New York, the *New York World* trumpeted the *Vaterland*'s arrival by declaring, "$6,000,000 Sea Monster *Vaterland* to Move Majestically into This Harbor Today." A tremendous crowd gathered at her Hoboken pier, the largest ever to witness the end of a maiden voyage. The ship sailed in gracefully, with celebratory flags aflutter, and not even the slightest hint of a list. As she approached her pier, she was immediately surrounded by a cluster of waiting tugs. One of them inadvertently crossed her bow, and the *Vaterland*'s pilot hastily gave the order "All Stop." The engines ceased, the errant tug was removed, and the pilot signaled again "Slow Ahead."

Nothing happened. The ship hung dead in the water, her engines not responding. Some unknown calamity had seized them. The tide began to pull the *Vaterland* inexorably downstream, farther and farther from the waiting pier. An army of tugs strained at her hawsers, but moving the 56,000-ton inert liner was a herculean task. The ship was in ever shallower water, and she would soon be aground. Her master faced the awful possibility that his ship might become the first in New York history to be beached next to her own dock. Finally, after over three hours' work, the *Vaterland* was coaxed back from disaster and into her pier. One chronicler called the poor *Vaterland* "an unhappy bumbler from the start."

Her departure five days later seemed to confirm this opinion. The pilot, like Captain Smith of the *Titanic* two years before, underestimated the power of the giant ship's propellers and sent her roaring out of her pier at full speed. She shot like a rocket clear across the Hudson, grounding herself in the mud at the foot of Greenwich Village, Manhattan. To extricate her, the pilot ordered full power astern. The *Vaterland*'s screws thrashed furiously in the water, dragging two smaller steamers from their berths. The backwash threw ships against their piers and swamped a nearby coal barge. One person, an engineer aboard a railroad tug caught in the *Vaterland*'s wake, fell overboard and drowned. The ship finally pulled free of the muck and resumed her course, but the two incidents coming one after another were remembered by New Yorkers for decades.

The *Aquitania*'s maiden voyage passed without incident later that month, and for that brief, fateful summer season of 1914 the three greatest liners in the world sailed majestically in concert: *Aquitania* from Liverpool, *Imperator* and *Vaterland* from Hamburg. It should have been a time of triumph for Albert Ballin—his two ships were both commercial successes, hailed as the mightiest on earth, and a third, the *Bismarck*, was on the way. But no one knew better than Ballin how fragile things had become. The *Vaterland* would have the briefest career of any liner, completing only a handful of commercial voyages before the war overtook her. When she re-emerged in 1920, it would be under a different name and a different flag. The *Imperator* was destined for the same fate. Only the *Aquitania* would survive the war unscathed, returning to her peacetime career and enduring long enough to participate in the outbreak of new hostilities in 1939.

Ballin may have sensed the disaster impending for his ships. Always a nervous, highly strung man, he became subject to fits of uncontrollable rage. His temperament swung dangerously between his usual bright optimism and complete despair. He added a little plaque to the clutter on his sumptuous desk; it read "Life is just one damned thing after another." In June 1914, he dined for the last time with Winston Churchill at Churchill's home near London. Ballin appeared anxious, almost desperate. "He said the situation was grave," Churchill later recalled. "He said, 'If Russia marches against Austria, we must march: and if we march, France must march, and what would England do?'" Churchill replied guardedly that England would have to judge events as they arose. But Ballin would not be put off. "Speaking with very great earnestness," as Churchill described it, he pressed the First Lord: "'Suppose we had to go to war with Russia and France, and suppose we defeated France yet took nothing from her in Europe, not an inch of her territory, only some colonies to indemnify us. Would that make a difference to England's attitude? Suppose we gave a guarantee beforehand.'" This was utter fantasy, and Churchill knew it. He gave an evasive response, and the dinner ended on an unsettled note. Shortly thereafter Ballin returned to Germany, having failed utterly in his last desperate attempt to preserve the peace. He would never see England again.

As the last cords of Anglo-German fellowship disintegrated, Albert Ballin experienced a moment of terrible clarity. He saw the ultimate fate of his ships, caught in the inevitable conflict that would annihilate his country, his friends, his Kaiser, and himself. But most of all he understood why it had all come about, and why even he—the peacemaker—was partly to blame. Recalling his earlier justifications for Tirpitz's fleet, he now said wistfully:

> My ships did not need the protection of a German fleet,
> and I should have emphatically said so to the Kaiser. But I
> could never summon the courage to do so. . . . We were all
> too weak toward the Kaiser. No one wished to disturb his

childlike, happy optimism, which could shift at once into an almost helpless depression if anyone criticized one of his pet projects. And among these, the fleet was the greatest. Now we have the result of our lack of courage!

Almost as if in a dream conjured by Ballin in the throes of his fitful insomnia, the Kaiser presided once again at the launching of the last and greatest of HAPAG's "Big Three," the *Bismarck*, on June 20, 1914. Ballin himself was there, looking grim. The great wall of unfinished steel that stood before him, seemingly solid, was in fact caught between two dimensions of time and space; conceived in a different age, it would be completed in a different world. The *Bismarck* would require over a year of fitting out before her maiden voyage, and Ballin knew better than anyone that the peace on the Atlantic would not survive long enough to allow it. Would she be finished as an armed cruiser, sent off to be torpedoed in some remote imperial backwater? Or would they simply wrench apart her steel beams, pry off her plates, and melt them down to be recast as ammunition or railway lines? Ballin didn't know; perhaps he no longer cared. He desperately wanted to return to the sitz baths of his mountain retreat, to his wife and daughter, to his sleeping draughts. Yet the formalities still had to be observed, and he pasted on a smile as the *Bismarck*'s godmother stepped forward to do her duty. The honor of the christening was given to the Iron Chancellor's granddaughter, Countess Hanna von Bismarck. At the appointed time the young Countess pressed the trigger, the crowd cheered, and the ceremonial bottle sailed down just as it had twice before. But this time it missed the ship entirely. Onlookers gasped; it was the very worst possible omen. Wilhelm stepped forward, seized the dangling bottle, and smashed it against the *Bismarck*'s hull. It was the last contribution Kaiser Wilhelm II would make to the race of the superliners.

Eight days later Archduke Franz Ferdinand and his wife were assassinated in Sarajevo, beginning the conflict that would soon be dubbed "the war to end all wars." By that time Ballin was back in Hamburg, writing despairingly to a friend: "Nothing can be done against the forces that are at work. One can only be resigned to watch the development of this frightful experience. I am seized by a deep melancholy from which I cannot deliver myself."

-11-

Descent

IT HAD BEEN A GRUELING RACE, BUT WILHELM FINALLY BEGAN TO BELIEVE he was gaining. The wheel of the *Meteor* was in his hands, and the lovely American-built racing yacht seemed to respond instinctively to his lightest touch. Sunday, June 28, 1914, was a splendid day at Kiel, the sort of day the Kaiser loved. Just over the horizon, off Laboe, lay the British Squadron: four battleships and three cruisers. Next to it, decked in equally gay flags, was the Imperial High Seas Fleet.

Wilhelm was supremely content that afternoon, for the symbolic presence of the British fleet seemed to reinforce his private conviction that relations with England were stabilizing. His last communiqués with the island nation had been cordial, and the coronation of his cousin King George V—succeeding the hated Uncle Bertie—did much to smooth over family relations as well. Moreover, England in the summer of 1914 was suddenly far more preoccupied with her own troubles than those of the Continent. The Irish Home Rule Bill had caused bitter schisms in Parliament, as riots spread across the Irish state. Civil war seemed imminent. A second coal strike loomed menacingly. England was turning inward, looking after divisions within itself. Even the most ardent supporters of the arms race with Germany were now inclined to cavil; Winston Churchill, erstwhile First Lord of the Admiralty, sent his genuine regrets to the Kaiser that he could not join the celebrations at Kiel and earnestly hoped the invitation would be extended again in the summer season of 1915.

On Friday, in an act of sheer jubilation, Wilhelm had donned the uniform of a British Admiral of the Fleet and boarded the new super-dreadnought *King George V.* If the sight of those unmistakably Prussian mustaches quivering above the stiff, high collar and epaulettes of the King's uniform caused some British officers to wince, they hid it manfully. Indeed, by virtue of rank and uniform, the Kaiser was the most senior officer present. Other men might have recognized the ceremonial aspect of their position, but not he. Wilhelm II was the sort of man who, if provided with a robe and miter, would have immediately begun pronouncing papal edicts. Thus, when outfitted as a British admiral, it was only his nature to out-Nelson Nelson. When he observed Sir Horace Rumbold, counselor of the British Embassy in Berlin, boarding the *King George V* in a top hat and morning coat, he dressed down the unfortunate diplomat like an errant midshipman. "If I see that again," snarled Wilhelm, gesturing at the top hat, "I will smash it in. One doesn't wear tall hats on board ship."

This scolding, as much as his selection of uniform, presented an image of the Kaiser at Kiel as supremely confident in himself, his nation, and the future. The joined fleets of Britain and Germany, lying side by side in the harbor, seemed to belie the gravity of the naval race, placing it on a par with the yacht races that were soon forthcoming, and the rest of His Imperial Majesty's worldview seemed almost as serene. Wilhelm had just returned from Konopischt, Austria, where he had visited his cousin, Archduke Franz Ferdinand. He, like all the family, found the Austrian heir a terrible bore. Shy, awkward, bullet-headed, and running to fat, Franz Ferdinand had none of the grace or polish a soon-to-be monarch should have. He spent most of the visit conducting Wilhelm through his rose garden, on which the Archduke lavished most of his time and affection. It was, Wilhelm had to admit, impressive.

Yet the interminable evenings spent with Franz Ferdinand and his wife, whose common lineage led her to be snubbed by the other royals, left Wilhelm drained and depressed. He received indifferently the news that the Archduke would shortly be visiting Sarajevo, Serbia, where he would be a spectator at military maneuvers by the Austrian army. The good news, from Wilhelm's point of view, was that this gesture was meant to placate tensions—for the Archduke was, despite his morose demeanor, a progressive man. Still, Wilhelm was glad to be quit of him.

Now, back in his natural element at sea, the Emperor was blissful. He observed with complete unconcern the little launch that had just departed the starboard flank of the *Hohenzollern* and was now bearing down on the *Meteor* with what seemed like intemperate haste. Whatever the message was, Wilhelm decided, it would not interfere with his race.

But unknown to the Kaiser, events had already assumed a momentum of their own. The message from the German consul at Sarajevo had reached the shore station at Kiel in the early afternoon, where it was hastily typed out and handed to a young officer with instructions to deliver it to His Imperial Majesty in person. This proved a difficult task. As his motor launch approached the glistening white flank of the *Hohenzollern*, a tart voice asked him to state his business. "An urgent dispatch for the All-Highest," the officer replied. The voice answered back gruffly, to the effect that the All-Highest was busy. In desperation, the young man placed the telegram into his silver cigarette case and hurled it onto the deck of the yacht. Then, his duty done, he departed. Admiral Müller, who had observed the whole performance, emerged from under the stern awning, picked up the shiny little square, pried it open, and extracted its contents. Moments later he himself was in a launch, bound for the distant billowing shape of the *Meteor*.

As the launch drew alongside, the Kaiser recognized his admiral and asked what the trouble was. "I am the bearer of grave news," Müller called back portentously. He refused, however, to speak it aloud, instead waving the telegram over his head, preparing to hurl it aboard the *Meteor* just as his junior officer had done aboard the *Hohenzollern*. But the Kaiser, irritated that his race was being interrupted, demanded that Müller stop this foolishness at once and tell him what it was all about. The answer that came back paralyzed him with shock: that morning Archduke Franz Ferdinand and his wife had been assassinated in their motorcar on a street in Sarajevo. Three bullets had been pumped into the fat body of the Austrian heir, and the details that emerged later were merely a footnote to the tragedy: doctors seeking to cut open his clothes and examine the wounds were foiled by a complex system of wires and harness that kept Franz Ferdinand's corpulence in check. By the time this apparatus could be taken apart, it was all over.

The Kaiser received the news with despair. "This unutterable misfortune has shaken me to the very depths," he would later write to the Grand Duchess Louise. In a moment, his serene universe had collapsed upon him. And the agent of its destruction was the one that was anathema to the Emperor's soul: an anarchist's bullet. Only a few years earlier he had confessed his fears of anarchy and socialism to J. P. Morgan, who could not understand them. Morgan's world—the world of finance—functioned on rational principles, from which it could not and did not diverge. Wilhelm's, on the other hand, was just as carefully constructed, yet vulnerable to the ever-present threat of revolution and anarchy. Now, just when his Byzantine system of allegiance and betrayal finally seemed to be bearing fruit, chaos moved to snatch peace from his very grasp. To the end of his life, Kaiser Wilhelm would insist that from this moment on he was maneuvered into a war he did not want and had no ability to control. Holding his head in his hands on the stern of the *Meteor*, he began muttering to himself. The British Ambassador, seated nearby as Wilhelm's honored guest, overheard his enigmatic words. To him they meant nothing, but for a man faced with the ruin of his life's work, they were apt indeed. "Now I shall have to start all over again," said Kaiser Wilhelm II.

The Singular Adventure of the "German Gold Ship"

The horrible destiny that Albert Ballin so deeply feared was finally coming to pass. Austria-Hungary declared war on Serbia on July 28, Germany declared war on France and Russia on August 3, and Great Britain declared war on Germany the following day. "The lamps," Sir Edward Grey famously said, "have gone out all over Europe."

The outbreak of war reduced the orderly schedule of the liners to

a state of utter chaos. Wireless sets crackled the length and breadth of
the Atlantic as ships were issued urgent new instructions. In a moment,
the vessels had gone from goodwill ambassadors to massive floating targets. Rumors of armed merchant cruisers (the submarine being as yet
an untried menace) added urgency to the ships' dash for shore. Yet their
destinations varied according to circumstance. The *Olympic*, three days
out of Southampton, remained on course for New York but increased
her speed. The *Mauretania* closed her wireless and raced to Halifax, her
Blue Riband engines sustaining an incredible speed of 28 knots. She
was followed shortly by the ancient *Cedric*. The *Lusitania* left New York
at 1:00 A.M., carrying only a handful of passengers. Ships' blankets were
draped over the portholes, and the passengers and crew suffered under
the dim glow of oil lamps—the first appearance of this ancient kind of
lighting in a luxury vessel since the 1880s. Hamburg and Bremerhaven
sent out anxious messages to all their ships, calling them home to the
Fatherland, or at least to a neutral port. For most German vessels, this
meant New York. The *Friedrich der Grosse*, whose captain was even
more cautious than the *Lusitania*'s, made the passage in complete darkness. On entering New York Harbor, she joined her sister ships the
Grosse Kurfurst and the oddly named *President Grant*, which had beaten
her there by a few hours. All in all, those two days in August saw a
frenzied migration of ocean tonnage unparalleled in earlier history,
equaled only by similar events on the North Atlantic in 1939 and in
American skies on September 11, 2001. In an age before radar, literally hundreds of ships altered their courses and sailed pell-mell for unscheduled ports on both sides of the Atlantic. To make matters worse,
a thick fog had descended over the Eastern Seaboard from Newfound-
land to New York. With wireless sets shut down for fear of enemy lis-
teners, signal lights blacked out, and engines running at full speed,
ships' captains were like blind men driving tractor-trailers through a
city at rush hour. Yet, miraculously, over the course of the next few
days, every ship arrived in harbor without serious mishap.

For those German ships berthed in New York, a long period of idleness began; many, in fact, would never see commercial service again.
Under orders not to endanger their vessels, and with the threat of Allied
warships cordoning off the East Coast, German captains had no choice
but to wait out events. Thirty-five liners, the bulk of the German

transatlantic fleet, rocked listlessly at their piers in Hoboken. The *Kaiser Wilhelm II*, flagship of North German Lloyd, was joined by fifteen of her sisters. Hamburg-Amerika's *Amerika* and *George Washington* lay close by. But by far the greatest vessel trapped in Hoboken was the enormous, still-new *Vaterland*, just arrived from her seventh voyage across the Atlantic. Her story was tragic: On July 31, three days after the outbreak of hostilities, her engines were busily building up steam in preparation for another eastward crossing. A record number of passengers, 2,700, were already picking their way along the *Vaterland*'s labyrinthine passageways toward their staterooms. Tons of baggage had been loaded aboard. Then a message reached the ship's bridge from Berlin, warning of French and British cruisers lying in wait for her just over the horizon. Regretfully, the baggage was removed, the irate passengers disembarked, and the engines closed down. So began a period of stagnancy for the giant vessel that would last for almost three years before a new master seized her for quite a different purpose.

Yet by far the strangest story in the early months of the war was that of the Lloyd liner *Kronprinzessin Cecilie*. Sailing with over a thousand passengers and a fabulous cargo of gold bullion and silver valued at eleven million dollars, the *Cecilie* was bound for Plymouth and Bremerhaven when her captain received the following message: "Erhard has suffered attack of catarrh of the bladder. Seigfried." Decoded, this silly missive meant that war was imminent, and Captain Polack must take every measure to prevent his ship's capture by the British. Polack, a cool man in an emergency, made up his mind at once. The *Cecilie* came about, alert passengers noticing that her engines had suddenly increased speed, while the moon—which had been hanging low to starboard—now blazed to port. Polack himself addressed the First Class passengers in the grand saloon. Silencing the orchestra, he said calmly, "Ladies and gentlemen, it is my duty to inform you that I have orders from the Imperial German Government to take this ship to a neutral port in the United States." After assuring them that the ship had plenty of stores to sustain the passage and admonishing them to "keep their heads," Polack turned on his heel and strode out.

The First Class passenger list on that voyage included several U.S. senators, numerous executives, and a shooting party of aristocrats en route to savage the grouse in Scotland. Their reaction to Polack's curt announcement—unanimous shock and outrage—was quickly replaced by wily Yankee cunning. A committee was formed, and in short order a contingent arrived on the bridge. Thereupon these men offered to an astonished Captain Polack to purchase the *Kronprinzessin Cecilie* for five million dollars, plus a bonus for the captain himself. He could then hoist the Stars and Stripes with a clear conscience and sail to England under a neutral flag. Polack, doubtless thinking of the Imperial Navy's reaction should this ever come out, demurred gracefully.

He did, however, concoct a scheme of his own. As the *Cecilie* sped westward, paint crews dangled from hoists on her four funnels. The signature color of North German Lloyd funnels was a yellowish dun; at a distance, it was virtually indistinguishable from White Star Line's yellowish beige. The difference, of course, was that White Star funnels were capped with black bands. The paint crews now affixed these bands to the *Cecilie*, as well as blacking out her name from the stern and bow. Polack, knowing the threat posed by English cruisers, was attempting to disguise his ship as the *Olympic*. But it was a specious plan at best, for the *Cecilie* was half the size of the British ship and her funnels—though now the same color as the *Olympic*'s—were paired in the German fashion. Even from a distance, there was no mistaking them for the *Olympic*'s evenly spaced quartet.

As it turned out, Polack's fears were not unfounded. The French liner *La Savoie*, hours ago a friendly competitor on the North Atlantic run, had spotted the *Cecilie* and relayed her coordinates and probable course to French and British warships stationed nearby. With a king's ransom in gold, which the American press had gloated over just days before, she was better prey than a Spanish galleon. The warships altered their course in pursuit, and the hunt was on for the *Kronprinzessin Cecilie*.

Her lights extinguished and traveling at full speed, the *Cecilie* tore through the fog in her bizarre disguise. Polack had abandoned hope of reaching New York: any port deep enough to accommodate the liner would do. Passengers feeling the frenzied vibration of the ship's engines and seeing the grim curtain of white outside their portholes became terrified and approached Polack again, this time demanding that he slow down. The captain brusquely refused, agreeing only to sound the foghorn more frequently. But the fog that imperiled the Cecilie may have saved her as well, for only in its murky half-light could the ship be mistaken for the bulkier, drastically different *Olympic*.

The *Cecilie* finally reached shore and safety on the evening of August 7—not in her Hoboken slip, but in the chillier latitudes of Bar Harbor, Maine. Residents of the sleepy summer colony, many of whom had never seen a vessel bigger than the night ferries from Fall River, Massachusetts, awoke to find a monstrous vessel resembling the ghost of the *Titanic* looming in their bay.

Having escaped peril on the high seas, Captain Polack and his crew now found themselves unwilling participants in New England's glittering social season. Invitations from society matrons poured onto the officers: invitations to tea, to dinner, to dance. Sailing parties were organized to give the officers events remininiscent of Kiel Week back home, while the entire Star Theatre gave up showing the "Perils of Pauline" and other favorites to entertain the *Cecilie*'s crew full-time. The Germans responded graciously by staging concerts featuring the ship's band on the village green. The band finished their first concert with "America," but the great crowd that had gathered clamored so lustily that they were forced to fall back on Teutonic favorites such as "Watch on the Rhine" for encores. With gestures such as these, Captain Polack and his crew became the undisputed social lions of Bar Harbor.

Yet the euphoria could not last. Summer changed to fall, and the transient vacation community of Bar Harbor dispersed. Trains and ferries spirited the resort's summer residents back to their inland homes, while the remaining townspeople closed their shutters, heated their wood stoves, and prepared for another fierce Maine winter. Fall changed to winter and still the *Kronprinzessin Cecilie* remained. By this time the American press had caught wind of her plight and was inclined to view the whole business as a tremendously good joke. "Captain Polack is penning his adventure with an ocean leviathan," wrote one journalist,

> to accessories of wireless, gun play, fog and foreign war. . . .
> All the elements of the popular novel are in the exploit: international complications, a huge treasure of gold bullion in the hold; the mystery of fog, the uncertain effects of wireless communication; a group of American financiers in the smoking room able and willing to buy the five million

dollar craft in order that they might go where they pleased.
The thing has a lordly sound. It has stupendous humor. . . .
The *Cecilie* is safe until further notice.

She was safe, to be sure, but idle as well. The changing seasons brought with them the war in earnest, and the crew felt the ties of the Fatherland tugging at them. Moreover, a complicated legal suit involving the famous bullion (now resting safely in the Manhattan bank from whence it came, having been returned by train that summer) ensued. Deputy Marshal Eugene C. Harmon, the acting force of law in Bar Harbor, was ordered majestically to "seize the ship." From then on the *Cecilie* was watched by a torpedo boat and cutter from the U.S. Navy, as though at any moment she would fire up her boilers and disappear with a derisive blast of her horn.

When the decision was finally made—by Assistant Secretary of the Navy Franklin D. Roosevelt—to move the *Cecilie* to Boston, all Bar Harbor figuratively draped itself in black. "The streets of the town have been made interesting by the presence of the officers and crew of the big liner," the *Bar Harbor Record* lamented, "and Captain Polack has been the recipient of many social courtesies and has proven to be a most delightful gentleman. . . ." Nostalgia mingled with commerce in the author's concluding comment, for the *Kronprinzessin Cecilie* had been good business for the town: "Bar Harbor citizens have hoped that the big liner would stay here until the conclusion of the big European war," he wrote, "for business and social reasons." Ironically, the latest turn of events delighted no one more than Captain Polack, who by then had grown weary of the cold Maine town and its parochial charms. "You know," he would later tell a Boston reporter, hand upon his heart, "down here I am glad that I am in Boston. It was getting to be cold and lonesome in Bar Harbor." Boston proved far more congenial for captain and crew, both in climate and entertainment. Crew members began taking night classes at Boston schools and checking books out of the Boston Public Library. The adventurous career of the *Kronprinzessin Cecilie* had ended, and a long period of listless somnolence had begun.

Still, it all made for a good tale. "Now that the Bar Harbor season is over," one American pundit wrote facetiously, "perhaps the *Cecilie* would enjoy Palm Beach."

The Liners Go to War: Trials and Tribulations of the Auxiliary Fleet

Their mad dash for safety was only the first of many problems to beset the British and German ocean liners. Once they were safe, what was to be done with them? To the Admiralties of both nations, the answer seemed obvious: they would be converted to armed merchant cruisers and sent off to harass enemy fleets.

The tradition of an armed auxiliary merchant fleet dated back to the sailing navy of Britain's second "Hundred Years War," the period of intermittent conflict with France beginning with the succession of William of Orange in 1688 and ending with the defeat of Napoleon at Waterloo in 1815. During this time, merchant and naval vessels resembled each other greatly, the differences between them often as trivial as the presence of cannons and a greater number of crew aboard navy ships. Conversion from one to the other was a simple affair and could be completed by a competent dockyard in a matter of days. Alongside purpose-built naval frigates there appeared a sizeable auxiliary fleet of former merchant vessels equipped with cannon and royal charter, whose job it was to seize and destroy enemy merchant vessels and disrupt enemy commerce. Often these ships kept their original captains and crews, adding nothing more than an extra cannon on the main deck. Canny heads at the Admiralty reasoned that such a navy would be not only effective but cheap: as merchant cruisers were allowed a share of their captured plunder, the voyages in effect paid for themselves.

The scheme was wildly successful. While the Royal Navy engaged in the destruction of its French nemesis and arranged troop transport, invasion, and the seizure of port towns, the auxiliary merchant fleet took on the humbler but no less vital task of robbing France of her supplies. By the end of the long war, France had been bled white.

Thus, when war broke out in 1914, it was immediately assumed that the liners would don the mantle of their ancestors and be sent off at once to confound enemy shipping. The idea of passenger liners as quasi-battleships, though it strikes the modern mind as ridiculous, seemed eminently reasonable to the Edwardians. It was cheap, effective, and a sure-fire morale booster. (After all, what could be more inspiring

than a beloved liner like the *Mauretania* slugging it out for Britain?)
A century of naval engineering and ballistics technology had, incredibly, done nothing to discourage this naïve optimism. In the tense
months preceding the war, German liners appeared festooned with suspicious mountings; an Imperial Navy Act two years earlier had proposed that all merchant vessels carry guns below decks. The *Kaiser Wilhelm II* caused a momentary uproar when she put into Southampton
for repairs following a Channel collision, and observant workers spotted a large cross-shaped crate on her foredeck. Anxious reports filtered
back to Whitehall that German liners were now boasting long-range
artillery.

The British were no less committed to assembling an auxiliary fleet.
In the first weeks of the war a rapid stream of communiqués flowed
out of the Admiralty, causing humor and consternation throughout the
merchant fleet. The *Olympic, Lusitania, Mauretania, Carmania*, and
other ships were issued orders to proceed to assigned docks and commence conversion to merchant cruisers. Typically, this meant strip-
ping the ship of her furnishings, reinforcing her exposed areas with
extra steel plating, mounting a few perfunctory guns forward and aft,
and covering the whole business in drab navy gray.

The larger process of conversion, however, obscured a plethora of
minor details intended to remove any vestiges of the ship's civilian purpose. Crews were trained in the proper salute and spent weeks drilling
under navy commanders. Ship's officers received similar treatment; resentment sprang up between navy officers and their civilian counterparts, many of whom had received overnight commissions. Both the
British and the Germans reasoned, quite sensibly, that the best people to
run these vessels were those who had already done so. It was a rare moment of clear thinking; naval officers, trained on board dreadnoughts
and cruisers, would be utterly lost on a 50,000-ton, 26-knot mastodon.

The transition from liner to cruiser was hardly as simple a matter as
guns and gray paint. The Cunard ship *Laconia*, undergoing conversion at Plymouth, was loaded down with seventy tons of cordite; the
crew, unable to find any other place for it, kept the munitions safe in
the cold storage rooms alongside barons of beef. Tons of plush furniture, miles of carpeting, and great slabs of marble flooring appeared
on the quaysides at Portsmouth, Southampton, and Liverpool, yet the

Aquitania's wartime hospital patients found themselves nursed to
health in a room that still bore the Adam paneling and bucolic land-
scapes of its former incarnation as the First Class Lounge. Some details of the transition from civilian to military roles crossed the line
from the reasonable to the superfluous or the outright bizarre—as
when, by direct order of the British Admiralty, the White Star liner
Oceanic's carpenter was solemnly equipped with a sword.

And yet the decision to arm these ships and send them out against
the enemy was not made on the spur of the moment. Rather, it was
something that had been planned for since the construction of the ships
themselves. When Parliament saved Cunard from the clutches of
J. P. Morgan, it was on the understanding that the massive grant bestowed on the line would be used to construct vessels capable of easy
wartime conversion. Also, all the vessels constructed by the Hamburg-
Amerika Line under the aegis of the German government were theo-
retically designed for rapid changeover to military utility. In reality,
however, Albert Ballin was so horrified by the thought of war that he
could not even contemplate the thought of losing his beautiful vessels
to its devastation. Thus the *Vaterland,* designed for service in peace,
with her marble bathtubs, Pompeian Bath, and myriad other luxuries,
would prove to be the most difficult conversion project of the war.

On August 3, the day before Britain declared war on Germany,
the British Admiralty issued orders for the immediate conversion of the
Lusitania and *Mauretania* to armed merchant cruisers. Their captains,
like Polack on the *Kronprinzessin Cecilie*, received coded instructions
at sea. New captains from the Royal Navy were appointed to command
the Cunard superliners; a third captain was dispatched to Liverpool to
oversee the conversion. The whole business was so rapid that Cunard
barely had time to catch its breath, much less protest. The General
Manager of the line was successful only in insuring the ships against
possible sinking as they returned from their aborted westbound voyages. It seemed as though the ultimate destiny of the dual-purpose liners was finally coming to pass. Gun platforms had already been constructed on their upper decks; the guns themselves awaited the vessels
in Liverpool. Admiralty orders called for the clearing of space around
the gun mountings, anticipating even more rapid conversion and
recommissioning.

But just as abruptly, the Admiralty changed its mind. On September 14, 1914, the merchant cruiser and ex-Cunarder *Carmania* was pummeled almost to extinction by another cruiser, the German *Cap Trafalgar*. The resulting carnage was so appalling on both sides that the practicality of using passenger liners as quasi-warships was questioned even before the conversion of the *Mauretania* and *Lusitania* could be completed. Ultimately the Admiralty decided to dry-dock the *Mauretania* for possible future use and allow the *Lusitania* to continue her civilian operations between Liverpool and New York. The decision was justified on the grounds of redundancy: with most German shipping already bottled up in neutral ports, the need for cruisers was less than anticipated. Thus, with a single stroke, all the tortured effort expended in making the *Lusitania* and *Mauretania* easily convertible to naval use had come to nothing. They were, for the moment, obsolete relics of another age.

The sad truth was that while the logic of an armed merchant fleet may have seemed perfectly sound to engineers in peacetime, the reality during war was quite another matter. Passenger liners, with their lounges and filigree and terrifyingly high fuel consumption, made miserable warships. They had none of a destroyer's nimbleness, a battleship's heavy armor, or a dreadnought's lethal array of artillery. With little more than a few stray guns (often without ammunition) and a new prefix—"HMS" for British ships, "SMS" for German—the liners sailed into a hostile Atlantic fraught with the hazards of a new technological age: submarines, sea mines, long-range weaponry. The best that can be said of their careers as armed merchant cruisers is that they were, without exception, short.

The Strange Voyage of the Kronprinz Wilhelm, "Mystery Cruiser"

The odyssey of the *Kronprinz Wilhelm* is a case in point. When war erupted the *Wilhelm* was in Hoboken, taking on her usual passenger load and supplies. Her orders came in the early afternoon, and at once the passengers were disembarked and far more stores were taken aboard. Only the officers were told the reason. The crew worked in silence, loading foodstuffs and extra coal into the ship's bunkers.

Finally, three days later, the *Kronprinz Wilhelm* slipped quietly out of her berth at 8:10 P.M., the late summer dusk still tracing her shadow across the bay. To prevent detection at sea, crewmen had nailed mattresses and tarpaulins over the portholes, giving the ship a ghostly, deserted feeling as she steamed through the Verrazano Narrows.

Her rendezvous lay halfway across the Atlantic with the supply ship *Karlsruhe*. Painters covered the hull, decks, and bridge in sea-gray camouflage while the ship's four funnels (paired, like the *Cecilie's*, forward and aft) were given black bands around their tops. The wireless carried almost hourly messages warning of imminent enemy presence, and it was with some relief that smoke sighted on the horizon proved to be that of the *Karlsruhe*, awaiting them. Once there the *Wilhelm* transferred mail and supplies and took on a navy captain, Lieutenant Commander Thierfelder, to replace the civilian Captain Grahn. This was the only change made in the ship's personnel; the *Wilhelm's* officers and crew—the bakers, stewards, stokers, trimmers, dining staff, and hairdressers—were now in the service of the Imperial Navy.

The commander called his officers into the recently vacated captain's cabin and explained their new duty. Their mission, he told them, was to capture and sink the enemy's merchant fleet. They would not put into port; they would draw their supplies and fuel from their prizes. Prisoners taken from prize vessels would be adequately treated and returned to shore on neutral ships as soon as humanly possible. The Admiralty had been most specific on this point. The *Kronprinz Wilhelm's* prisoners were to be treated as guests, accorded First Class accommodation and the full services of the ship's staff. Captured crews would be berthed in Second Class. Prisoners would receive the same food as the crew of the *Wilhelm* herself. (Though in practice the eager dining staff, more at ease with peacetime passengers than wartime service, were grateful for their unexpected guests and often treated them better. The situation would eventually become so divisive that complaints were made to the captain, who assured his men that "no partiality was being shown" to the enemy "guests.")

With his officers thus brought up to speed, Thierfelder addressed his crew. "Men of German blood," he said proudly, "your Fatherland has chosen you for a high duty—that of harassing the commerce of the enemy, thus making it harder for him to continue war against your brothers in the trenches. Our duty is to sink merchant ships, at the same time taking due care for the safety of their passengers and crew. Remember, men," he cautioned them, "we hope soon to begin our captures; then the time of temptation and self-control will begin. On the ships we take will be valuables, intoxicants, and women. . . ." Derisive laughter was quickly stilled by the commander's forbidding scowl. "Let not one drunken seaman disgrace the voyage of the *Kronprinz Wilhelm*," he growled. "Remember your mothers, your wives, your sisters. I need say no more."

A properly chastised crew now began the arduous task of converting their liner into an armed warship. Mattresses, carpets, and bags were strung over the ship's sides as supposed protection from shrapnel. Mattresses became a priceless commodity, and only the most vulnerable areas of the ship—the hospital and the bridge, for example—were awarded the dubious security of "mattress protection." Target practice began with the ship's two short-range guns, small-caliber weapons mounted on the bow and stern. This was complicated by the fact that there was currently no ammunition aboard the *Kronprinz Wilhelm*; consequently, as each gun was trained on imaginary targets, the crew raised and lowered their hands to indicate when the shot had been fired, and the officers on watch covered their ears against the imaginary explosion. The classic phrase "clear for action" also took on unexpectedly comic overtones, as the crew scurried about securing wicker chairs and greenery, taking up their stations under the beveled glass skylight in the First Class lounge, or peering through peepholes hastily erected through mattress barricades on the shuffleboard court.

Count Alfred von Neitzychowski (known to his friends as Neizy), the *Wilhelm*'s first officer, described a more poignant spectacle. In acts of destruction repeated throughout the merchant fleets of Britain and Germany, the luxurious trappings of the *Kronprinz Wilhelm* were ruthlessly gutted to make way for military necessities. The smoking room became a hospital, while the glorious grand saloon was dismantled entirely to become an auxiliary coal bin. "I remember with what a pang I suddenly came upon the beginning of this work," Neizy wrote.

> Just as I appeared at the grand stairway, the great mirrors were
> being taken down, and the empty walls behind them looked
> as if they were gasping for breath. I felt like a man who

watches the workmen begin to tear down his old home. . . .
Only the day before I had sat back in the plush cushions
gazing around me with a feeling of unlimited possession,
while only the faint and far-off rumble of the engines and
the never-ceasing tremor of the ship as she rose and fell on
the unstable sea reminded me that I was not in Eden or
Empyrean but on the tempestuous war-darkened ocean.

    "This is war," I grumbled when I saw all this splendor
vanish. "War alone would permit this blasphemy—war, the
destroyer."

Neizy's expulsion from the plush-cushioned Eden of the First Class
lounge, a blasphemy in 1914, would hardly impress veterans of the
Somme or Passchendaele. But few accounts so vividly recall the loss of
innocence, the transition from peaceful security to wartime anxiety, or
the sense of grim irony that was the beginning of the First World War.
Neizy, like so many others, would lose friends and relatives in the war.
But it was that first image that remained with him—his ship suffering
indignities beyond imagining. The liners were thus unique: the transition from peace to war could actually be witnessed in them. Imagine,
by comparison, the London Ritz being converted to a barracks or Atlantic City to an armed fortress, and one might appreciate the singular
role of the *Kronprinz Wilhelm* and her fellows.

In due time, the *Kronprinz Wilhelm* took her first prize—a tiny
Russian fishing vessel, the *Pittan* of Riga. Lieutenant Fix clambered
aboard the trawler, drew himself up before its bedraggled captain, and
announced, "You are a prisoner of war. Give us your papers. We are
going to sink your ship."

The Russian's reaction took Fix aback. "Sink my ship?" he said un-
believingly, looking around him. He then threw his head back and cried
aloud in Slavic despair. "This ship is all I have," he wailed. "I have
worked years—saved, starved myself—to buy this ship. Now I'm
ruined. My wife, my children—they will be penniless. I'm a ruined man.
I'm a ruined man." The Russian then sank into inarticulate sobs.

The Germans were mortified. The *Kronprinz Wilhelm* loomed lu-
dicrously over the tiny trawler, looking like a grim gray giant deciding
whether or not to squash the vessel under foot. Fix himself went to
Thierfelder, explaining the situation and asking for leniency. The commander, his severe expression unchanging, agreed. Fix went back to

the *Pittan*, beaming with good news. The Russian, now equally moved to tears of gratitude, promised not to disclose his encounter with the German cruiser, assured them of his perpetual hospitality should they ever visit Riga, and presented the astonished captain with two jugs of fiery homemade brandy. It was the *Wilhelm*'s first prize; the crew divvied it up accordingly.

After this first rather anticlimactic encounter came a number of successes. The British liner *Indian Prince* sailed right under the *Wilhelm*'s lee, her commander mistaking the vessel—not surprisingly—for a neutral passenger ship. This minor triumph was quickly followed by a quick succession of French captures, the liner *La Correntina* and the barks *Union* and *Anne de Bretagne*. In each, the pattern repeated itself. The enemy ship approached unaware, then struck her colors at once as the *Wilhelm*'s guns swiveled to face her decks. It mattered little that the weapons were unloaded; not one of the prizes had so much as a signal gun to answer with. Once alongside, passengers and crew were transferred aboard the *Wilhelm*. There the astonished prisoners were greeted with smiles, warm blankets, and First Class staterooms. "There was a total absence of grumbling as the men came aboard, dragging their baggage or bearing it upon their shoulders," Neizy noted. "The passengers accepted our courtesies with thanks—indeed they were gratified to be treated as free men and given first class berths—while the officers and crew, bowing to the lot of war, took their second class quarters, glad not to be given worse."

In fact, many of these unexpected guests regarded their being taken prisoner by the *Kronprinz Wilhelm* as a happy accident, like winning a luxury cruise in a sweepstakes. Comforted by the promise of transfer to the first homebound neutral ship, the *Wilhelm*'s ragtag captives created a warm camaraderie below decks, not far removed from that of passengers in a round-the-world peacetime cruise. Sporting events were organized, and the ship's band entertained prisoners and crew alike with spirited renditions of *The Merry Widow* waltz and other favorites. The *Wilhelm*'s staff delighted in encouraging this jovial fiction. When the London-bound *Highland Brae* was found to carry a large number of women and children, the crew outdid themselves; the children were immediately treated to ice cream and cake made specially under the supervision of the head chef, while the awestruck ladies, expecting a quick and dirty end under the apish hands of the Hun, were presented with needlework fashioned by the *Wilhelm*'s crew. The poor women were so overcome with relief that they became hysterical.

Not everything was tea and cakes, however. A contingent of captured British merchant officers considered themselves poorly treated; on reaching the bridge, they promised, if released, to unload their cargo ashore and then return to a given position and let the *Kronprinz Wilhelm* capture them again. Thierfelder refused. This was still a ship of war, not a ferry boat. The *Wilhelm*'s crew underlined this distinction by making a grand show of searching each prisoner on arrival for weapons, pilfered valuables, and alcohol. "We took these articles from them," says a pious Niezy, "assuring them that all *legitimate* possessions would be given back later on." Women, of course, were immune from such tactics. The gallant crew merely accepted their assurance that they carried nothing seditious; those who looked suspicious—"and there were a few later on"—were segregated and kept under observation.

The *Wilhelm*'s crew was also not above a little playful teasing when the occasion warranted. The temptation was enormous; prisoners, primed by newspaper propaganda to expect a bloodthirsty crew of pirates, were easy prey, and some waggish crewmen couldn't resist. One of the crewmen on the captured ship *Anne de Bretagne* was a Dane. Scholke, the ship's comedian, fell upon the man and pronounced him his long-lost brother. He cried. They embraced. The Dane, nonplussed, did some quick thinking. After the first flush of complete nonrecognition, he declared that yes, it was true, this man was indeed his forgotten kinsman. At once Scholke stepped back, looked at him quizzically, and said this man was not his brother, but instead an old acquaintance who owed him money. He demanded the sum. The poor Dane then burst into jabbering incoherencies, and the crew exploded with laughter.

If captivity on the *Kronprinz Wilhelm* was not exactly a seagoing carnival, it was still a far cry from prison. Niezy would later describe the scene as a new complement of prisoners from the *Bellevue* arrived on board: "The prisoners already quartered there from the *Union* and the *Anne de Bretagne* welcomed the newcomers cordially and fraternized with them in their common misfortune. Some seemed to regard the

whole business as a good joke; others were incensed over their deten-
tion; still others merely shrugged, looked cynically content, and confined themselves to borrowing tobacco and playing cards. Once the
tiresome business of taking prisoners aboard was completed, a far more
vital task began. The *Kronprinz Wilhelm* was at sea for over a year, never
once putting into port. Her engines consumed several tons of coal per
day. It was imperative that each captured ship deliver up its fuel to the
Wilhelm's bunkers, and every shovelful was precious. Coaling at sea is
a tricky business; the two ships must be brought alongside one another,
gunwale to gunwale. Then the lower ports are opened, a conveyer is
stretched between them, and the process begins. In calm seas this is
merely cumbersome; on the North Atlantic in a heavy swell, it's often
impossible. The two ships pitch and rock out of synch, the coal is
heaved into the sea, and the ports—which are only one deck above sea
level—are continually awash. Coaling was the bane of every merchant
cruiser, a dangerous, time-consuming, and frequent ordeal that kept the
ships perpetually in search of fuel.

Therein lay an additional difference between the *Kronprinz Wilhelm* and the armed merchant fleet of Nelson's day; while a frigate
needed only the wind and a star to steer by, a twentieth-century passenger liner owed every knot of speed, every nautical mile of distance,
to the coal in her bunkers. Without it she was as helpless as a kitten, as
was the *Wilhelm*'s famous elder sister, the *Kaiser Wilhelm der Grosse*,
when her nemesis finally caught her in the Rio de Oro, Spanish West
Africa. The liner had, like the *Kronprinz Wilhelm*, recently undergone
a conversion to armed merchant cruiser. In her brief career, she sank
three British ships and detained three others for inspection. She was
tied alongside a supply ship, receiving her precious fuel supply, when
HMS *Highflyer* approached from out of nowhere. Tethered and vulnerable, the *Kaiser Wilhelm der Grosse* could not escape. A brief pitched
battle ensued, while the crew of the stricken liner frantically tried to
complete her coaling and start her engines. Strafed, exhausted, and
out of ammunition, the captain ordered her scuttled. Scarcely one
month after the war began the first of the great liners was lost.

Once coaling was complete, if indeed that was possible, and every
remaining valuable had been removed from the prize ship, Lieutenant
Thierfelder would give the order to sink her. For some vessels this was

as simple as venting her seacocks—valves located in the bottom of the hull—and letting her settle gradually into the water. Older ships, however, were often, oddly, harder to sink. The *Anne de Bretagne*, for example, clung to life with a Rasputin-like tenacity; she resisted firing, ramming, and a charge of dynamite, and was finally abandoned as a broken but still defiant derelict. When a prize proved particularly difficult to submerge, the sharp prow of the *Kronprinz Wilhelm* was brought into action. Cleaving into the ship like a giant knife, she rammed and sank the French steamer *Mont Agel*, a livestock hauler from Brest. The little ship proved remarkably resilient; the *Wilhelm* struck her amidships first to port, then to starboard, and again in the stern before she finally gave up the ghost. It was at that moment that a tiny figure appeared at the *Mont Agel's* stern. Efforts had been made to locate and remove every animal from the ship, including two dogs, several cats, and a few canaries. But one had apparently been overlooked: a small tabby pacing up and down the shattered deck, mewing despondently. The crew were so unnerved by the sight that one actually volunteered to row over to the vessel and rescue the terrified feline, but the commander—probably fearing the suction of the dying ship—refused. Moments later an explosion from the submerged boilers suddenly engulfed the *Mont Agel* in an inferno of smoke and debris, and both ship and cat were gone.

The Last Duel

Throughout her year-long tour of duty, the *Kronprinz Wilhelm* never fired a single shot in anger, partly because she had no ammunition for much of her cruise but also because her prizes were, without exception, undefended. The *Wilhelm* and her consorts preyed on the weak and the defenseless; tramp steamers, fishing boats, and the like. This was not cowardice; had the *Kronprinz Wilhelm* met any resistance, she would likely have been annihilated. Her first officer was clear on that point—her standing orders were to flee at the first sign of danger. With two paltry guns forward and aft and little else but mattresses and cotton wadding in between, her sizeable bulk made her a sitting target for even the most lightly armed ship of the Royal Navy. The guiding principle of the armed merchant cruisers was to live to fight another day;

hence it is not surprising that their entire history furnishes only one recorded instance of actual combat.

The Cunard liner *Carmania*, once the "wonder ship" with Parson engines, was now eleven years old and showing her age. She had been on the short list for refurbishment when war broke out, and plans were hastily redrawn to convert her to a cruiser. Much of the refitting was done at the expense of the ship; as in the case of the *Kronprinz Wilhelm*, as many of her fittings and furnishings as could be pried loose were heaved over the side or burned. Eight 4.7-inch cannons were mounted on her decks, and she was painted battleship gray—exactly the same color as the German merchant cruisers. Thus equipped, the *Carmania* steamed into a remote corner of the South Atlantic to begin her patrols.

At Trindade Island off Brazil she encountered the *Cap Trafalgar*. Newly built by the Hamburg-Amerika Line, the German ship had, like the *Carmania*, undergone a frantic conversion: her dummy funnel removed, two 4-inch guns and six machine guns fitted aboard. When the *Carmania* spotted her she was engaged in the same tiresome business that had doomed the *Kaiser Wilhelm der Grosse* and threatened the *Kronprinz Wilhelm*: coaling. At first, neither ship recognized the other. Then Captain Grant aboard the *Carmania* ran Royal Navy white ensigns up all the halyards; the *Cap Trafalgar* responded with the ensign of the Imperial Navy. As per rules of engagement, Grant put a warning shot across her bows. The *Trafalgar* answered, rather surprisingly, with a burst of machine gun fire aimed at her enemy's bridge.

Already the *Cap Trafalgar* had flouted the rules; now she went further. Throwing caution to the winds, she closed the distance between herself and her opponent and began strafing the *Carmania* with her machine guns. But the machine guns' range was a fraction of the *Carmania*'s artillery, and Grant was able to bring five of his cannons to bear. The duel had begun.

The effect of sustained firepower on both ships was soon horribly apparent. Though roughly equal in munitions, neither enjoyed the customary protections of a warship. Their fragile steel hulls buckled and splintered, and their decks were soon laid waste. As the range closed to a mile and a half, the *Carmania*'s fire control was lost, her bridge utterly destroyed, and her superstructure a twisted wreckage. The *Cap Trafalgar* was in worse shape. While she had aimed her guns at the *Carma-*

nia's decks, the *Carmania* had pounded away at her waterline, which proved the wiser course. Though apparently more intact, the *Cap Trafalgar* was listing heavily and moving sluggishly through the water. A single shell fired from one of the *Carmania*'s cannons blew a great hole in the *Trafalgar*'s deck amidships, landing just twenty feet from a dazed engineer named Powell. As Powell approached the gaping hole in shock, a burst of compressed air from behind vaulted him into the sea. From there he watched as the giant, looming bulk of the *Cap Trafalgar* settled more and more into the ocean around him. He was picked up several hours later. As if belatedly aware of her orders, the *Trafalgar* abruptly ceased firing and attempted to escape. But the pressure of turning around and increasing steam merely exposed more of her fractured hull to the sea, and she foundered. "More and more," said one eyewitness on the *Carmania*, "the big liner fell over until at last her funnels lay upon the water, and then, after a moment's apparent hesitation, with her bow submerged, she heaved herself upright and sank bodily. It had been a good fight . . . and when, as she vanished, the men of the *Carmania* raised a cheer, it was hardly less for their own victory than as a tribute to the enemy."

The English crew had good reason to honor their enemy. Though the *Carmania* was still afloat, she was in scarcely better condition. Her steering controls had been shot away, she was plagued with fires, and her upper decks were almost unrecognizable. No fewer than seventy-five rounds had punctured her sides. Frantic SOS signals from the *Cap Trafalgar* had brought every German ship for miles racing to her side—among them the *Kronprinz Wilhelm*—and the *Carmania* was in no condition to continue the fray. Joined by the cruisers *Bristol* and *Cromwell*, which had arrived that night in response to her urgent summons, the *Carmania* limped for shore. She was in such a sorry state that both cruisers were virtually stripped of their extra steering components just to patch up the *Carmania*'s heavily damaged controls. Weeks of refitting at Pernambuco, Brazil, were required simply to make her capable of a single Atlantic crossing, and when she was back on patrol two months later she was almost a completely different ship.

The battle of Trindade proved more than the unfitness of liners for wartime action; it was a symbol that the great race, which had begun almost thirty years before, had finally reached its tragic conclusion.

Built to surpass each other in speed and luxury, the Atlantic liners were now pressed into a very different role: pitted against one another in a struggle to the death. Though this would be the only actual battle between liners, it was symbolic of the cold, harsh reality underneath the gray war paint and coltish awkwardness of the merchant cruisers. Once built to compete, they were now poised to destroy. Jocular parallels between the liners and the sporting events at Cowes and Kiel were now defunct, as the role of the liners became secondary to that of the dreadnoughts.

What had begun in 1889 as a race ended, in 1915, as a duel.

Life on Board a Merchant Raider

The fleeting excitement of chase and capture punctuated an otherwise dull existence aboard the *Kronprinz Wilhelm* and her fellow cruisers: long periods of aimless wandering on an empty sea made even more unpalatable by the nagging urgency to replenish foodstuffs and coal bunkers. Homesickness was as endemic as seasickness, and boredom slowly sapped morale. The *Wilhelm*'s crew were not navy sailors hardened to long stretches of sea duty, but merchant mariners accustomed to a regular schedule of departure and arrival with the certainty of shore time once every six days. There was also widespread pessimism over the fate of the *Kronprinz Wilhelm*. When an eager boy from the supply ship *Walhalla* attempted to enlist on the *Wilhelm*, one of the officers kindly dissuaded him. "We're all doomed men on this ship," he told the boy, "a kind of forlorn hope out here on the Atlantic."

The men of the armed merchant cruiser *Kronprinz Wilhelm* were indeed forlorn, understanding only too well the peculiar vulnerability of their craft and the impracticality of her purpose. "It cannot be too strongly emphasized how serious an encounter with an enemy warship would have been," Niezy records. "For the *Kronprinz Wilhelm*, with her two small guns and spare supply of ammunition, would be shot down almost without reply as soon as she came within range of a hostile warship." It was more than a hopeless mission (for that would have been perversely appealing to the sort of heroism glorified by men); it was an inherently silly one.

The crew coped with their lot in a variety of ways. Target practice with the ship's two guns, once ammunition finally arrived, became a way to pass the time. When that flagged, officers took turns shooting down sea birds with their service revolvers or blasting away at the friendly porpoises that tracked the ship's wake. The primal instinct seemed particularly strong during these long doldrums, almost as if hunting prey under the sea could replace the lack of enemy prey on its surface. Christmas brought a new diversion: shark hunting. Bait was strung on chains over the ship's side as binoculars anxiously scanned the sea's surface. Once a shark took the bait in its mouth, lifeboat davits were employed to hoist the unfortunate, wriggling beast out of the water and past seven rows of portholes until it reached the boat deck. If hooks were unavailable, the men waited for the shark to flip over on its back, shooting it through its exposed belly and watching "with grim satisfaction the stream of blood which stains the water behind the rapidly careening body." At least fifty sharks were disposed of in this manner, the carcasses covering the whole fireman's deck. But the highly superstitious crew would not touch the meat; instead, the teeth and fat (used for lamp oil) were removed, and the rest was thrown overboard.

Not all the crew's leisure activities were as brutal, however. Indeed, there seemed to have been a consensus on board the *Kronprinz Wilhelm* to retain as many of the prewar shipboard shenanigans as possible, admittedly under constrained circumstances. The former ship's purser organized tug-of-war contests, sack races, and other sporting events dear to the hearts of travelers; a small coterie of intellectuals began publishing a daily ship's newspaper; and the ship's barber passed the time with a steady stream of good-natured gossip ranging from dubious war bulletins to the unwholesome pasts of the *Wilhelm's* prisoners.

Yet perhaps the most tangible link with an earlier, gentler time was the Ritual of Line Baptism. It was a cruise ship tradition that began in the late nineteenth century and survives to the present day. The baptism, a silly sort of ritualized hazing for passengers and crew, occurs on the ship's top deck as she crosses the equator. Those who have not crossed the equator before must be "baptized"—that is, smeared with various condiments and then dumped ceremoniously into the ship's pool.

An almost identical ritual occurred on board the *Kronprinz Wil-*

helm. Sailors stripped to the waist, decorated themselves with burnt cork, and wrapped a length of rope around their midsections—the total effect being to turn them into "savages." Neptune appeared in full regalia, joined by his wife (a lanky youth crowned with hemp braids), and—rather incongruously—a "pastor's wife," also a seaman in drag. What followed then was a rather bizarre and not a little blasphemous hodgepodge of pagan rituals, cruise ship deck games, and the Book of Common Prayer. "These men shall be cleansed of their earthly dust by the baptism!" Neptune bellowed. "Our will be done!" "Amen!" answered the crew. Thereupon the initiates were brought forward with all the solemnity of a sacrificial rite. More incantations: "We, the rulers of Neptune's realm . . . polluting traces of unbaptized landsmen . . . good ship *Kronprinz Wilhelm.* . . ." et cetera, et cetera. Thierfelder, entering into the spirit of things, endured an arch dialogue with the Chief Astronomer and Neptune himself as he begged their respective graces' permission to cross the equator. Permission duly given, the long-suffering commander looked on as the first of the pledges was brought forward. "Miller!" Neptune thundered, with a voice of doom. Miller stepped forward hesitantly. "Miller," said Neptune, "you lack one lung, have a treacherous taste for strong drink, and cannot withstand the pipe and the cards. And, before I forget it, I see that your brains have turned to sponge. Wherefore, O Miller, I prescribe for you seven pills from the pill boxes in the pharmacy of Neptune."

The "pills" were oiled plums, a powerful laxative. Seven in all were forced down the poor man's throat as he struggled to escape the grasp of two burly seamen. Here the narrative turns rather grisly, and one is reminded that this is not a pleasure ship bound for the Caribbean, but a ship at war. No self-respecting purser would allow this force-feeding or what was to follow. Once Miller had swallowed the last plum, the ship's barber was called forth. Provided with a paintbrush and a bucket of tar, he proceeded to slather the horrible stuff all over Miller, then scrape it off again with a giant wooden razor. Throughout Miller struggled pitiably against the bonds of his tormentors. Finally he was carried hand over hand to the dunking tank, dropped in head-first through a cloth-wound hoop, and half drowned. "I, pastor of Neptune, here pronounce thee a new-borne follower of the sea," said that personage weightily, "and thy name hereafter shall be 'Canned Salmon.' Arise, Canned Salmon, and salute your brothers!" But by this time Miller was insensible; his limp carcass was carried away, and the next man brought forward.

What are we to make of these antics? Certainly there is an element of sadism in this ritual not found in its prewar incarnation. Yet there is also a heady dose of escapism; at one point in the long recitative, Thierfelder warns the assemblage that enemy ships may cut the ceremony short. "I, wizard of Neptune's realm and especially of this baptismal procession, do command all the enemies of the *Kronprinz Wilhelm* to stay away until the ceremony is over!" bellows the master of ceremonies. And so it continues.

Yet what is most interesting to note is not the latent barbarity, but its rather ironic schoolboy innocence. There is an element reminiscent of the pirate "trials" once held in seventeenth-century Madagascar, bloodcurdling farces in which random crew became the "accused," the "jury," and the "judge." Such trials were often conducted with a terrifying semblance to reality, and occasionally the "accused" had good reason to fear for his life. Yet, like the pirate trials, the baptisms aboard the *Kronprinz Wilhelm* were a way to face the nameless, dragging fears of drowning, capture, or torture in enemy hands. They were also a desperate attempt to keep alive the receding traditions and gaiety of a lost age. Finally, and most importantly, schoolboy prankishness defused tensions among the crew, brought them closer together, and fostered egalitarianism between them and their captain. In sum, the Ritual Line of Baptism on board the *Kronprinz Wilhelm* served as a symbolic melding of the bizarre dual role of the liner, the effect of her wartime transition on her crew, *their* nostalgia for lost Edwardian customs, and their fears of death and capture.

The *Kronprinz Wilhelm* steamed more than 37,000 miles, consumed more than 45,000 tons of coal, and remained at sea 251 consecutive days, from August 3, 1914, to April 11, 1915. At no time did she put in to shore for repairs. Even by January, the ship was rapidly deteriorating. Boiler tubes exploded, electrical wires short-circuited, and a steady leak on the port side was contained only by constant caulking and ceaseless pumping. Great rust streaks trickled down from the *Wilhelm*'s portholes like tears. Even her engines, which remained strong to the last, spewed noxious clouds of black smoke. It was horribly apparent to even her most junior seaman that the *Kronprinz Wilhelm* was not designed for such service and would not hold out much longer.

A hasty consultation was held on the bridge, and it was decided to head for the nearest American port. A wave of fever had broken out on board, and the captain did not trust his ship to reach Germany—another week's travel. There was also the never-ending problem of coal. The *Wilhelm* had barely enough to reach the American shore, not even a fourth of that needed for the journey home, and no prospects of further supply. Accordingly, on Sunday, April 11, 1915, the *Kronprinz Wilhelm* arrived at Norfolk, Virginia, within full view of the American naval squadron. At seven o'clock that morning two officers from the United States Navy presented their compliments and arranged for shore visas. Formalities having been dealt with summarily, the Americans were all smiles. The *Kronprinz Wilhelm* was a minor legend, having sunk fourteen craft, having been declared sunk herself by the Allied press three times, and having earned herself the dashing title of "Mystery Cruiser" in the bargain. More than anything else, like the *Kronprinzessin Cecilie*, she was a novelty. As the *Kronprinz Wilhelm* steamed slowly up the bay, coming abreast of the American fleet, the respective warships of Germany and the United States greeted each other in friendly salutes for the last time in the Great War. Niezy recounts:

> Now the first guns of the American vessels boomed out in salute, until each ship had fired. Then the bands of the battleships began playing "Heil dir im Siegerkranz," one picking up the tune as the last finished it. "The Star Spangled Banner" followed, pulsating across the bay until we had passed the whole review, when our men dropped their salute and lined the rail, waving and cheering in return to the American sailors. . . . Shortly afterward we cast ashore to await events.

Events would soon overtake them. Like the *Kronprinzessin Cecilie* and a score of others, the *Kronprinz Wilhelm* and her crew remained captive in America, waiting for favorable conditions to attempt the return voyage home. Those conditions would never come. English warships continued to monitor the Eastern Seaboard, and relations between Germany and America grew increasingly strained. Two years later, the *Wilhelm's* crew suddenly found themselves declared enemy aliens. Their valiant ship, which had nearly destroyed itself in the last dash for safety in American waters, was seized, refitted, and recommissioned as a troopship for the American Expeditionary Force.

The Decline of the Merchant Cruiser and the End of the "Good War"

There is a comic-opera quality to the story of the *Kronprinz Wilhelm*. It resonates in the irony of prisoners being given First Class cabins, the crew fighting their lethargy by shark-baiting and pantomime, the captain sparing a Russian trawler out of sheer embarrassment, even the ludicrous story of the stranded cat; all in all, the tale of the voyage is rich in pathos and humor, if not in gun smoke or adventure. But the story of the *Kronprinz Wilhelm* is very much a story of the early days of the First World War, when archaic Edwardian notions of gallantry and sportsmanship still held sway and the Battle of the Atlantic was conducted with as many rules and protocols as a yacht race at Kiel. The *Kronprinz Wilhelm* was thus a symbol, simultaneously, of chivalry's last gasp, the uneven effects of modern technology on warfare, and—most poignant of all—the decline of late Victorian serenity in the face of a world going slowly mad.

The tension between the ship's civilian and military roles produced a strange hybrid of adventurism, apathy, prankishness, heroism, kindness, and servility in her crew. One can only look to operettas to find their like: Gilbert and Sullivan's pirates of Penzance, who were so absurdly compassionate toward their victims that they made perfectly dismal brigands. So did the crew of the passenger ship-turned-warship *Kronprinz Wilhelm* find themselves playing a buffoonish role, with an all-too-obvious luxury liner playing the role acting as their "pirate ship."

The *Kronprinz Wilhelm* represented a watershed in naval history, the last time a civilian vessel of any size would be converted to a warship while retaining her original crew. Her bizarre history proved once and for all the utter impracticality of an armed merchant fleet; the same technology that built ships the length and breadth of the *Kronprinz*

Wilhelm likewise made them incapable of fulfilling any other role but the one for which they were designed. A new role would be assigned them, one for which they were eminently suited, but it would not come to pass for another two years.

In the meantime they waited: the *Kronprinz Wilhelm, Kronprinzessin Cecilie, Kaiser Wilhelm II, Grosse Kurfurst, Vaterland,* and a score of others. Tethered side by side in the muck of Hoboken and Norfolk, the great German passenger ships sat idle, their furnishings covered with dust cloths, as the world for which they had been created disintegrated. The "good war" was ending. German submarines, the dreaded "U-boats," had formed a cordon around the British Isles and were threatening the Atlantic seaway. The scale of Allied merchant losses increased exponentially. Far more than the anachronistic armed merchant fleet that had so titillated Admiralty engineers at the turn of the century, it was these small, fragile, pencil-shaped vessels that would constitute the greatest menace to supply lines throughout the war. With the advent of the clandestine submersible attack, traditional concepts of surface sea battles unchanged since Trafalgar—battles in which an armed merchant cruiser had a raison d'être—became obsolete. The British Admiralty, which had as recently as two decades before still clamored for auxiliary sails on their vessels, viewed the submarine as sneaky, treacherous, and utterly unfair—just the sort of weapon, they told themselves, the spoilsport of Cowes would employ.

As the war escalated and new forms of technology came into play, notions of chivalry receded further into an idyllic past. The era of the great liners was ending, and nothing could have demonstrated that more effectively than the career of the *Kronprinz Wilhelm.* The Kaiser's fleet sat forgotten at their anchorages, as their sponsor grappled with the more immediate problems of being Supreme Warlord. As the submarine campaign intensified, relations between Germany and the neutral powers—most notably the United States—cooled. Had the *Kronprinzessin Cecilie* consented to stay in Bar Harbor, as the townspeople hoped, her crew would soon have found the climate even chillier than they had bargained for, and the enthusiastic reception given to the *Kronprinz Wilhelm* in April 1915 would have seemed both inappropriate and seditious only a few weeks later, on May 7, 1915, a day that would forever change the history of passenger travel on the Atlantic as well as bring the United States and Germany far closer to war.

On that day, as Kapitanleutnant Schweiger surfaced his U-boat just south of Ireland's Old Head of Kinsale and found a great passenger liner squarely in his sights, the comic-opera war on the Atlantic officially ended, and a new era began.

-12-

Armageddon

THE STANDING JOKE ON BOARD THE *LUSITANIA* WAS THAT THIS, HER TWO
hundred second crossing, would be her last. "[T]he idea came to be
regarded as a mild joke for lunch and dinner tables," one passenger
wrote later. Indeed, some even anticipated it. "I hope we see *something*
exciting," passenger Dorothy Conner exclaimed wistfully. "It would
be too bad to have to go home and admit that the trip was no more
thrilling than going to Coney Island." Unlike the *Titanic*, which sailed
to her death on a buoyant wave of hubris, dire warnings and grim predictions had clustered around the *Lusitania* for months. As the last
great express steamer still operating on her peacetime schedule, she
was an object of curiosity and perhaps disproportionate attention: her
sailings, still as regular as clockwork, were a tenuous link to a gentler
past when the only menaces on the Atlantic were rogue waves, icebergs,
and indigestion. Much has been made of the warnings sent to passengers before embarkation and the host of predictions of her demise. Yet

these were, in the context of war, both natural and expected. When Alfred Gwynne Vanderbilt received a telegram signed "Morte" that read "Have it on definite authority the *Lusitania* is to be torpedoed. You had better cancel passage immediately," he correctly dismissed it as a hoax.

Overshadowed by the melee of cranks and lunatics, genuine warnings were ignored. A notice appearing in the *New York Times* the day before the *Lusitania* sailed read as follows:

> NOTICE!
> Travelers intending to embark on the Atlantic voyage are reminded that a state of war exists between Germany and her allies and Great Britain and her allies; that the zone of war includes the waters adjacent to the British Isles; that, in accordance with formal notice given by the Imperial German Government, vessels flying the flag of Great Britain, or any of her allies, are liable to destruction in those waters and that travelers sailing in the war zone on ships of Great Britain do so at their own risk.

It was signed "Imperial German Embassy." Either by accident or design, this notice appeared prominently beside the Cunard advertisement for the *Lusitania*'s sailing schedule, the "N" in "Notice!" being almost exactly parallel to the tips of the *Lusitania*'s funnels. There is no evidence that it had the slightest effect on her passengers. Perhaps it appeared too late; such warnings might discourage booking but would be far less likely to prevent someone with ticket in hand from going. In fact, the passenger complement on the *Lusitania* was the largest since the outbreak of the war, probably due to a recent drop in fares as well as the imminent approach of clement spring weather.

Alfred Vanderbilt, perennial world traveler and sportsman, was off to the annual meeting of the International Horse Breeders' Association. Charles Frohman, the rambunctious little man who had brought *Peter Pan* to the stage and been dubbed "the Napoleon of Drama," had his eye on new productions in Drury Lane. Welsh coal baron D. A. Thomas was returning home with his daughter, the spirited suffragette Lady Margaret Mackworth. Perhaps the most colorful figure on this May crossing was the self-styled "sage of East Aurora," Elbert Hubbard. An early precursor to the yokel philosopher typified by Will Rogers, Hubbard extolled homely virtues and homespun humor in his books while sporting long hair and floppy bow ties in the manner of Oscar Wilde.

Also like Wilde, Hubbard had a certain genius for self-promotion. He met reporters in his stateroom in New York and informed them loftily that he was traveling to Germany to interview the Kaiser—with the intention, he said, of giving his readers the straight truth about foreign affairs. "If the Emperor won't see me in Berlin," said Hubbard, shrugging genially, "I'll be patient a while and see him later in St. Helena." When one reporter tactfully inquired whether such a voyage was wise, given the dangers on the Atlantic, Hubbard gaily replied that he hoped for nothing more than a torpedo, as it would give a tremendous lift to his book sales.

This brief list of luminaries disguises a less glamorous reality, that the vast majority of the *Lusitania*'s passengers were neither famous nor rich. Despite Cunard's resolute attitude of "business as usual," the approach of the summer season in Europe had lost its allure for American travelers. The Atlantic voyage had reverted, for most, to what it had once been for all: a measure of necessity. The *Lusitania*'s three classes were occupied primarily by British subjects of all walks of life answering the call of their beleaguered homeland. In an era when passenger lists were published regularly in the *New York Times* in the way that scandal sheets now cover the doings of movie stars, the *Lusitania*'s last passengers made poor copy indeed. One can almost sense the palpable frustration of writers in the aftermath of the disaster, searching vainly for the stories of heroism and sacrifice among the titled and notorious that had kept editors busy for months after the *Titanic* went down. This desperation was reflected nowhere more absurdly than in the headline that appeared after the sinking on the front page of a Welsh newspaper and caused many a chuckle among the downtrodden miners: "GREAT NATIONAL DISASTER! D. A. THOMAS SAVED."

Those who had braved the risks of war and booked passage on the *Lusitania* found themselves ensconced at once in familiar surroundings. While world events seemed to have spiraled out of control, life aboard the *Lusitania* was as slow, contemplative, and rigidly Edwardian as ever. The ship's orchestra still serenaded passengers in the lounge; her galleys still turned out *boeuf Bourguignon,* tournedos, and those rich sauces so dear to the aristocratic palate. The ship's newspaper, assembled from tidbits collected off the wireless, provided a relentlessly cheery and optimistic view of the war—alarmism was in poor taste. One First Class gentleman who paraded around the deck every day in a life preserver was regarded as a harmless lunatic. Those who had harbored misgivings in New York were quieted by the reassuring presence of the staff, and most of all by their captain, William Turner. "A torpedo can't get the *Lusitania*," he repeated, again and again. "She runs too fast." Faced with the absolute confidence of this gruff and salt-sprayed old mariner, even the most fearful passenger came away reassured.

Indeed, Captain Turner seemed at times almost *too* unconcerned. A host of Admiralty instructions had reached his desk via the Cunard office before sailing, intended to safeguard the *Lusitania* and her passengers from calamity. They included the posting of extra lookouts, frequent boat drills, and the necessity of steaming a zigzag course near shore (intended to confuse U-boat commanders attempting to plot her direction). Turner blithely ignored almost all of them. A merchant commander with over thirty years' experience at sea, he regarded Admiralty directives as so much bureaucratic, meddlesome nonsense. The *Lusitania*'s safeguards lay in her speed and her stature. As the fastest ship afloat (sharing this distinction with *Mauretania*—which, incidentally, Turner had captained during her record-breaking twelve-day round-trip crossing in 1910), she could outpace anything, even a torpedo. Moreover, as the most famous merchant carrier still in harness, her distinctive four funnels made her instantly recognizable from any distance. She could not possibly be mistaken for anything else. And as a passenger liner still in commercial service, she was presumably inviolable. In spite of the warnings from the German Embassy, the sinking of a famous liner was still considered a remote possibility. Possibly it could happen by accident or by the overzealousness of a submarine commander, but the combination of circumstances and the rules of naval war made any attack on the *Lusitania* almost unthinkable. And even if such an attack did occur, there were rules for that, too. The submarine must surface, announce her intentions to her victim, and allow time for the passengers and crew to be evacuated. This was the time-honored tradition of wartime courtesy, which surface raiders such as the *Kronprinz Wilhelm* had obeyed scrupulously.

Despite indications that such courtesies were increasingly being ignored, Turner was untroubled, and his attitude was shared by the Cunard Line itself. A representative at its New York office assured one nervous passenger that the *Lusitania* was "perfectly safe; safer than the trolley cars in New York City." When the German notice appeared, one Cunard agent angrily declared that it was just another attempt "to annoy the line and make its passengers uncomfortable." Captain Turner may even have been acting on an unspoken company policy. Though it had willingly passed on the Admiralty's instructions, it did so without any comment, additions of its own, or instructions on how the orders were to be implemented. Indeed, the company may simply have handed over the message with a wink-wink-nudge-nudge.

Whatever the reasons, the *Lusitania* put to sea woefully unprepared for danger. Her usual crew had been largely replaced by an unruly gang of recruits; most of the original seamen had already returned to enlist. Her lifeboat drill was "a pitiable exhibition." A small group of seamen in life jackets swung a boat out on its davits, clambered aboard—looking self-conscious—then returned quickly to the ship. No attempt was made to test the davits or tell passengers to which boats they were assigned. When an American traveling in First Class asked Turner whether this was sufficient, given the war, his answer was brusquely affirmative. Any further discussion was forestalled; it was well-known that Captain Turner (unlike Smith of the *Titanic*) thoroughly disliked his passengers and found most of them a damned nuisance.

As the *Lusitania* approached the Irish coast on May 7, 1915, the early morning fog had lifted, revealing a perfect spring day without a hint of wind. The sight of shore was immensely reassuring. The *Lusitania* had made it across unscathed; she was safe. The anxieties that may have perturbed her passengers in New York were forgotten. Passengers dawdled over lunch, read bulletins of news ashore, contemplated catching the 6:15 train to Waterloo. A few remained on deck, watching the Irish coast slide by as the *Lusitania* steamed her doggedly straight course en route to Liverpool. For most of them, the voyage had, in effect, already ended. The veil of shipboard life was dissolving rapidly, as it always does, into anticipation of the coming disembarkation.

Yet the *Lusitania* was not moving away from danger, but into it. As she approached the shore, she steamed directly into the path of German submarines cordoning the British coast. Circumstances, as well as the willful ignorance of her operators, had conspired against her. Her passengers did not and could not know that she was courting danger with her undeviating course and that she was running slower than usual with two of her boilers closed down. And even Captain Turner did not know that twelve Allied ships had been sunk in these waters in the past week alone.

The traditional mores of war were rapidly being abandoned, and Kriegsmarine Kapitanleutnant Walter Schwieger knew that all too well. And he knew that it was not entirely Germany's fault. Winston Churchill, then First Lord of the Admiralty, had openly flouted long-standing tradition by ordering surface ships to disregard a submarine's orders to heave to, and attempt to ram her if possible. He further authorized the construction of a number of "Q-ships," submarine hunters disguised as harmless merchant vessels. When a sub surfaced and came alongside, giving the ship's crew a chance to evacuate, guns sprang from hidden mounts aboard the ship and strafed her. The net result of these aggressive tactics was to drive German submarines underwater, ultimately making them a far more deadly opponent. On February 4, 1915, the Kaiser announced a policy of unrestricted submarine warfare in the waters surrounding the British Isles. "If it is possible to save the crews," he told his captains, "do it. . . . If you cannot save them, then it cannot be helped."

Thus, when Schwieger spotted the *Lusitania* steaming a direct course toward his position, he ordered his sub, the *U-20*, to dive at once. It was 12:45 P.M., GMT. The *U-20* disappeared beneath the surface, her periscope leaving a wake above. One of Schwieger's fellow officers recognized the ship as either the *Lusitania* or *Mauretania*. That was enough for Schwieger. Both ships were registered as adjuncts to the Royal Navy; both were known to carry armaments and munitions. Schwieger took the bearing of the enemy vessel and ordered a torpedo to be readied. Seconds later, he depressed a small brass switch on the control panel, and a sound of escaping air filled the sub. Like a child's bathtub toy, the little projectile hurled itself across the sea, followed by a thin wake of bubbles. The torpedo struck the *Lusitania* just aft of the bridge, sending up a flume of water and debris. Schwieger, in his precise manner, recorded the next eighteen minutes in his log:

> Torpedo hits starboard right behind the bridge. An un-
> usually heavy explosion takes place. . . . The ship stops
> immediately and heels over to starboard very quickly, im-

mersing simultaneously at the bow. Great confusion ensues
on board; the boats are made clear and some of them are
lowered to the water. . . . The ship blows off; on the bow
the name "Lusitania" becomes visible in golden letters. . . .
Since it seems as if the steamer will keep above water only a
short time, we dived to a depth of twenty-four meters and
ran out to sea. It would have been impossible for me, anyhow, to fire a second torpedo into this crowd of people
struggling to save their lives.

Though Schwieger's clinical description of the liner's last moments
was largely accurate, the experience on board the *Lusitania* was quite
different. The initial impact of the torpedo was variously described as
a thud, a clap, or a shudder. Captain Turner likened it to the sound of
a door being slammed. A second explosion followed, much louder and
far more sustained than the first. It rose up from the bowels of the ship
in a low rumble, tearing through the decks like a volcanic eruption. At
the time, most thought a second torpedo had struck the ship, but that
was not the case. The explosion has since been variously attributed to
coal gas igniting in the bunkers, a boiler eruption, or the sudden conflagration of munitions, which the *Lusitania* was rumored to be carrying. Whatever its cause, it was lethal. A gaping hole appeared in the side
of the ship, and she heeled over dramatically. Turner, who had raced
back to the bridge from his cabin, made a desperate attempt to beach
the vessel on nearby shoals. But it was this, ultimately, that doomed her.
When the *Titanic* sank, her engines were still. Thus, she went down
slowly and on an even keel. By keeping up steam, Turner quite literally drove his ship into the water. She listed heavily to starboard, making her portside boats all but useless. Her bow was driven beneath the
surface in mere seconds.

Chaos reigned aboard. The electrical current flickered, then died.
Thousands of passengers struggling through the ship's labyrinthine passageways suddenly found themselves fumbling in absolute darkness.
Many never reached the top deck. D. A. Thomas and his daughter
had been about to enter one of the *Lusitania's* famed latticework elevators when the torpedo struck. Not fully knowing why they did so,
they stepped back. Moments later, when the lights went out, the elevators halted between decks; their terrified occupants were entombed
within them; so too were three suspected saboteurs who had been ap-

prehended in New York attempting to stow away on board. They had been locked up in a holding cell deep in the ship's bowels, and there they remained.

Things were scarcely better on deck than below. The ship's crazy list made launching the boats a near impossibility, and the terrified, untrained crew were in no position to organize an orderly evacuation. To make matters worse, Turner had expressly forbidden any attempt to abandon ship: he was still attempting to beach her. Those officers disposed to disobey these mad orders were confounded by circumstances. As the *Lusitania* plowed remorselessly ahead, boats that reached the surface capsized at once in the swell or were dashed to shreds against the ship's sides, their occupants spilled into the sea. Only two portside boats even reached the water, and both had been so damaged by projecting rivets of the ship's plating that they sank instantly. On the starboard side, the gap between deck and lifeboats necessitated a long jump to reach them. Passengers leaped, missed their footing, and hurtled into the sea.

On deck, confusion bred anarchy. Stokers and other crew members stormed the boats, elbowing aside men, women, and children in their desperation. Soon nearly everyone was shoving their way to the rail, and the ship's officers could do little more than look on in despair. One deranged First Class passenger, Isaac Lehmann, brandished a revolver and ordered his lifeboat launched immediately. "To hell with the captain!" he screamed. "The first man that disobeys my orders to launch this boat I shoot to kill!" A sailor unwillingly knocked out the retaining pin, and the five-ton lifeboat lurched horribly inward, skidding along the decks and crushing some thirty passengers in its path. When it hit the water it heeled over at once and sank. Lehmann, unfortunately, survived. Lady Mackworth watched the sorry situation disdainfully and remarked to a friend, "I always thought a shipwreck was a well-organized affair."

Not everyone lost their heads. In the midst of the maelstrom, Alfred Vanderbilt was unperturbed. Fellow First Class passenger Oliver Bernard spotted him standing quietly apart from the crush on deck, dressed faultlessly in a gray suit and polka-dot bow tie. He was smiling faintly, as though amused by all the turmoil around him. "In my eyes," said Bernard, "he was the figure of a gentleman waiting for a train."

Later, another passenger saw him order his valet to "save all the kid-
dies you can." At last sight, Vanderbilt was attempting to tie life jackets to baby bassinets. His own life jacket had been casually given away,
and he could not swim a stroke. Not far away, Charles Frohman smiled
beatifically as he helped his lady friends into a lifeboat. "Why fear
death?" he told them. "It is the most beautiful adventure in life." Even
Dorothy Conner found her situation strangely amusing. Recalling her
earlier comment, she remarked lightly to a friend, "Well, I wanted some
excitement."

The last few moments on board the dying *Lusitania* were hellish.
Open ventilator shafts on deck echoed the panic-stricken cries of those
still struggling in the depths of the ship. Hundreds remained on deck as
the sea closed over them. The forward funnel hit the surface of the sea
with a hiss, sucking in nearby passengers. Moments later an explosion
from within the ship shot them out again as though from the mouth
of a cannon, covered with soot but otherwise unscathed. Everything
that could move hurtled toward the bow as the ship settled into her
final descent, loose debris scything through the thin bulkheads on her
decks and sending up a low, rumbling, almost seismic growl. Then the
stern finally disappeared, taking with it a congregated mass of struggling humanity that was pulled remorselessly under by the suction.
Moments later, as the wreck slammed against the sea floor and broke
apart, the surface erupted briefly in a mass of glutinous white bubbles.
Then it became calm.

The water temperature was 55 degrees Fahrenheit, twenty degrees
warmer than it had been when the *Titanic* sank, yet still lethal. A fully
grown man could not expect to survive more than twenty-five minutes of immersion; children were carried away almost at once. Hy-
pothermia is a deceiver. The feeling of intense cold gives way to an
illusory, pleasant sensation of warmth. The brain enters a dreamlike
state, and the victim spends his or her last moments hovering in an ec-
static euphoria while the mechanisms of the body shut down. When
the sea closed over the *Lusitania*'s stern and almost a thousand people
were suddenly immersed in the cold water, a great cry went up: "a long
lingering moan," said one survivor, as "those who were lost seemed to
be calling from the very depths." It was the same eerie sound that had

reverberated over the *Titanic's* grave just three years earlier. And just as before, it lingered only a few minutes before gradually quieting into a terrible, unnatural silence. The sea was clotted with a seething mass of detritus and passengers, "an undulating horrible mattress of deck chairs, oars, boxes, and human heads." Survivors clung to paneling torn loose from the ship's lounge, to fragments of planking wrenched from the deck, to the wrecked lifeboats. Captain Turner remained at his post to the last and finally floated away clinging to a chair.

In the few surviving lifeboats, passengers clung to one another and waited for rescue. It was long in coming. The *Lusitania* had been given no escort (an omission that would dog the Admiralty for years), and the time it took for the signal to be relayed and rescue vessels to be dispatched was several hours. Crews had to be found among Queenstown pubs; steam had to be raised. The Royal Navy cruiser *Juno*, stationed nearby, made at once for the wreck—but Admiralty orders turned her around again. The Admiralty later justified this extraordinary command by claiming it did not want to put "live bait" into an area known to be infested with German submarines. Thus, the first vessels on the scene were tiny fishing trawlers, their sails set to catch the faint breeze. They seemed terribly slow. Quarrels broke out in the boats, and passengers scanned the cluttered sea for signs of lost relatives and friends. "You have perhaps lost your husband," said a gentleman with a French accent to a young nurse seated next to him in a boat. "Do not worry. I am wealthy. I will look after you."

The Queenstown harbormaster was not as accommodating. As the motley flotilla of vessels bearing survivors made for his dock, he stood at the water's edge, an obstinate expression on his face, demanding to see their papers. The dazed, bedraggled, oil-slicked survivors looked at him with vacant eyes. No papers, no admission, he told them—no unscheduled landings allowed. But as the flotilla became a small armada, the harbormaster's resolve finally broke down. Reluctantly, and still grumbling, he allowed the *Lusitania's* survivors to land.

As the afternoon waned and evening approached, rows of dead were laid out on the harbor piers, each succeeding boat adding its share to the grisly collection. Townspeople, drawn by morbid curiosity, eyed them with disbelief. Survivors picked their way among the dead, searching upturned, bloated faces for the features of loved ones. Everyone spoke in a whisper.

Through muted tones of shock and horror, a single irate voice sounded the clarion call. On board the rescue ship *Bluebell*, Lady Mackworth was startled to hear a man angrily, vehemently decrying the whole situation. It was a disgrace, he bellowed, an absolute disgrace! Sounding for all the world like a customer given shoddy service in a restaurant, he enumerated his complaints, concluding with a loud promise that everyone on earth would soon know who was responsible for this appalling crime. Only as he moved aside did Lady Mackworth see the person to whom this diatribe was addressed. Draped in a ship's blanket and still in his shrunken uniform, Captain William Turner stared blankly at the deck.

"A Dirty Business"

When the grim census was finished, 1,198 people had lost their lives. Bodies continued to wash ashore for weeks, after drifting along the Irish coast like so much flotsam. When the *Titanic* had gone down, little had remained to mark her place but her boats, the occasional deck chair, and corpses. The restless wreck of the *Lusitania* churned up a seemingly limitless supply of horrors.

Among the British public, shock gave way to outrage, spurned on by these daily reminders of an atrocity. Vacationers on shore had actually watched the explosion and seen the great ship heel over and sink before their eyes. Not since the *Great Harry* capsized within sight of shocked onlookers in the late sixteenth century had England witnessed so horrid a maritime catastrophe so close. The loss of the *Titanic* had plunged Britons into grief, but it was a stately, detached bereavement, as of someone attending the funeral of a great man he barely knew. Nothing was left of the ship but survivors and photographs: even most of the bodies had disappeared into the North Atlantic by the time vessels attempted to retrieve them. But the *Lusitania* was, as Lord Mersey privately termed it, "a dirty business."

The serried rows of contorted dead on the Queenstown quayside seemed to cry aloud for justice. For some, the end had come quietly: Charles Frohman lay as peacefully as if asleep. But most of the bodies and facial expressions testified to the ravages of a violent death. Corpses grappled with invisible obstacles or clung to nonexistent wreckage. Lips were drawn back in the rictus of a long scream. No one viewing the spectacle could walk away untouched, for every lost soul told its own story: "Men broke down when they looked upon a young mother lying there with her baby . . . folded in her protective arms," wrote the *London Times* correspondent. "Nearby were two baby twins . . . [and] a sailor, who was found with a body of a little child strapped to his shoulders. Two children who went down together with their arms around each other were still folded firmly together. . . ."

Such descriptions, disseminated to a horrified English public over their toast and tea beside graphic images of the slain, had their desired effect. Through the iconography of the dead, the British press worked its alchemy on the public mind, transforming the sinking of the luxury liner into propaganda of unparalleled utility. "A number of babies, I should say about thirty, were laid out stark and stiff on the floor of a temporary morgue," one survivor told a reporter. "I never saw anything quite so ghastly and harrowing, and it filled me with an insensate desire for vengeance. I hope those tiny mites will be fully avenged."

Again and again the image of the *Lusitania*'s dead would surface in the national propaganda campaigns of the Great War. "Take up the sword of justice!" proclaims Britannia in one poster, standing above the waves as the liner disappears in the background. Hands emerge from the surface, grasping at the hem of her skirt. One enterprising photographer even took an old dory, painted *Lusitania* in enormous black letters on its side, and assembled local actors to play the roles of dead bodies being extracted from a lifeboat. The veracity of the image was somewhat compromised by a precocious child "victim," playing dead and clearly enjoying his role. But by far the most evocative and effective poster was one depicting a drowned young mother clutching her baby in her arms, suspended in gray-green water with her skirt fanned alluringly around her. There is no image of the ship, nor need there be. A single word appears in the caption: "ENLIST."

Yet the symbolic significance of the *Lusitania* disaster was greater than the propaganda surrounding it. On May 7, 1915, the serene presumptions and sportsmanlike platitudes of the Edwardian era were finally revealed for what they had become: hollow, brittle husks of a world that was now utterly gone. Never again in the brutal conflict that followed would anyone speak of it as a "good war." The horrors of war had been brought home to those taking part, as well as to those who still stood on the sidelines. The most common question asked by appalled observers on both sides of the Atlantic was, "How could this happen?" The sinking of the *Lusitania* represented a collision between two distinct and antithetical concepts of the race of the superliners.

To the admiralties of both Germany and England, the thirty-year race had always acknowledged the potential of war. The subsidies provided for the construction of the *Mauretania* and *Lusitania* were given expressly because these ships were seen as essential adjuncts to the Royal Navy. Hence, both ships had reinforced decks for gun mounts and shell-resistant plates hammered to their superstructure. Not until William Francis Gibbs designed the SS *United States* in 1951 would any liner be so explicitly constructed for swift military conversion.

Since the British Admiralty regarded them as potential weapons, it is not surprising that the German Admiralty should regard them as potential targets. The *Lusitania* was known to be carrying munitions, and there were rumors that she herself was armed. Thus, despite her apparently civilian role, she seemed very much an enemy vessel to the Germans. But even had she *not* been carrying ammunition, she was perceived by both navies as a potential warship; she was, in fact, on the Royal Navy register. Since the *Teutonic* had been fitted with cannons and shown off to the Kaiser in 1889, the British Admiralty constantly reminded its German counterpart of the dual purpose of its passenger fleet. The rhetoric of the time amounted to almost a taunt: even if Germany succeeded in crippling England's navy England could still fight the Hun with every merchant vessel at her disposal. By 1914, the German Admiralty had become so paranoid about this possibility that it was likely to regard almost *any* British vessel as a threat—an attitude that was deliberately encouraged by the British themselves. Thus, when Schwieger found the *Lusitania* in his sights, he had every reason to regard her as a viable (and legal) target.

But the race between the German and British liners had also been a peaceful one, as much a counterpoint to the naval race as an adjunct to it. Thus civilians came to see passenger ships as a separate species from warships—herbivores, if you will, to the navy's carnivores. It was this perspective that had been enthusiastically embraced by Albert Ballin, himself an avid proponent of naval rearmament. He did not see the two as dichotomous; the buildup of Germany's navy would keep her safe from foreign aggression, protect her possessions overseas, and enhance her prestige in global politics. But her merchant fleet would be the floating embodiment of Germany herself. Ballin's ships were, above all, ambassadors. They carried Germany across the Atlantic, providing foreigners with their first glimpse of that nation, both its technology and culture. The race, as he saw it, was not between two competing governments, but two competing cultures. It was thus an almost brotherly rivalry. Central to this concept was the underlying legitimacy and inviolability of both nations: they were competitors, not enemies.

This was the image that had been popularly disseminated in both Germany and England. Naval efficacy remained important to the admirals, and was occasionally reported in long and tedious detail in *The Shipbuilder*, but civilian perspectives on the liners were derived from being either spectators or passengers. Thus, when Britons spoke enthusiastically about the reinforced plating on the *Lusitania's* decks, they spoke with equal animation about her Adam paneling, hydraulic barber's chair, and gutta-percha tiling in an overall catalog of the ship's technological and architectural wonders. Passengers embarking on the ships saw only those aspects designed for their comfort or amusement; the ship's warlike aspect remained, if vaguely reassuring, very much out of sight.

Hence the presumption that passenger ships were essentially immune from being targeted, entirely removed from the horrors of war. A ship is a self-contained universe, operating on its own physical laws and fostering its own reality. As technology gradually allowed the construction of bigger, faster, and steadier liners, the connection between ship and sea became more and more tenuous, until finally the Atlantic itself was little more than a panorama to be viewed from behind the double-glazed safety of windows in the First Class Lounge. The menaces that lurked in the Atlantic during wartime were likewise remote. And the Cunard Line, for its part, actively encouraged this false sense of security. Though acutely aware of the dual status of their liners, the publicists for the line presented to the traveling public an image that was resolutely serene and peaceable. Worse, like any good salesman, they came to believe their own sales pitch. In eighty years of continuous operations, Cunard had never lost a life. This came to be the leitmotif of the line, a talisman of safety against storms, icebergs, and submarines. Not only would the *Lusitania*'s engines protect her; the favor of the gods seemed to follow her as well. This was perhaps why Cunard did not wholeheartedly embrace the Admiralty's directives and why Captain Turner deliberately disregarded them. Even after the disaster, the company saw the tragedy not as a result of its own folly but rather as "the moment when God Himself seemed to forsake us."

The shock and disbelief that registered in the public mind after the *Lusitania* went down show how entrenched this presumption of inviolability had become. The two races, naval and merchant, had finally collided, with horrible results. In hindsight, it seems inevitable. As the battle of the Atlantic grew more aggressive and the realities of total war settled on the minds of both admiralties, the *Lusitania*'s crossings became increasingly absurd and dangerous. Neither fish nor fowl, built for an alternative nineteenth-century form of war wherein merchant ships had a role alongside their navies, she was a floating anachronism. Within she retained the antebellum status of a technological marvel and passenger ferry—the turbine-powered supership that dazzled the world in 1907. But without, she was a quasimilitary vessel of an enemy nation carrying munitions across a contested battle zone. Her ultimate destruction was absolutely assured.

On the day after the sinking, rioting mobs in London, Liverpool, and Manchester vented their revenge on German businesses, ransacking stores, overturning tables in restaurants, looting, even setting fires. Newspapers bristled with quotes from British notables decrying the sinking as "the ghastliest crime in history" and "the foulest of many foul crimes that have stained German arms." Headlines fanned the flames: "Huns Sink the *Lusitania*," growled the *Daily Sketch;* "The Huns Carry Out Their Threat to Murder: Famous Cunarder Sunk Off the Irish Coast," the *Daily Mirror* wailed. Improbable stories of unspeakable barbarity were attributed to survivors: how Schwieger and his men stood on the deck of the *U-20* and cheered as the *Lusitania* went under; how Schwieger sent a torpedo into the struggling crowd of survivors. The *New York Times* reported with absolute sincerity that the torpedo that struck the ship contained poisoned gas. As time went on, shocked protestations of inhumanity were replaced by dark hints of conspiracy. Why did the *Lusitania* sink so fast?, the London papers asked. Was she carrying explosives? Was she sabotaged?

Nearly everyone agreed that dark deeds were afoot, but that was as far as the consensus went. If there was indeed a conspiracy to sink the *Lusitania*, nobody was sure of its author. The easiest answer, of course, was the Kaiser himself. He loathed and despised the English liners, it was said, as they represented a challenge to his own. The *Lusitania*, who with her sister held the coveted title of fastest ship on earth, was therefore particularly irksome to him. It was not long before cartoons appeared depicting him as a comic opera villain in top hat and cape; the waxed, pointed moustaches didn't help, either. British propaganda seized upon him in this context as the embodiment of German barbarity, as it had already done and would continue to do throughout the war. The Kaiser was shown awarding medals to a slavering dog marked "U-20," offering a laurel wreath of apology on the point of a sword, recoiling in mock horror from a group of naked, spectral babes with outstretched arms crying "Why did you kill *us*?" When the coroner's court of Queenstown met in sacred splendor to inquire into the crime of the *Lusitania*, it returned a unanimous verdict of willful murder against Wilhelm Hohenzollern. But while it was true that the Kaiser made the perfect stalking horse, there was not a shred of evidence against him. What, then, of Grand Admiral Tirpitz, master of the fleet, or Captain Schwieger himself? Again, while the destruction of the liner might be a crime against humanity, there was nothing to suggest it had been premeditated.

Then, as details of the disaster emerged, even more sinister villains appeared from the woodwork. How did the *Lusitania* come to be steaming a direct course right into the path of a German submarine?, people wondered. Where were her escorts? What of all the Admiralty instructions? Why did the *Juno* turn back? Why, above all, was a civilian passenger liner sent steaming blindly in the middle of a war into an area infested with submarines? The suggestion arose that Winston Churchill himself might have engineered the sinking to push the Americans into the war—an accusation almost identical to that leveled against Franklin Roosevelt after the bombing of Pearl Harbor. In the case of the *Lusitania*, however, the evidence was not entirely circumstantial. A letter Churchill sent to Walter Runciman, President of the Board of Trade, on February 12, 1915, reads almost like an invitation to murder. "My dear Walter," Churchill writes,

> It is most important to attract neutral shipping to our shores in the hope especially of embroiling the United States with Germany. The German formal announcement of indiscriminate submarining has been made to the United States to produce a deterrent effect upon traffic. For our part, we want the traffic—the more the better and if some of it gets into trouble, better still.

Even the Kaiser wondered if the Admiralty might have deliberately left the *Lusitania* exposed. He told an American visitor one year later that "England was really responsible, as the English had made the *Lusitania* go slowly in English waters so that the Germans could torpedo it and so bring on trouble." But although Churchill might have earnestly wished for a torpedo to bring the Americans into the fray, there is little to suggest he acted on this desire. Indeed, Churchill's letter suggests the hope that some harm may come to "neutral" (read "American") shipping, not the pride of the Cunard Line and the embodiment of Britain itself. The number of Americans killed, 128, was a small fraction of the overall number of dead. It seems unlikely in the extreme that, should Churchill have desired to effect his Machiavellian schemes, he would have chosen the *Lusitania* as bait.

Finally, once all the greater villains had been considered and dispensed with, attention turned to the pitiable figure of Captain Turner. Having been chastised by the British Inquiry for recklessness, he now faced public murmurings of bribery by the German government. It nearly broke him. Appearing at court in a borrowed uniform several sizes too large, he looked old, tired, and penitent. He defended the company loyally, endured the cynicism and often downright hostility of his interrogators, and returned as quickly as possible to obscurity. Two years later a second Cunard liner, the *Ivernia*, was blown out from under him. Shortly afterward he retired.

England, though hardest hit by the loss, was more prepared for it than the United States. Though Americans accounted for just 10 percent of those killed, the attack on the *Lusitania* came to be viewed as a deliberate attack on American neutrality. Theodore Roosevelt crustily termed the sinking "piracy on a vaster scale than any old-time pirate ever practiced," and this view was more or less shared by the majority of the American public. It was, said one lyrically inclined observer, "a deed for which a Hun would blush, a Turk be ashamed, and a Barbary pirate apologize." Some believed that war was imminent. "The U.S. must declare war or forfeit European respect," the American ambassador to the Court of St. James's cabled President Wilson. Wilson himself was in no position to handle the tragedy. His affection for a certain Mrs. Edith Bolling Galt, culminating in a marriage proposal just three days before, had been spurned. When the news reached him via cablegram, the President was striding through the garden on the way to a comforting round of golf. He broke down and sobbed as the cable was read. But Americans were not yet ready for war. Wilson drafted a sternly worded yet deliberately vague complaint, to which the German government responded with an abject yet equally vague apology. The matter was then tacitly dropped. America would not enter the war for another two years, but when it did, "Remember the *Lusitania*" became a rallying cry. The most direct effect of the *Lusitania* disaster was to harden America against the German cause and propel it more firmly into the Allied camp. Interventionists within the government were handed a potent weapon to further their claims, and pacifists like Secretary of State William Jennings Bryan were left wringing their hands in despair. Even the German ambassador in Washington grimly informed his superiors that the outrage over the sinking made efforts to ameliorate his country's image all but impossible.

But by far the most interesting and revealing response to the *Lusitania* was Germany's. Angry English newspapers reported that Germans celebrated the sinking with an orgiastic holiday, but this was a fabrication. Indeed, the attitude that best describes the German reaction was one of quiet satisfaction. The *Lusitania* was universally depicted as a "fully armed munitions carrier"; her passenger complement was regarded as secondary at best. In fact, many Germans laid the blame for the disaster on Cunard, for cluttering their warship with innocent human shields. Karl Goetz, a Munich metalworker, fashioned a small bronze medallion commemorating the disaster, which featured a portrait of the *Lusitania* going down, her decks packed with armaments; the opposite side displayed an image of Cunard, as skeletal Death, selling tickets to innocent passengers under the heading "Business Above All," while a distinguished-looking German standing nearby attempts to dissuade them. The medal had very limited circulation in Germany, but was picked up by British propagandists almost at once. "And they struck a medal for *this!*" one outraged poster cries.

Yet Goetz's satiric medal raises several very real issues. First, Cunard's blithe disregard of wartime conditions did indeed smack of "business above all." One Berlin newspaper acidly remarked that the lost souls aboard the liner were, "if we wish to call things by their right names, a sacrifice to Great Britain's frivolity and avarice." Nor was blame limited to Cunard. "It was criminal of the British Government," declared Franz von Papen, "to allow Cunard to carry passengers on a ship transporting explosives and munitions." The question of whether the *Lusitania* did in fact carry munitions remains open to this day; it is quite likely that she did. Above all, the medal—and its symbolic representation of German opinion—reinforced the German perception that the *Lusitania* was, unequivocally, a naval vessel. While British propaganda correctly displays the ship sinking by the bow, German depictions (from the earliest newspaper accounts to posters much later) almost all imagine her sinking by the stern. Thus her murderous sharp prow is highlighted, a prow that could slice a submarine in half. Moreover, the broad expanse of foredeck is almost always shown littered with gun mounts, munitions, and other paraphernalia of war.

Not only was the sinking of the *Lusitania* thus made legitimate by her warlike trappings and the depravity of her operators; she was also the greatest demonstration of the Fatherland's new weapon. The *Lusitania* was by far the largest "kill" in those early days of the war, and her destruction was lauded as demonstrative of the "splendid," "extraordinary," and "exceptional" U-boat campaign. This attitude found a surprising proponent in Albert Ballin. "Whether it was right to torpedo the *Lusitania* with 1,600 passengers, most of them neutral, is a question I will leave aside for the moment," he wrote dismissively:

> But every intelligent man will admit that our entire U-boat
> action has contributed to reducing the arrogance of the
> English and to complicating enormously the situation in
> England. It was certainly the only thing we could undertake

against England. . . . If the British are not completely god-forsaken, this action must show them how necessary it is for them in the future to engage in a form of World policing with Germany.

Ballin's enthusiasm reflected another, less discussed aspect of German satisfaction. Aside from being a successful coup for U-boats, the sinking of the *Lusitania* had deeper national significance. The destruction of its greatest liner was a stunning blow to English national prestige, just as much as her construction had been a cause for consternation in Germany eight years earlier. One could not fault the Germans for feeling a little smug that this sinecure of England's maritime glory had been so cruelly and swiftly humbled. One imaginative front page of *Der Tag's Illustrierte Unterhaltungs-Beilage* hints at this; it portrays the sinking of the *Lusitania* from the familiar bow-on position, yet the ship shown is, unmistakably, the *Titanic*. This not-so-subtle device made the obvious comparison between the two distasters, almost as if an invisible tally sheet stood above them.

The *Kolnische Volkszeitung*, an organ of the Catholic Center Party, did not bother itself with niceties. "The sinking of the *Lusitania* is a success of our submarines which must be placed beside the greatest achievement of this naval war," it stated baldly:

> The sinking of the giant steamship is a success of moral significance which is still greater than material success. With joyful pride we contemplate this latest deed of our Navy. It will not be the last. The English wish to abandon the German people to death by starvation. We are more humane. We simply sank an English ship with passengers who at their own risk . . . entered the zone of operations.

Hence the race was, at least in the realm of propaganda, still very much on. Even as the German liners rusted away at their piers in forced isolation, their mere existence above water gave Germany superiority. Ballin, whose mood now fluctuated wildly between euphoria and despair, exulted over the loss of the *Lusitania* as one less competitor for his ships to reckon with after the war.

Yet the general sense of satisfaction in Germany was allied to a feeling, particularly among her leaders, that she may have gone too far. The Kaiser himself would say later that "he would not have per-

mitted the torpedoing of the *Lusitania* if he had known, and that no
gentleman would kill so many women and children." Even Ballin seemingly reversed his own earlier jingoism when he wrote to a friend:

> I think it unfortunate . . . if we officially justify our sub-
> marine action in the light of the depravity of the English
> and of starving German women and children. I consider it a
> mistake to present the use of submarines as retaliation since
> we thereby admit that this form of military operation is ille-
> gal in international law. . . . I believe that we would do well
> to emphasize that our strategy is based on the novelty of the
> weapon.

What accounts for this apparent inconsistency? On the one hand
Germany regarded the sinking of the *Lusitania* as a triumph, both mil-
itarily and politically, but under this blanket patriotism ran a current of
murmured anxiety. Germany, too, had finally realized that "gentlemanly" rules had no place in modern war. Thus within the conflicting
strands of German opinion one finds ultimate expression of the dual
quality of the passenger liner race. Germans could exult over the destruction of an enemy cruiser carrying munitions, and they could
blame the attendant loss of civilian life on the arrogance and avarice of
the British. They could even celebrate the destruction of an irksome
symbol of English maritime superiority. But try as they might, they
could not fully shout down their own horror at seeing the *Lusitania*—
epitome of peaceful competition between the two nations—obliterated
by the ravages of total war.

The essential incompatibility between the two concepts of the liner
race, one peaceful, the other warlike, had been finally and irretrievably
demonstrated. The mantle of unquestioned security on the Atlantic liners would never again appear. Years later, a chronicler who had lived
through the horrors of World War II at sea wrote,

> It seems inconceivable that in 1915 the faith in "humane"
> war according to the rules was so great that a ship of such size
> and value voluntarily had her speed reduced for economic
> reasons; that in a danger zone speed was further reduced in
> order to pick up a pilot at a suitable time; that it was still fur-
> ther cut down by fog; that there was no zigzag and no escort
> of any sort to meet her and finally that in spite of warnings so
> many people should elect to risk their lives in her.

In truth it was not inconceivable at all. Reliance on the rules of "humane" war only partially accounts for the false sense of security surrounding the *Lusitania*'s last voyage. Equally important, though rarely credited, was the almost universal image of the liner as a surviving product of a peacetime race that followed gentlemanly rules of competition, and the notion that those rules still applied despite the war that gripped the competitors. It was this basic misconception that motivated the Cunard Line to continue to operate the *Lusitania*, and her passengers to purchase tickets.

Only the admiralties fully understood the *Lusitania* for what she was. Thus, while paying obligatory lip service to their respective nations, they remained largely unperturbed throughout the whole debacle. The British Admiralty took heavy fire for allowing the liner to maintain its peacetime schedule; it responded that, although the ship had been designed for conversion to military use, no such conversion had yet been attempted. Hence she retained her peacetime guise. Interestingly, the Admiralty did relatively little to challenge the sinking on military grounds. It centered the brunt of its criticism on Turner's failure to obey its instructions, regarding the torpedoing as almost preordained given the monumental series of blunders preceding it.

The position of the navy throughout, from the construction of the *Lusitania* to her sinking and after, was pithily summed up by former Admiral John "Jackie" Fisher in a private letter to his old friend, Admiral von Tirpitz. When the *Lusitania* had been sunk, Tirpitz was Grand Admiral of the German Fleet and Fisher was First Sea Lord. But by 1916 both men had been jettisoned from their navies: Tirpitz for criticism over his submarine policies, Fisher for extreme old age. "Dear old Tirps!" Fisher wrote exuberantly,

> Cheer up, old chap! . . . You're the one German sailor who understands War! Kill your enemy without being killed yourself. I don't blame you for the submarine business. I'd have done the same myself, only our idiots in England wouldn't believe it when I told 'em. Well! So long! Yours till hell freezes, Fisher.

-13-

A New Mission

EMPTY, CAVERNOUS, AND STILL, THE GREAT ATLANTIC LINERS WAITED like iron sentries to be awakened for a purpose, a cause. But none came. As war raged around them they sat at their piers, rusting. The *Vaterland*, *Kaiser Wilhelm II*, and *Amerika* rose and fell on the tides of the Hudson; the *Mauretania*, *Aquitania*, and *Olympic* bobbed listlessly in Liverpool and Belfast. The loss of the *Lusitania*, whose shattered wreck now fouled the nets of Irish fishermen, had abruptly ended commercial service on the Atlantic. The short, expensive, abortive careers of the *Kronprinz Wilhelm* and *Carmania* proved likewise that liners had little utility as merchant cruisers. Denied both of their designed roles, the British ships' enlistment in the Royal Navy now seemed a cruel joke; it was almost certain that they would sit out the rest of the war in obsolescent ignominy.

Then Winston Churchill had an idea. In mid-1915, the First Lord of the Admiralty conceived a bold plan to alter the fortunes of war by launching a peripheral attack on the Ottoman Empire, Germany's weakest ally. By so doing, England would force her enemies to divert troops and resources to a different field of battle, improving the chances of final victory. Churchill's plan called for a massive invasion through the straits of the Dardanelles, augmented by the bulk of the Royal Navy, converging on the tiny peninsula of Gallipoli in the Aegean Sea.

The problem was transportation. For the invasion to succeed, sixty thousand soldiers would have to be ferried past the coasts of France and Spain, through the straits of Gibraltar, across the Mediterranean Sea, then into the Aegean past Salonika and Athens, through Mudros Bay, and into the Dardanelles. But that was only the beginning. Ships must also remain on hand to maintain supply routes, tend the wounded, and ultimately return the victorious army of St. George to London, covered in glory.

As if called by trumpet blast, the British liners were stirred from inactivity. Dust covers were hastily removed, and swarms of workers poured through their hatchways. In weeks, the great liners of Cunard and White Star appeared ready to assume their third and ultimate role, as troopships. It was a rough business for the ships themselves. Passenger capacities were doubled, tripled, or quadrupled as nearly every fitting and unnecessary partition was dumped unceremoniously on the dock. Ships that had retained their peacetime colors were repainted drab navy gray, making them almost indistinguishable from their naval escorts. The *Mauretania* was completed first. Even as her sister was blown apart in the Irish sea, the *Mauretania* was carrying 3,182 troops through the Dardanelles. She continued service as a troop ferry throughout July and August, averaging over 3,500 military personnel each trip. She was soon joined by her sister, *Aquitania*, and the two worked in tandem for the rest of the year.

The *Mauretania*'s career was punctuated with more than its share of excitement and escape, never more harrowing than on one afternoon in the fall of 1915 when her master, Captain Dow, spotted a telltale streak of bubbles heading straight for her starboard bow. The torpedo was going to strike her exactly where the *Lusitania* had been hit, and with a full complement of soldiers exceeding 3,500, the results would be catastrophic. Acting with lightning speed, Dow seized the wheel and turned the *Mauretania* hard a-port, slamming the ship into a breakneck turn that tumbled bunks, troops, and everything not nailed down. The torpedo streaked by the *Mauretania*'s bow a mere five feet away.

The *Olympic* was the last of the great prewar liners to be converted. With no small regret, the same Belfast firm that had built her five years before now took on the onerous task of gutting those lovely Louis XVI interiors in the name of wartime necessity. Not surprisingly, since the *Olympic*—unlike her Cunard rivals—was never designed for military conversion, the task took longer. She departed Belfast in October 1915, en route for Mudros via Liverpool, Gibraltar, and La Spezia. There she joined the *Mauretania* and *Aquitania*, picking her way carefully through mine-strewn seas to deliver the British forces safely.

The Dardanelles campaign was short-lived. Logistical problems and tactical errors confounded the British. First, the Turks proved surprisingly resistant to invaders; second, the climate worked against them. Vessels designed for the arctic blasts of North Atlantic winters were ill-equipped to cope with the rigors of a Mediterranean summer. Men fainted, sometimes even died, from heat stroke in the sweltering, low-ceilinged caverns of the Atlantic ferries. As autumn approached, Churchill's brilliant plan proved to be a terrible disaster.

At this point the role of the liners changed yet again. The *Mauretania* and *Aquitania* were hastily reconverted from troop carriers to hospital ships in grim recognition of the changing realities of war. A snapshot taken on the *Aquitania* around this time shows the incongruity of her new position. The Palladian elegance of the First Class lounge is nearly crowded out of the frame by a cluster of hospital beds, from which wounded men lift their heads and gaze with lackluster eyes at the photographer. Nurses in crisp white smocks circulate among them, and a single officer—poised strangely in imperial fashion, hand on hip—seems very much master of the situation. Ionic columns and gilt filigree complete the odd spectacle.

It was at this inauspicious moment that the third of Ismay's ill-fated trio, once to be called the *Gigantic*, made her brief appearance. Her hull was completed quietly in November of 1915, by which time the tide in the Dardanelles had already turned. Requisitioned by the Admiralty even before she was finished, the ship, now called *Britannic*, received orders for immediate conversion to a hospital ship. Since she was little more than an iron shell to begin with, the conversion proved quite simple. As the largest of the White Star trio, in her vast interiors she could hold an average of 3,300 sick and wounded servicemen, tended in a fully equipped ship's hospital staffed by 52 doctors, 101 nurses, and 336 orderlies. When she put to sea for her trials in December, it was obvious even from afar that the lessons of the *Titanic* had been learned. Virtually every inch of deck space was covered with lifeboats, some even stacked threefold at the ship's fourth funnel. Giant davits cluttered the graceful lines of the ship, now painted an unflattering white with the green and red markings of the Red Cross. After a brief shakedown cruise, the *Britannic* left to start her active duty in the Mediterranean just two days before Christmas 1915.

Apart from a brief reprieve in the summer of 1916, the *Britannic's* wartime service continued unabated, as thousands of injured servicemen were carried home from the carnage of Gallipoli. She was steaming eastward into the Aegean on November 21, 1916, en route to collect another three thousand soldiers, when the ill luck of her sister finally caught up with her. At approximately 8:00 A.M. a mine exploded along the starboard flank of the ship, not far from where the iceberg had pierced the *Titanic* four years earlier. Unlike then, however, there were few people on board, a great surplus of lifeboats, and absolutely no panic. Indeed, the loss of the *Britannic* was a textbook case in marine safety. Many of her crew had been recruited from the White Star Line and included some, like stewardess Violet Jessup, who had been through this once before in 1912. Nurse Jessup was so unfazed by the explosion that she continued making breakfast for a sick colleague, delivered it to her, and finally helped her up to the boat deck. Crew members calmly donned lifejackets, then went to their appointed stations on deck. The ship might not have sunk at all but for Captain Bartlett's mistaken attempt—chillingly similar to Captain Turner's—to beach the vessel on nearby shoals. She took water fast, through portholes that had been unwisely left open in the heat, and settled by the head. Once it was clear that the attempt to beach her was folly, Bartlett ordered the engines shut down and all persons to abandon ship. The evacuation could not have been more orderly. The only casualties resulted from the lowering of two lifeboats without permission—again, like those of the *Lusitania*—which were then drawn into the churning wake of the still-revolving propellers and dashed to pieces. Captain Bartlett remained on deck to the end, then stepped calmly into the warm Mediterranean Sea and swam to a nearby collapsible lifeboat.

The *Britannic*, the largest vessel to be sunk in the First World War, capsized in a mere fifty-five minutes. She went down, said Nurse Jessup, "like a lady."

The *Mauretania* and *Aquitania* remained in service to evacuate the remainder of the expeditionary force, and then returned to their Liverpool anchorages. The *Olympic* was already back in Belfast, nursing her wounds. Though the Dardanelles campaign was a failure, it had been a brilliant victory for the Atlantic liners. By ably fulfilling their duties as troopers and hospital ships, they provided a vital service to their government. It was a lesson the Admiralty would not soon forget. As cruisers, the liners were oversized, under-armed, and clumsy. But as troop carriers, the same circumstances that rendered them unfit for any other military service—their size and the thirst of their engines—made them sublime. The Atlantic race had accelerated the natural growth of the British liners, making them exponentially bigger and faster as they locked horns with their competitors in Hamburg and Bremen. Thus it produced a fleet of ships capable of carrying vastly greater numbers of troops at far higher speeds than could have been imagined in 1890. Little wonder that the Admiralty failed to recognize their potential at first. For them, passenger liners were still the four-masted, single-funneled, 15-knot, 5,000-ton Lilliputians they remembered—the kinds of ships that had ferried troops to Crimea and the Boer War. When they came to the belated realization that a 50,000-ton ship could not fulfill the same wartime duties as one scarcely a tenth her size, they saw only the disadvantages, not the opportunities. Yet, after the Dardanelles, passenger liners would be the primary means by which troops were carried overseas. Just as the *Olympic* and *Mauretania* served in World War I, the *Queen Elizabeth* and *Queen Mary* would be vital as troopships in World War II (Winston Churchill maintained vehemently that their combined contribution shortened the war by at least a year), and the *Queen Elizabeth 2* and *Canberra* would serve England in the Falkland Islands in 1982. With scarcely enough time to clean the rust from their portholes and service their engines, the British ships were requisitioned again, this time to carry Canadian soldiers from Halifax to Liverpool and onward to the Western Front. The *Mauretania* carried a total of 6,214 enlisted men in two voyages in the fall of 1916; then she was retired again, though temporarily, to Liverpool. The

Olympic was employed on the Canadian run throughout 1916 and 1917. The Admiralty originally proposed that the ship be protected by a convoy of cruisers to encircle her and keep watch for submarines. But Captain Hays, her master, demurred. The maximum speed of a convoy is exactly equivalent to its slowest member—in this case, 12 knots. At top speed, the *Olympic* exceeded 22. Thus she was allowed to streak across the Atlantic unaided, placing herself and the lives of her soldiers in the hands of her superior speed and maneuverability. This time the gamble worked. Her unblemished record of safe crossings almost eclipsed the grim memories of her sisters, and she was fondly dubbed "Old Reliable."

But by 1917 the transport of Canadian soldiers had declined, and the *Olympic* was left to handle the remaining traffic alone. The *Mauretania* and her confreres were back in Liverpool, out of work and collecting dust once again. Churchill had been ousted from the Admiralty, and it was doubtful whether his love for peripheral war games, such as the Dardanelles, would ever again be pursued. The war was entrenched along a single front, and the troops needed to maintain it were mostly ferried across the Channel. While P&O liners continued to bring in reinforcements from far-flung imperial outposts, the Atlantic liners seemed redundant once again.

But then, in the spring of 1917, the long period of unrestricted submarine warfare on the Atlantic finally reached its inevitable crescendo, and a reluctant President Wilson (whose re-election campaign had ended in victory with the slogan "He kept us out of war") committed the American military to the defense of the Allies and the defeat of Germany. In a moment everything changed. The British liners would be called out of retirement once again, for this last, greatest push, and this time they would be joined by some unlikely counterparts.

"The Fleet the Kaiser Built for Us"

The events of April 5, 1917, read like the script of a bizarre spy farce. The United States was on the eve of war; diplomatic communications with Germany had ended two months before, and the President was drafting the declaration that would thrust his nation into the fray. Yet the first battle of the American-German conflict took place not on the

Western Front, but on a darkened New Jersey pier where the HAPAG liner *Vaterland* lay moribund and decaying.

The fate of the ship had been a topic of speculation for some time. In the early months of the war, as the *Kronprinzessin Cecilie* reveled in Bar Harbor and the *Kronprinz Wilhelm* scoured the seas, the *Vaterland* had been an object of sympathy and curiosity for New Yorkers: an orphaned, benevolent giant towering over Hoboken. Her crew, those that remained, amused themselves by skating on the frozen Hudson, arranging concerts, and enjoying the boisterous hospitality of New York's thriving German population. Meanwhile Albert Ballin, with his intuitive sense of impending disaster, frantically attempted to secure her release. He pleaded with the German Admiralty to declare the *Vaterland* a relief ship, bringing medical supplies to the front. Herbert Hoover, then relief commissioner in Belgium, concurred, but the German Admiralty did not. They feared to risk the big ship; hence she remained under self-imposed exile in America, perpetually awaiting orders.

Then the *Lusitania* went down. Ironically, it was the *Vaterland*'s formidable wireless set that first picked up the news, then rapidly sent it on to the Cunard Line's Manhattan office. After that, everything changed. The *New York Times* recommended seizing all German liners in response, an action that was considered but not then adopted by the U.S. Navy. The status of Commander Ruser, his men, and his ship suddenly became tenuous. Crew members defected in droves, until finally only 300 remained of the original 1,234. The *Vaterland* herself, formerly a reassuring presence, now seemed vaguely threatening; her fierce prow jutted over the Hoboken docks as though ready to eat them.

Matters reached a head on the evening of April 5. It was, appropriately, a "vicious, bitchy night . . . raining like the devil," as one officer recalled. No fewer than two hundred U.S. soldiers sent to capture and secure the *Vaterland* skulked about the docks in comical secrecy, concealing themselves behind crates and popping out suddenly from behind barrels, rather like the timid policemen in *Pirates of Penzance*. Shortly after midnight, they sprang into action. The seizure of the rusted, nearly abandoned liner was accomplished with the bravura of a commando raid, Captain John Baylis and his men storming en masse up the *Vaterland*'s gangway and brandishing pistols. Commander Ruser, faced with a cavalry charge on his bridge, said quietly, "I protest." He and his men were arrested, interrogated, and finally sent to plush imprisonment at the Mountain Park Hotel in Hot Springs, North Carolina. The *Vaterland* became official property of the United States Navy.

Just ten hours later, President Wilson asked Congress to declare war.

The seizure of the *Vaterland* was quickly followed by those of the *Kaiser Wilhelm II, Kronprinzessin Cecilie, Kronprinz Wilhelm,* and two score other vessels from Norddeutscher Lloyd, as well as the *George Washington, President Grant, President Lincoln, Amerika,* and thirty-one lesser ships of HAPAG. Secretary of the Navy Josephus Daniels, a jovial cherub of a man and cheerful mentor to Franklin Roosevelt, rubbed his hands together with glee. Just look, he said happily, at "the Fleet the Kaiser built for us." Rarely had the fortunes of war been so fortuitous; the problem of transporting the two million doughboys of the American Expeditionary Force was painlessly and effortlessly solved—and in the most ironic way imaginable. Navy dockyards were given the bizarre task of converting the German merchant fleet to wartime use as American troopships, and they seized the task with intemperate enthusiasm. Mewès's delicate interiors were gutted and demolished, and the light creations of Johannes Poppe on the Norddeutscher Lloyd liners disintegrated rapidly under the swinging axes of American servicemen. Few of these ships would ever see commercial service again, and no thought was given to any postwar utility. Although they retained the paired funnels and raked hulls that marked them as once-vaunted German wonderships, within they became floating barracks with as little finery or finesse as Fort Bragg. In months the soft recruits emerged from their harsh retraining looking like hardened veterans. Their hulls, decks, and funnels were coated in uniform navy gray; the Stars and Stripes fluttered at every stern. Even their names had been Americanized: the Lloyd ships became, respectively, the *Monticello, Mount Vernon,* and *Von Steuben*; the transformation of the HAPAG liners, thanks to Ballin's predilection for American-sounding names, was accomplished by the changing of a single letter: *Amerika* became *America,* and the rest remained the same.

The *Vaterland* was the last and most difficult conversion of all. "You will never run her," Chief Engineer Otto Wolf hissed at his American usurpers. At the time, Wolf's remark was interpreted to mean sabotage; later, after the full extent of the *Vaterland*'s decline had been assessed, it was thought he might well have been referring to her overall condition. The ship was a derelict. Had she been a building rather than a liner, she would have been condemned. Nearly every surface was pocked with rust, some patches extending right through the metal. Her hull had not been scraped in over two years, and every manner of marine organism now clung to her underbody. Her paneling sagged and buckled; disuse and neglect had reduced most of her furnishings to congealed rags.

The ship's mechanical condition was, if anything, worse. One of her turbines had fractured at high speed—a catastrophic event that was not recorded anywhere in the *Vaterland*'s log—rendering her practically inoperable. A completely new turbine would have to be built, requiring a new set of blades—38,000, to be precise—and all new machinery. None of her forty-six boilers functioned properly, either. Frayed wires and fractured pipes ran the full length of the ship, playing havoc with heating and lights and sending harassed engineers on wild-goose chases throughout the vessel. The restoration process was almost unimaginable. Every inch of pipe and wire had to be examined, tested, and if necessary replaced. The ship's wireless set, hastily smashed by departing crewmen, took three months to put back in order. And nowhere aboard the *Vaterland* was there a complete set of plans. Engineers groped and fumbled through pitch-dark crawl spaces, peered anxiously into open ventilators, and gazed mystified at an array of levers, gears, and switches clearly marked in brass lettering, all in German.

And there had been sabotage. Behind innocuous paneling, water lines were cut; the ends were then squeezed back together, creating slow leaks that confounded engineers. A similar ruse had been employed with the steam lines: threads of bolts were filed smooth to give way under pressure, and the pipes themselves were surreptitiously plugged with brass and soldered again. Some vandalism was less subtle—as if a rampaging giant had run amok through the ship. Telegraph lines, gauges, and electronics had been smashed and wrenched apart. While the overall damage was minimal, the potential threat remained: engineers moved gingerly about, waiting for the inevitable booby traps to fall upon them.

Once the mechanical restoration was deemed feasible, the physical conversion began. It was, like everything else about the ship, a nightmare. The *Vaterland* was the largest, most opulent liner in the world. The sheer weight of her marble alone was so great that it had once threatened her stability. Moreover, Ballin's designs had conspicuously avoided any consideration of a possible wartime conversion. Thus the design of the ship's interior spaces—terraced decks, alcoves, and awkward (though aesthetic) angles everywhere—made transformation to a troopship almost unfathomable. Yet, as they had with the other German prizes, eager demolition crews went to work on the *Vaterland* with gusto. One wistful observer, reminiscent of Baron von Neizychowski on the *Kronprinz Wilhelm*, described the ensuing process as "the gutting of the German whale." Busts of the Kaiser were gleefully dashed on the pier, and portraits of himself, his family, and German dignitaries were mutilated, defaced, and then discarded. More than 1,200 cabins were demolished. Tons of marble from bathtubs, sinks, and tiles were knocked loose with sledgehammers and tossed in pieces over the side onto the dock. Inside storage sheds the size of airplane hangars a sad, motley pile of the *Vaterland*'s furnishings accumulated. In a tangled heap lay the mechanical horses from the gymnasium, the leather-upholstered seats from the barbershop, cutting boards from the bakery, friezes from the dining room, and four mammoth oil paintings from the First Class Lounge depicting the legend of Pandora. All were thrown together pell-mell with ten thousand other bits and pieces, each one a separate fragment of Albert Ballin's shattered dream.

Seven months to the day after her seizure, on November 17, 1917, the *Vaterland* was ready to sail. All the other German liners had preceded her, but she was the titan among them, and it was popularly assumed that the real business of troop transport would not begin until she was complete. The ship was practically unrecognizable. Her interiors could hold ten thousand troops at a time; in a pinch, she could carry even more. This miracle had been achieved by transforming the entire vessel into a great steel shell and packing every square inch with beds, three bunks high. The dining saloon now had standing room only for eight thousand men; the swimming bath was drained and fitted with shelving as a baggage hold.

The only task left was the easiest of all, to give the new ship a new name. Though registered on the navy list as "USS *Vaterland*," the name "Fatherland" seemed both ironic and unlucky for an American troop-ship. The choice ultimately fell to President Wilson, who with a Puritanical turn of mind supplied the name from an unlikely, though strangely appropriate, source. When considering what to call the largest seagoing object on earth, now being hurled like a battering ram against her creators, he did not hesitate. "Call her *Leviathan*," he said, without looking up from his papers. "It's in the Bible. . . . It means 'monster of the deep.' "

"The Greatest Ship in the World"

Like prima donnas perpetually giving their last performances, the British liners were called out of retirement once again. The *Mauretania* had suffered a full year's idleness and took several weeks to put to rights. The *Olympic* was transferred off the flagging Halifax run to be joined soon after by the *Aquitania*, *Andania*, and a host of intermediate vessels. The entire passenger fleets of England and the United States (including the captured German ships) were rapidly commissioned, ranging in size from the *Leviathan* of 54,282 tons to the Orient Line's tiny *Ormonde*, of 14,853. New York and Liverpool bustled as never before with a constant stream of itinerant humanity; to the casual observer it seemed almost like old times again. German, English, and American ships sailed in and out on regular schedules for the first time in nearly four years.

There were distinct differences, however. Embarking passengers, who had once been saluted by brass bands, tinkling bells, and confetti, now marched in double-quick step to bugle calls and shouted orders. Fond farewells from the rail had a double poignancy, for it was all too apparent that of each congregated mass of doughboys now crowding the decks, only a fraction would return. The most startling difference, however, was in the ships themselves. Originally, both the American and English navies had adopted the traditional procedure of painting the liners battleship gray. Not only did this make them obviously identifiable as navy vessels, it also—allegedly—made them harder to spot on the horizon. But while the first line of reasoning was true (for better or worse), the second proved painfully false. U-boat crews had little difficulty distinguishing the gray smudge in the periscope from its background of sea and sky, and the folly of attempting to make a 40,000 ton vessel invisible was belatedly acknowledged. Then, in an unprecedented burst of creativity, the British Admiralty decided to tack in the opposite direction. Rather than conceal their liners, they would instead make them as glaringly obvious as possible. Marine artist Norman Wilkinson was employed to concoct paint schemes that would obscure each vessel's profile in a maze of seemingly random blocks and patterns, thus making it harder to plot her course. This device, known as "dazzle painting," was immediately applied to every troopship in the Allied fleet. Though its utility has never fully been proven, its aesthetic value was dramatic. By a single order, the drab gray troopships were transformed into strange and wonderful geometric fantasies, a decade ahead of the Cubist movement. No two were alike or even akin. The *Empress of Russia* had two sets of imperfectly aligned zebra stripes running across her flanks; the *Mauretania* boasted a diagonal checkerboard of grays, blacks, and blues; the *Olympic*, anticipating the 1960s "go-go" style, went to sea with psychedelic swirls and dips; the *Leviathan*, the most daring of all, sported a jagged row of grinning shark's teeth across her bow.

In the single year of 1918, these ships ferried across the Atlantic an astounding two million men, breaking the stalemate in the trenches and pressing on to final victory. The role of the liners cannot be overstated, for without them this logistical triumph would have been impossible. Moreover, had not the Anglo-German superliner race engendered a fleet of ships of disproportionate size and speed, each one exponentially larger than the last, the business of troop transport would have been unimaginably more cumbersome, time consuming, and dangerous. Consider, by way of illustration, the difference between the capacities of the *Vaterland*, built in 1914, and the *Amerika*, of 1905. Both were, at their inception, the largest ships in the world. Scarcely a decade had passed between their respective constructions. Yet the *America*, reconditioned, held fewer than 3,000 troops—which was in itself a vast improvement over ships built just two or three years before her and capable of carrying barely half that number. The *Leviathan* carried over 10,000 at speeds half again faster. One ship doing the work of three meant fewer voyages in total, which in turn meant coal, time, and lives saved. So prodigious was the carrying capacity of this single vessel that 1 in 20 servicemen in the entire AEF crossed aboard her—a dazzling record when one considers that over two hundred liners were employed as troopships at the time. With English and German steamers yoked together in the task, the workload was effectively halved. From Germany's *Kronprinz Wilhelm* to its *Vaterland*, and from England's *Oceanic* to its *Olympic*, the liners that had once been prize entries in the race for Atlantic supremacy claimed the lion's share of troop-ferrying. The peacetime competition between them ultimately succeeded only in greatly augmenting the tonnage the Allies now had at their disposal. Thus, it is no exaggeration to state that the liner race between Britain and Germany helped speed Allied victory in the Great War.

This miracle of transport was not, however, accomplished without incident. Nearly every ship had her own tales of near loss, none more than the *Olympic*, which seemed to have absorbed all the lost luck of her sunken sisters much as aboriginals once ingested the spirits of their dead. On May 18, 1918, the *Olympic* approached the Scilly Isles on the southwest coast of England carrying more than 6,000 American servicemen for Liverpool. Four British destroyers formed a convoy around her for this last leg of the journey. In the uncertain half-light of incipient dawn, a lookout in her crow's nest spotted a submarine surfaced some distance away on the horizon, her engines idle. Captain Hays, the same commander who earlier had spurned offers of escort for his beloved ship, now turned the *Olympic*'s bow to face the enemy. Her 6-inch guns blasted away from the foredeck, but the ship's powerful engines had already closed the distance between them. The shots went wide. The submarine likewise altered course, turning to port in a desperate attempt to bring her torpedo tubes to bear. Then, with a sickening crash, the bow of the *Olympic* sliced into the submarine, venting her pressure hull to the sea. The U-boat trailed along the flank of the ship, suffering further damage from the huge brass propellers. Moments later it up-ended and sank out of sight. The stem of the *Olympic* was as battered as a prizefighter's nose, but she made the rest of the trip otherwise unscathed, her crew and passengers celebrating wildly the first and only instance in the entire war of a merchant ship sinking an enemy vessel.

It was not until months later, when the ship was hauled out in dry dock, that a huge dent was discovered in the double hull amidships. Several plates had sprung, but the honeycombed hull had contained the leakage and concealed it from her crew. It was clear that at some point a torpedo had struck the ship and failed to explode. Did the lost sub get off a single Pyrrhic round after all? Or did another U-boat steal quietly upon her—unknown to anyone—fire its abortive missile, and disappear again unseen?

The *Olympic* was far from the only great liner to court danger. The HAPAG standard-bearer *Vaterland* might have become the American troopship *Leviathan*, but she was still a hoodoo ship. On her first crossing under the Stars and Stripes the intense cold caused a steam whistle to contract, sending a great blast of sound reverberating over the Atlantic and announcing her presence for all to hear. Despite the frantic efforts of a score of engineers, the appalling din continued throughout the night. Shortly thereafter she went aground for several anxious hours off Liverpool, the largest sitting duck in the world. On a later cruise the port steering engine broke suddenly, sending the ship steaming in aimless circles. Finally, as if in retaliation against her captivity, the ventilating system began, for no apparent reason, to work backward, sending toxic fumes throughout the ship and nearly suffocating her crew. The threat of illness was likewise ever present, all the more so on a ship the size of the *Leviathan*. On one voyage in late September, an epidemic of flu killed ninety-one soldiers within a week, turning the entire ship into a floating quarantine.

External threats were no less terrifying. Her captain once spent nearly seventy hours on the bridge navigating through thick fog, scanning the surrounding wooly blankness for enemy vessels, afraid to sound his own horn for fear of betraying his position to a nearby sub, and thus running the constant risk of collision with the escort vessels blundering about in the murk.

Some ships were even less fortunate. Over one-third of Cunard's fleet and nearly as much of White Star's was sunk by the end of the war, contributing to the over two million tons of Allied shipping sent to the bottom by German submarines. By 1919, both companies had lost one of their flagships—the Cunarder *Lusitania* and the White Star *Britannic*; curiously, the only great trio to survive the war unscathed were Ballin's *Imperator*, *Vaterland*, and still unfinished *Bismarck*.

Once the liners were safely retired to their home ports, the incredible tally of their contribution could finally be assessed. Even today, the numbers are staggering: the *Leviathan* held the record for greatest number of passengers ever embarked in a single voyage: 14,416; the *Olympic* was a distant second at 6,148, then the *Aquitania* at 6,090, and finally the *Mauretania* at 5,703. Though the smallest of the quartet, between March and November of 1918 the *Mauretania* made seven roundtrips, fourteen voyages in all, and carried 33,160 troops. After the Armistice, she carried home another 19,536. In total, from 1915 through 1918, the *Mauretania* carried some 69,751 troops and 8,605 wounded. The *Olympic*'s record was no less impressive—the only great liner to remain in continuous military service throughout the war, she steamed a total of 184,000 miles and burned 374,000 tons of coal.

Yet no ship emerged from her duties more covered in glory than the *Leviathan*. Her ability to carry almost twice as many troops as any of her counterparts set her apart from the rest, and her implausible history was legendary. No ship had done more to win the war, and it was a delicious irony that the same qualities that once made the *Vaterland* a fierce competitor to the British—size and speed—were instrumental in their aid. Her ten round-trip voyages carried over 100,000 American troops into combat. On her very last, she was awarded the singular honor of bearing home General John J. Pershing and his famed Rainbow Division. The *Leviathan* then retired as the "glory of the transport service." Speaking to an assemblage of newsmen on the docks, Secretary of War Newton Baker said fondly, "It is a great career, worthy of the greatest ship in the world."

"An End with Dread"

When a dream is destroyed, it often seems as though the men who conjured it disappear as well, vanishing from the pages of history as if their whole life and purpose was exhausted in pursuit of that single goal.

But the truth is crueler still, because more often the dreamers survive, sometimes for many years, to watch in horror as everything they built and stood for is dismantled, ridiculed, and finally forgotten.

So it was for Albert Ballin. The capture of the *Vaterland* was only one in a series of tragic disappointments for the embittered visionary. As early as August 1914 he declared, "At this moment, my life's work lies in shreds." He did not know how right he was. The HAPAG fleet still existed, on paper at any rate, and he still enjoyed the favor of the Kaiser. But circumstances had already conspired to sour both those graces. Of the 175 ships of the Hamburg-Amerika Line, only 80 were currently in German ports. Most of the rest would never see Germany again. Ballin's perpetual schemes to free the ships seized in Hoboken, ranging from Red Cross sponsorship to relief efforts, came to nothing. Still convinced that the war would be concluded in months, he strenuously objected when the Admiralty seized his vessels and began affixing guns and armor plates to them. Once again, he was overruled. The bulk of his fleet remaining in Germany was refashioned and sent out to its certain destruction as armed merchant cruisers.

Faced with the dreadful realization that he no longer controlled his own line, Ballin changed tactics. Taking a leaf out of Lord Inverclyde's book, he proposed a scheme to the Admiralty remarkably similar to that presented by Cunard in 1904. In return for a government subsidy equaling 42,000,000 marks, HAPAG would construct three liners over five years, each easily convertible to auxiliary cruisers. When completed, they could be pressed at once into military service; at the conclusion of the war they would revert to their civilian roles. Thus, instead of losing his fleet, Ballin would augment it. But times had changed, and the government was no longer receptive to Ballin's entreaties. They had neither the money nor the facilities to undertake such a project. Though Ballin did gain a substantial indemnity, enough to nurse his ailing line through the war, his grandiose scheme to preserve intact the great liner race had failed once and for all.

Ballin's relationship with the Kaiser likewise declined. In some ways this was inevitable, for in Wilhelm's eyes Ballin represented an era of competition and pageantry, not wartime necessity. Their friendship had always been based on the Kaiser's love of pomp and his vanity, and on Ballin's willingness to play on those traits. In peacetime their interests coincided, and Ballin persuaded himself that the Kaiser viewed foreign relations as he did: a vast and intricate game of peaceful one-upmanship, always ending with handshakes all around. But when the situation changed, Ballin increasingly found himself removed from the charmed circle at court.

There were other reasons for this besides the inherent differences between the two men. Ballin had, not surprisingly, been a passionate advocate for peace in the summer of 1914. He was so convinced of his position that he erroneously believed it to be shared by the British as well, and conveyed his firm belief in their neutrality to the Kaiser after returning from a visit to London in August. At the outbreak of war, he was ridiculed. There was also the perennial problem of his Jewishness. Wilhelm held this factor in small account; he shared the nascent anti-Semitism common to nearly all German royals, but not particularly virulently. A man who genuinely enjoyed conversation and new perspectives, he was quite willing to extend his circle of friends to include many who would otherwise not move in the rarefied circles of Hohenzollern nobility. But this sympathy was not shared by his colleagues. Most had always regarded Ballin, the dapper Hamburger with his pearl stickpins and egg-shaped head, with thinly veiled Prussian contempt.

The worst offender was the Kaiserin. A poisonous woman who hated Jews and Englishmen with equal fervor, she found in the pacifist Ballin an embodiment of her loathing. As Ballin drifted into the reputedly anglophilic circle of Baron Holtzendorff, her barbs became more frequent and spiteful. At first Wilhelm turned a deaf ear: "The Kaiser spoke about you in the nicest and most charming way," Holtzendorff reassured Ballin after one stormy encounter, "and *der hohe Herr* repeatedly stressed, particularly to the Kaiserin, that he could fully understand your opinion and your standpoint, since you certainly had to represent the interests of your life's work, the greatest shipping line in the world!"

But the Kaiser's resistance was crumbling. While he might acknowledge that Ballin was valiantly trying to save his line, this goal seemed paltry in comparison to the weighty matter of war. His wife became a sort of Lady Macbeth, constantly stoking his dreams of total victory against the English. Soon any talk of compromise or conciliation was not only unwanted but treasonous. Ballin's continuing efforts to foster mediation between the two great powers suddenly looked very suspicious. As the Kaiser's mood hardened, the two drifted apart. There was never anything so dramatic as a break—they remained cordial, even affectionate, to the very end—but there was certainly a greater distance between them.

Ballin, with some justification, blamed the courtiers. "The men around the Kaiser have cut me off," he wrote gloomily. "I have seen the Kaiser only in the company of other guests. He has been completely removed from my influence and he would be exceedingly mistrustful of it now. . . ." Worse yet, it became horribly apparent that the Kaiser's sycophantic circle were so desperate to curry favor with him that they withheld any potentially disquieting news and censored any dissenting opinions ruthlessly. "No one," said Ballin, "tells him the whole truth, most people do not even tell him half the truth, and very many lie to him. That is the situation." It did not occur to the naïve Ballin that perhaps the Kaiser preferred this sort of treatment. Instead he regarded himself as the only man in Germany capable of bringing the Kaiser to his senses. Yet, as he became more and more convinced that he could speak truth to power, he found himself utterly cut off by suspicious yes-men.

The fault, however, was not entirely theirs. Once Wilhelm had been able to sustain two separate images of himself: on the one hand, benevolent, peace-loving Father of the Nation; on the other, Supreme Warlord. But the time came when he could not maintain both, and he was forced to choose. What Albert Ballin did not and could not understand was that the Kaiser had already made his choice by the summer of 1914, and remained unwaveringly committed to it thereafter. This was, in essence, what the courtiers were attempting to communicate to him through their rebuffs. Even Wilhelm, by his conduct, made it plain. He frequently left Berlin to be with his troops—a place where Ballin's presence would be neither appropriate nor permitted—and on returning seemed more interested in battle plans and ballistics than old dreams of cultural supremacy. When they met, he treated Ballin with the detached courtesy one gives an old college chum, once very close, whom one has not seen for many years and now has little in common with.

The irony of his position moved Ballin to despair. No man, he acknowledged, had done more than himself to "wrest so much from the British" in peacetime. If the Anglo-German liner race was not precisely his invention, it was certainly he who had given it shape, direction, and impetus. And, to cap it all off, he had won! The *Imperator*, *Vaterland*, and *Bismarck* were greater vessels than the British had ever built, or would build for another twenty years. Yet now he was branded an anglophile! Ballin began to write long though not particularly sensible letters to all his old friends and colleagues. Each missive was filled with dread—for his line, for his country, for all of Europe, for himself. "The course of these great, splendid events unfortunately strengthens me in my fear that this greatest war in world history will be ended not by governments and armies but by revolution," he predicted grimly. When the Americans entered the war, his worst anxieties were realized. He watched helplessly as his beautiful fleet was snatched from him—the fault of the blundering Admiralty, which had foolishly let it remain in American waters despite his frantic entreaties—and turned into troop ferries for enemy soldiers. He must have winced at the thought of the lovely *Vaterland*, in so many ways his own child, stripped and gutted and filled with American doughboys with their pocket knives and chewing gum.

Ballin's health began to fail. He spent less and less time in Hamburg and more in curative spas. Professor Dapper's sanatorium in Bad Kissingen became a sort of second home. His temper, always mercurial, was increasingly erratic. He could no longer sustain his old incorrigible optimism, and the valleys between the peaks were greater than ever. He snapped at his friends, threw objects around the room, and slept for days at a time. In short, Ballin was showing classic symptoms of manic depression. A combination of drugs including morphine and veronal—some prescribed, some not—further sharpened his mental decline. His face, which even in moments of despair had retained its expressive elasticity, tightened into a look of perpetual worry. Sometimes when acquaintances came to call he did not recognize them.

Still, to the very last, Ballin persisted in his attempts to foster amity between Germany and England. Though by September of 1918 he was a virtual outcast from Berlin society, he resolved to make a final appeal to his beloved Kaiser's reason. In a letter to Admiral Müller—the same man who had brought the news of the Archduke's death to Wilhelm four years before—he announced his intention to meet with the Emperor and tell him frankly that the only choice left to him was peace or revolution. That night he presented himself at Wilhelmshöhe, looking determined. The Kaiser received him with his usual boyish exuberance. "The Kaiser made a very lively impression, Ballin a very dejected one," an observer recalled. Wilhelm's ignorance of the military situation, both willful and through the misinformation of his advisers, staggered Ballin. "His Majesty was in such a sunny disposition that it seemed to me quite impossible to spell out, or even to intimate, the seriousness and frightful danger in which Germany found itself," he said later, admitting "My determination collapsed." The two men made forced conversation for over an hour, then broke off abruptly. Ballin returned to his spas and his sleeping draughts, the Kaiser to his Olympian dreams of victory. They would never meet again.

"Better an end with dread than dread without end," Albert Ballin was fond of saying. On November 8, 1918, he acted upon this conviction. That night, riddled with insomnia and depression, he swallowed a huge quantity of sleeping tablets and collapsed into a coma. Whether it was deliberate suicide or merely a rash miscalculation would never be known. Terrified friends rushed him to a nearby clinic, where his stomach was pumped and various restoratives were administered. For a while it looked as though Ballin might pull through. But then on the following day an ulcer, which had been aggravated by the drugs, suddenly hemorrhaged, and his body went into extremis. Albert Ballin died of heart failure in the early afternoon of November 9.

Two days later, the Armistice was signed.

-14-

The
Lion's Share

A LION AND AN EAGLE. THE LION, SPRINGING WITH CLAWS BARED AGAINST a blood-red banner; the eagle, its sharp talons covetously clutching the globe. It was no accident that Cunard and HAPAG chose the national symbols of England and Germany to represent them, for each had become, by 1914, the apotheosis of nationalism. It mattered little that their flagships' interiors owed more to French décor than their own country's, or that most passengers continued—despite the best efforts of both lines—to book passage based on sailing schedules, not patriotic impulse. It was an enduring paradox of the great race of the superliners that while the ships themselves reflected little of their national heritage, they remained the most tangible and recognizable symbols of their respective nations before, during, and even after the First World War. Thus it was with no small sense of satisfaction that the English hauled down the imperial flag from the *Imperator*'s stern and raised the red ensign of the British merchant marine. In a single moment, all the *Imperator*'s cultural significance to Germany vanished, and she became, within and throughout, a British ship.

The 1920 Cunard Line company dinner was held with vindictive triumph in the First Class dining room of the *Imperator*, like Norse warriors bivouacking in the halls of a fallen enemy. The Cunard lion flew from the mainmast, just fifty or so feet back from the bows where the great bronze eagle had once perched. By the terms of the Versailles treaty, the *Imperator* was theirs, the United States Line took the *Leviathan*, and White Star received the still unfinished *Bismarck*. This was seen as eminently sensible reparations. Cunard had lost the *Lusitania*, White Star the *Britannic*. The two Germans would fill the gaps left by their sunken flagships. The Americans received the *Leviathan* as well as the bulk of the Norddeutscher Lloyd fleet—the *Kronprinzessin Cecilie*, *Kronprinz Wilhelm*, *Kaiser Wilhelm II*, and others—simply because they were already under American control. It was all very reasonable, save for one fact: the Germans themselves were left with nothing. After England and America had taken their shares, the largest vessel in the German mercantile fleet was the *Gröss Gott*, a 781-ton coastal steamer.

The race was over, the victor decided. Yet the men who now congregated to claim their prizes were nothing more than a second-string team. The visionaries, those who had worked the technological and financial miracles that conjured these behemoths into being, were all gone. J. P. Morgan, Lord Inverclyde, and Albert Ballin were dead. Kaiser Wilhelm and J. Bruce Ismay were both exiled from their countries: Wilhelm in forced seclusion in Utrecht, Holland; Ismay in self-imposed reclusion in Galway, Ireland. Both would live on for decades, little more than living ghosts of their lost age.

Similarly, the ships themselves entered a new decade looking very much like relics from the past. Most, in fact, never saw active service again: the *Kronprinz Wilhelm* was scrapped in 1923; the *Kaiser Wilhelm II* and *Kronprinzessin Cecilie* were docked alongside one another in a remote backwater of Chesapeake Bay, still technically under U.S. Navy commission. Like forgotten monoliths, they wasted slowly away throughout the 1920s and 1930s. In 1940, the Lend Lease plan might have reinstated them to active service, albeit merely as troopships. President Roosevelt offered the German ships to England in conjunction with the mothballed American destroyer fleet, but the cost of updating the liners was so extensive that England refused. Once the navy realized they could not even give the ships away, their utility was ended. The last survivors of the great German fleets (ironically, the former *Imperator*, *Vaterland*, and *Bismarck*—which enjoyed commercial service while their older cousins languished in port—had all been scrapped by this time) were finally towed to a secluded anchorage and obliterated.

After World War I, the *Imperator* underwent several months of reconditioning and refurbishment, emerging in 1921 as the Cunard flagship *Berengaria*. Charles Mewès's predilection for French interiors meant that relatively few changes were necessary to effect the transformation from German to English—the *Berengaria*'s interiors were, in fact, a stylistic counterpart to those of Arthur Davis's *Aquitania*. Still, traces of the past remained. Ashtrays in the First Class lounge had "Zigarren" stenciled on their sides; the bathroom taps and other valves, buttons, and switches were still labeled in the original German.

Likewise, no amount of English camouflage could conceal the liner's unwieldy tendencies. All the infamous marble bathtubs had been removed, replaced by lighter steel models, and one thousand tons of iron was added as ballast, but all this accomplished little. The *Berengaria* continued to list alarmingly at the slightest cause and rolled her passengers dreadfully in a heavy sea. To the end of her productive life, she remained a "tender" ship. The ex-German's speckled career also seemed to haunt her. While the *Mauretania* and *Aquitania* radiated English reserve and aristocracy, the *Berengaria* was always seen as rather flashy, even vulgar. "Everybody on the *Berengaria* was 'socially prominent,' " said one of her officers, "even the dogs." The glitter of nouveau riche excess seemed to draw one to the other. "Everything about the *Berengaria* is on the grand, the opulent, scale," one brochure frothily declared. "She is sensational. Sensational people board her. . . . No one who is amused by encounters with celebrities should deprive himself of the chance acquaintances of the *Berengaria*." The first of Ballin's glorious trio enjoyed a long and active service until a combination of financial straits and advanced age ended her career in 1936. Her replacement, already being fitted out as the *Berengaria* made her last voyage to Rosyth, Scotland, was the *Queen Mary*.

In 1920, the *Bismarck* was still an unfinished shell in the Hamburg building yard of Blohm and Voss. The ship that the Kaiser had once intended to carry him on his victory tour had suffered numerous delays and setbacks throughout her six-year fitting out, including strikes, steel shortages, and a fire. After the war, when the White Star Line took possession of the vessel, Blohm and Voss was ordered to complete the ship, now titled *Majestic*, with greatest dispatch. The proud German firm, which had also built the *Vaterland*, regarded their new employers with undisguised contempt. Work proceeded as slowly as humanly possible, and it was not until 1922 that the *Majestic* was reluctantly ready for trials. When White Star officials arrived to take possession, they were given a shock. The enormous liner, at 56,551 tons the largest in the world, had been defiantly titled *Bismarck* in great brass letters at the bow and stern; her three funnels were likewise painted in HAPAG colors. The intent was obvious: even if it was only into a lifetime of alien servitude, the *Bismarck* would have at least one voyage under her true identity. White Star officials, incensed, posted guards to prevent any possible sabotage of their new flagship. But the transfer occurred without incident. Captain Hans Ruser, who had been on the bridge the night the *Vaterland* was seized, handed over the *Bismarck* to Captain Bertram Hays, who had charged the *Olympic* into an enemy submarine. Then the German crew departed the port side of the vessel, and the English crew boarded to starboard. The red ensign was raised, and the ship departed Blohm and Voss as the *Majestic*. Crowds of workers and townsfolk lined the piers, waving mournfully. Some sang laments.

By far the most difficult conversion was, predictably, the *Leviathan's*. Decommissioned from troop duties in 1919, she returned to Hoboken and sat untended for three long years. Once again, the great German ship slid rapidly into decay. Her dazzle paint peeled in long strips down her sides, revealing prewar colors of white and black. Great teardrops of rust streaked from every porthole, and windows shattered in their frames. By 1922, the *Leviathan* was in much worse shape than she had been as the *Vaterland*. Though technically she was the second largest ship in the world, many believed the United States had been given a pig in a poke. One editorial suggested that she be converted to floating apartments; others suggested that she merely be destroyed.

That would have been the likely fate of the liner had it not been for the perspicacity and downright stubbornness of a marine architect named William Francis Gibbs. Gibbs, who would go on to design the SS *United States*, the fastest liner in history, was a young and rather arrogant architect at the Newport News shipyards. For two years, Gibbs pestered the Shipping Board to give him the *Leviathan*. A hard, austere man unaccustomed to finesse or even common courtesy, he relied instead on a veritable barrage of memos, which flooded the office until even the exorbitant price of ten million dollars—Gibbs's estimate for the *Leviathan* conversion—seemed a small price to pay to get this infernal man off their backs. Victorious at last, Gibbs sent off immediately for a set of blueprints from Blohm and Voss. His timing was inopportune: the firm had just watched the last of its beloved liners sail away under an enemy flag. They answered back with acid politeness that they would be happy to provide a set of plans for one million dollars.

Thwarted, Gibbs and a crew of engineers embarked on their own survey. Nothing like it had ever been attempted. With only old brochures to guide them, they began slowly, methodically to examine every inch of the *Leviathan*, intending to formulate their own set of plans. "There was nothing to go on but the ship herself," Gibbs said later. "We knew nothing about her." The survey took a full year, but a final set of plans was drafted. Then Gibbs and his men got to work. Furnished with a generous government subsidy (the first since Edward Knight Collins had presented his case to Congress in the 1850s) the newly formed United States Line set out to win the Atlantic for the Stars and Stripes. The design of the interior spaces was drastically altered, eschewing ancien régime for art deco. The ship's three funnels were painted a cheerful red, white, and blue; in the library, where once Prince Ludwig had stared imperiously at First Class denizens, a portrait of President Warren G. Harding—looking misleadingly decisive—now presided.

The newly rechristened *Leviathan* departed on her first commercial voyage on July 4, 1923. The next three voyages were solidly profitable, and her owners began to congratulate themselves. But their relief was premature. Rarely would so many varying circumstances coalesce to confound a ship's career. Some were anticipated, some not. Of the former, there remained the fact that, unlike the Cunard or White Star ships, the *Leviathan* had no comparable running mates. Without them, her every-other-week sailings could not compete with the weekly service offered by her competitors. Second, a ship of her size and dimensions relied on the emigrant trade for support. After the Dillingham Immigration Restriction Act of 1921, that safety net was gone. The *Leviathan* frequently put to sea with as few as five hundred paying customers, less than half her total number of crew.

Then there were the imponderables. Of these, the most damaging was yet another act of Congress, the Volstead Act of 1921. Alcohol became an illegal substance, a prohibition that extended to all American liners but not, for obvious reasons, to those under foreign flags. For every other passenger firm, it was an unexpected windfall. Americans began booking passage to Europe solely on the expectation of satisfying their thirst, and the companies were happy to comply. The French, in particular, took transatlantic tippling to a new level, introducing the longest bar afloat and marketing their ships as little more than floating gin palaces. The *Leviathan*, fettered by the last feeble bonds of American Puritanism, was doomed. Her First Class became the refuge of dowdy Midwestern matrons, anxious to escape the perception of sin and frolic aboard "foreign" ships. Fourth and finally, there was the ill luck of the ship herself. Frequent accidents, mishaps, and even small fires cost the line uncounted thousands in repairs. The *Leviathan* was also the victim of one of the worst storms in Atlantic history, rolling 15 degrees to port and starboard while her captain spent seventy-two consecutive hours on the bridge.

Somehow the *Leviathan* limped on for another decade, hemorrhaging cash from every seam. When the Great Depression settled on the Atlantic trade and reduced even the Cunarders to half-filled lounges and penury, no ship was harder hit than the *Leviathan*. Finally, in 1938, she was withdrawn from service. Had she been given the same three-year dormancy that she twice endured, the ship would have been worth her weight in gold for a new generation of troop crossings, but it was not to be. The great liner that left its Manhattan pier for the last time already showed signs of age and neglect. A persistent leak in the stern required the operation of the pumps throughout the entire voyage, pipes burst everywhere, and the food was rancid. As the temperature dropped in the mid-Atlantic, the same freakish contraction occurred in the *Leviathan*'s whistle that had imperiled her in 1917. This time, with nothing around her but miles of empty sea and nothing ahead but demolition, she seemed to be sounding her own funeral dirge.

There is a surreal quality to this, the last chapter of the Anglo-German race for supremacy on the Atlantic. In the fevered battle, who could have predicted that superliners built to compete with each other would someday fly the same flag; that in fact the flagships of both Cunard and White Star, the largest vessels on earth, would be the very same German ships that had once sought to humble them? In the wake of total war, irony succeeded irony. To trace the path of the Atlantic liners in this period, 1914–1919, is to watch the whole world sink into madness by degrees, like a ship going down slowly, but inevitably, by the bow. English and German liners built in a spirit of friendly competition first fled and hunted one another, then decimated each other with hastily erected guns; German liners, seized in their American ports, were yoked with their English rivals in the traitorous business of ferrying troops across the Atlantic to destroy their own countrymen; finally, the German titans were transformed into English and American liners, replacing those the Germans themselves had sunk. "*Britannia* ruled the waves" once again, one author wrote, but "with a gleam of Prussia in her blue eyes." It was well that Ballin did not live to see this final humiliation of his fabulous fleet, for the shame of it surely would have killed him anyhow.

The German fleet had been stolen by their erstwhile rivals even as some ships rested in their dry docks unfinished. The offices of the Norddeutscher Lloyd and Hamburg-Amerika lines were sparsely staffed, like underfunded charity organizations; the vast, cavernous passenger sheds of Bremen and Hamburg were ghostly still. The very few liners that the great shipyards now built were for their enemies. The two men who had been the driving force behind the German mammoths, Kaiser Wilhelm and Albert Ballin, were gone from the scene. Germany settled into deep fiscal depression, fueled in no small part by the vengeful war reparations dealt by the Allies at Versailles. Germany was beaten, exhausted, defeated.

BY AUGUST 1924, THE HAMBURG SHIPYARD OF BLOHM AND VOSS HAD BEEN a virtual tomb for two years, since the beautiful captive *Bismarck* had been hauled away. The ceaseless sound of hammering had stilled, and the shipwrights who had defiantly lined the piers in salute to their exiled creation were unemployed. Germany herself was on her knees, crushed and dispirited by the staggering burden of reparations imposed by the victorious Allies. It began to look as if the venerable yard would soon close its gates forever, but then, miraculously, a contract arrived. The Hamburg-Amerika Line, re-formed under a new chairman and struggling to keep afloat without any of its former government subsidies, commissioned their first liner since 1914. She would service Hamburg, New York, Southampton, and Cherbourg, making the trip across the Atlantic in a leisurely ten days. All the hopes of her beleaguered nation would sail with her.

Yet the lean black hull that took shape in the stocks was, in many ways, a disappointment. At only 20,607 tons, she was less than half the size of the *Bismarck*, closer in fact to a third. Her profile also seemed strangely retrogressive: four masts, two squat funnels, and a small superstructure crammed between large expanses of open deck. The new German ship, in fact, looked most of all like a barely upgraded version of the *Oceanic* of 1870. She was slow (15 knots), small (627 feet), and dumpy—her interiors were both dated and curiously austere, like the Second Class of an old ship like the *Kaiser Wilhelm der Grosse*. As the liner that would single-handedly reintroduce Germany to the Atlantic trade, she seemed a poor showing indeed.

There was only one indication that this new ship might represent something greater, and a small indication at that. Her name, chosen by her Hamburg directors, was painted in large letters on the bow and stern of the new ship in clear, bright capitals. It was an odd choice, not euphonious and scarcely impressive-sounding. Yet within its four syllables the whole panoply of the Anglo-German liner race was writ large: her name, if not her shape, would sound the trumpet for a new generation of competitors. Defiantly, and with all the bravado of a gauntlet thrown, she was the *Albert Ballin*.

Afterword

"TRANSPORTATION IS CIVILIZATION," WROTE RUDYARD KIPLING, HIMSELF a traveler of some renown. His words echo down the thirty-year history of the Anglo-German liner race, resonating on multiple frequencies even as they sum up the age. "Transportation"—that is, the liners themselves—was "civilization" in that their interiors and furnishings were mirror images of life ashore. The great liners were certainly floating embodiments of Edwardian fashions and fads, from the Louis XVI paneling in a writing room to the electric-powered camels in a ship's gymnasium. "Civilization" might also embrace the microcosm of class strata that the liners reproduced in their serried decks. Nowhere else could one find so many disparate social classes confined in a shared environment. To recreate on shore the economic disparities within a single Atlantic steamship, one would have to circumscribe an entire metropolis—New York, for example—from the brownstones in Manhattan to the tenements in Brooklyn. Yet in the *Olympic* they were all contained within an 850-foot hull, within sight, and in some cases, even within reach of one other. But despite such unique proximity, the Atlantic liners also reflected the stark divisions among classes, all the more rigorously for their close quarters. First Class looked down—quite literally—on Second Class, and Second Class looked down on Steerage. Beneath them all, hidden within the darkest depths of the ship, were the stokers and trimmers whose labor kept the rest of this tight little society safe and comfortable.

Perhaps the most compelling interpretation of Kipling's maxim, however, is its pithy depiction of the transformative effect of increased mobility on the structure and geography of twentieth-century society. It would be an exaggeration to claim that the liners created modern America, but not much of one. In the great migration to America in the late nineteenth and early twentieth centuries, the pivotal role of steam travel has for too long been ignored. America needed immigrants, and other nations were anxious to send them. In the 1880s the United States had vast tracts of open, arable land and a burgeoning industrial complex. It needed men and women to till its fields, lay its rails, and work its factories. In Europe, economic and political crises propelled a near-exodus of potential labor across the Atlantic in search of opportunities and more hospitable conditions in the New World. Yet this cause and effect, long considered axiomatic by historians of the period, pointedly ignores the vast expanse of hostile ocean separating the two continents. Until the Anglo-German race produced liners capable of carrying thousands of immigrants in a single crossing, the treacherous sea passage was an enormous bottleneck. Ships before 1890 could carry only a fraction of would-be emigrant passengers, a few hundred at most, in conditions so appalling that many succumbed to and died of seasickness, malnutrition, and disease. Yet the demand for emigrant ships was overwhelming: men like Albert Ballin built fortunes on this tidal mass of emigrating humanity. And the United States, until the third decade of the twentieth century, had more than enough room for all.

Thus the most crucial and tangible result of the great liner race was not to fashion greater thrills for rich clientele—though that is by far the most discussed—but rather to increase exponentially the carrying capacity of ships for emigrant trade. As hulls exceeded 700 feet and 30,000 tons, passenger numbers rose from 1,000 to 4,000 and more. The oceanic bottleneck was thus widened, and countless thousands—even millions—of new Americans arrived in the crucial fourteen years before the First World War. Had ships continued to expand in the much smaller pre-race increments, this would not have been possible.

It could be argued, of course, that the race was only one among several contributing factors: that the demand for emigration, as well as increased technological advances, themselves supplied the necessary conditions for rapid expansion. Yet this approach quite overlooks the intense nationalism surrounding the liners' construction, reflected in everything from their mascots to their press coverage. While sound business practices might have encouraged the construction of somewhat larger ships over a greater period of time, they cannot account for the meteoric growth seen in both German and English shipbuilding (but no other nation's) during this period. The race for the Atlantic required more than sound business decisions; it demanded leaps of faith. Nothing else can account for Cunard's gamble on Charles Parsons's turbines or Norddeutscher Lloyd's unique ultimatum to the German ship-yards.

Finally, if transportation is indeed civilization, it too can be contorted and destroyed by the awful spectacle of war. And so it was. The reconditioning of the Atlantic liners from peacetime ferries to wartime cruisers and troopships was one of the most poignant, tragic symbols of civilization's decline into chaos. The seizure of the German liners by the U.S. Navy, symbolic on a host of levels, represents most of all the frail inadequacy of peaceful pre-war rivalries when confronted by their logical conclusion, military expediency. Yet their role was not merely symbolic. The giant ships, which had been built to showcase the glories of their respective nations, were placed in tandem, facilitating the incredible transport of over two million American and Canadian soldiers to the trenches of Europe. Just as most historians consider the immigrant boom without regard to the logistics of transport underlying it, so too do they regard the American influx as greatly influencing the outcome of the war without thought as to how the U.S. military got its men over there in the first place. The role of German and British liners was absolutely central, for without them the problem of transporting such a vast number of men on vessels of 15,000 tons would have been practically insoluble.

The liners that plied the Atlantic from 1889 to 1919 transformed both the Old and New Worlds. They were the lifeline between continents, bringing their respective cultures to sea and meeting in a symbolic point halfway across the ocean, in the lounges and dining saloons of a dozen majestic ships. Like embassies, they carried with them the mantles of their respective nations, yet also provided a forum where all nationalities could meet in amity. Fifty years before the creation of the United Nations, Atlantic liners were practically the only place where such international harmony and diversity could be found. The rivalry that produced these wondrous vessels would eventually destroy them, but their symbolism as national icons had already been superseded by something much larger. Though the English and German superliners were conceived in symbolic opposition to one another, their greatest effect would ultimately be achieved in tandem. Together, they carried a new generation of citizens to the United States; together, they transported a vast American Expeditionary Force that changed the course of the First World War; together, they introduced innovations and technologies that would revolutionize the business of sea transport forever after. The melding of the two fleets in the postwar period may be regarded as a crowning irony, but only when viewed from the perspective of Anglo-German rivalry. Perhaps the greatest irony is this: in quite another way, they were sisters all along.

Notes

Chapter 1: The Gauntlet

10 **will of the king."** Cookman, Scott. *Atlantic: The Last Great Race of Princes*. New York: John Wiley, 2002.

11 **three years old.** Massie, Robert. *Dreadnought*. New York: Ballantine, 1991.

14 **"the man nobody liked,"** Cookman, 52.

14 **bottom of the sea."** Massie, 158.

16 **sleeping, except coffins.** Brinnin, J. M. *Sway of the Grand Saloon*. New York: Delacorte Press, 1971.

17 **the rag bag,"** Coleman, Terry. *The Liners*. New York: Putnam, 1977, 18.

17 **for decades to come.** Brinnin, 170.

19 **seasickness and fright.** One might also add the number of unfortunate souls who take their lives while aboard ship, a rare but recurring event vividly depicted in John Maxtone-Graham's *Crossing and Cruising*. Stephen Fox, in his recent work *Transatlantic*, is quick to point out other departures from Cunard's maxim, including the loss of the early steamers *Columbia* and *Oregon*, freak storms, and other calamities. Yet none of these events diminishes the extraordinary and indeed unprecedented record for safety which the company has enjoyed.

20 **racing to be run."** Hughes, Tom. *The Blue Riband of the Atlantic*. New York: Scribners, 1974.

20 **miss the boat trip!"** Maxtone-Graham, John. *The Only Way to Cross*. New York: Macmillan, 1972.

22 **best that can be had."** Coleman, 33.

24 **not even the sea."** Brinnin, 287.

24 **every way excellent.** Coleman, 35.

Chapter 2: "The Delightfulest Ship I Ever Saw"

27 **to hold us both."** Fox, Stephen. *Transatlantic*. New York: HarperCollins, 2003.

29 **book was finished."** Brinnin, 313.

29 **of the Cunard Lines.** Clemens was even more explicit in a letter home to his wife. "I do so regret taking you in the *Batavia*," he wrote, "your journey [on a German ship] would have been a hundred times pleasanter." Stephen Fox, *Transatlantic*, 275.

30 **—by the other.** Cecil, Lamar. *Ballin*. Princeton: Princeton University Press, 1967.

31 **depending on him."** Brinnin, 314.

35 **miscellaneous machinery.** The use of a dummy funnel would persist long after the funnel craze subsided, though for practical rather than competitive reasons. Its hollow

shell was invaluable for concealing unsightly encumbrances. Some held machinery, others dog kennels or storage space. The third funnel of the 1930's French superliner *Normandie*, for example, housed the officer's lounge. Later, aesthetics trumped other considerations, and funnels became unique (if bizarre) vantage points, with 360-degree lounges perched on top. The most recent manifestation of this phenomenon is the aft funnel of Disney Cruise Line's *Disney Magic* and *Disney Wonder*, which contains, of all things, a sports bar.

35 **four-funneled—*Deutschland*.** Maxtone-Graham, 31.

37 **the English public."** Brinnin, 316–317.

37 **over 23 knots."** Hughes, 91.

39 **never saw the *Deutschland* again.** Hughes, 95.

40 **"millionaires' boat."** Maxtone-Graham, John. *Liners to the Sun*. New York: Sheridan House, 2000.

41 **new German menace.** They were egged on a great deal by the press, who kept the issue very much in the public mind. Even the staid *London Times* surrendered itself to taunts and lamentations, in an article published in the fall of 1900: "The swiftest Cunarders can neither catch the Germans nor run away from them, still less can the White Star ships. If, then, the Germans know how to build record-breaking Atlantic steamships and run them at a profit, have the English lost that art? . . . Do the English lines mean to contend with the German, or do they leave to them their present supremacy on the Atlantic unchallenged?" *London Times*, November 6, 1900.

42 **none ever existed before."** Massie, 297.

45 **adventuresome young lady."** Brinnin, 319.

Chapter 3: Morgan's Gambit

49 **"a squashed strawberry."** A very apt description of Morgan's nose appears in the novel *Ragtime*, by E. L. Doctorow. See also, generally: Sinclair, Andrew. *Corsair*. Boston: Little Brown, 1981.

50 **a raucous cough.** Duveen, J. H. *Collections and Recollections*, quoted in Sinclair, 193.

50 **American business structure."** Sinclair, 192.

50 **a wonderful man.** Sackville-West, Lady Victoria. *Diary*, quoted in Sinclair, 199.

50 **that nose," she lamented.** Sinclair, 198.

54 **benevolent, Christ-like employers,** Morris, Edmund. *Theodore Rex*. New York: The Modern Library, 2001.

54 **tyranny of plutocracy,"** Roosevelt, Theodore. *Autobiography*, quoted in Sinclair, 140.

55 **find his price."** Sinclair, 125.

55 **richest man in the world."** The two men would later meet again, ironically on a transatlantic liner, and Carnegie would admit to Morgan that he should have increased his selling price by another hundred million. One version of the story holds that Morgan responded, "If you had, I should have paid it," while another claims that he instead growled "I'd have given it, if only to be rid of

you." Either way, said the *Wall Street Journal*, Carnegie was so "soured in his soul" as a result of this conversation "that he could take no more toast and marmalade."

57 **be," he mused.** Coleman, 48.

58 **and lost badly.** Carosso, Vincent. *The Morgans*. Cambridge: Harvard Press, 1987.

58 **bill of lading."** Brinnin, 324.

58 **over the Atlantic.** Coleman, 48.

59 **voyage each year.** Maxtone-Graham, John. *Crossing and Cruising*. New York: Macmillan, 1991.

60 **and *President Grant*.** Miller, William. *The First Great Liners in Photographs*. New York: Dover Publications, 1985.

61 **take it or leave it."** Coleman, 47.

61 **businessman, to refuse.** Sinclair, 143.

62 **another vessel in 1909.** McCluskie, Tom, Michael Sharp, et al. *Titanic and Her Sisters Olympic and Britannic*. London: PRC Publishing, 1998.

62 **turn of the century.** White Star Line was also in some respects the spiritual descendant of the failed Collins line, discussed supra. White Star ships employed the distinctive straight-stem Collins bow, the lavish interior appointments, and even the names: *Adriatic, Baltic, Atlantic, Arctic, Pacific* (in a further bow to the disastrous fate of the Collins ships, the names *Arctic* and *Pacific* were quietly changed to *Republic* and *Celtic*). As if to make the link all the more palpable, White Star chose Digby Murray, a former First Officer aboard Collins liners, to serve as the fleet's commodore. The reawakened challenge to Cunard Line was thus solidified. Stephen Fox, 241.

62 **a glorious prize.** As Morgan himself could attest. As early as 1880, traveling aboard the newly built *Britannic*, Morgan vowed never to travel on any other line. A confirmed gastronome, he was delighted with the culinary skill of White Star's kitchens. "Of the eleven at our table I don't think anyone except Mrs. Egleston missed a single meal although it was very rough," he wrote. He would cross the Atlantic a dozen times between 1880 and 1893, each time on a White Star vessel. Perhaps, given his imperious manner of declaring "I'll have it," it was inevitable that he would one day own the line which he so ardently favored.

62 **partners in 1900.** Carosso, 482.

63 **declaration of war."** Brinnin, 325.

63 **reaction to this was mixed.** Carosso, 483.

64 **attention to Germany.** Cecil, 49.

64 **simply astounding."** Brinnin, 326.

66 **every single item.** Quoted in Brinnin, 327.

67 **an obstinate Frisian.** Cecil, 52.

67 **"second class with crown."** Brinnin, 327.

68 **maintain their independence."** May 13, 1902, quoted in *London Times* May 14.

72 **Morgan, the businessman.** Sinclair, 150.

73 **neatly folded.** E. L. Doctorow, in his splendid novel *Ragtime*, offers a strange and

moving postlude to this story. Though fictional, it offers a keen insight into the
man and his world:

> [Morgan] fled to Europe, embarking on the White Star liner *Oceanic*. He had com-
> bined the White Star Line, the American, Dominion, Atlantic Transport and Ley-
> land lines into one company numbering 120 ocean-going ships. He despised com-
> petition no less on the seas than on land. He stood at night by the ship's rail,
> hearing the heavy sea, feeling its swell but not seeing it. The sea and the sky were
> black and indistinguishable. A bird, some sort of gull, appeared from the blackness
> and lighted on the rail a few feet from him. Perhaps it had been attracted by his
> nose. I have no peers, Morgan said to the bird. It seemed an indisputable truth.

Chapter 4: The Old Man and the Sea

74 **their bank vaults."** Sinclair, 148.

75 **ocean from this on."** Maddocks, Melvin. *The Great Liners.* Alexandria: Time Life
Books, 1982.

75 **signed J. Pierpont Morgan.** Brinnin, 329.

75 **afther nex' week."** Quoted in Sinclair, 140.

75 **the civilized world."** Brinnin, 330.

76 **in recorded history.** As of writing, Morgan's ambitious attempt remains singular,
yet an unlikely challenger has arisen. Carnival Cruise Lines, founded by Israeli entrepreneur Ted Arison as a cut-rate "party ship" line in the late 1970s, has become a
behemoth. In the late 1990s the company acquired Seaborne, Windstar, Holland
America, Costa, and, incredibly, Cunard lines. It has recently added the even more
venerable P&O/Princess Cruises. Norwegian Cruise Lines and Royal Caribbean are
the last major firms not yet under the Carnival moniker, and both have spurned offers. It remains to be seen whether another American—in this case, Micky Arison,
son of the late Ted Arison—can finish the work begun by Morgan a century before.

76 **value of their shares.** Coleman, 48.

76 **profit for the shareholders.** Brinnin, 328.

77 **tremendously entertained.** Coleman, 51.

77 **have hitherto done."** Brinnin, 328.

78 **the Profits Thereof.** Cleveland, *Plain Dealer* (1902), quoted in Sinclair, 147.

78 **President and Kings."** Quoted in Myers, Gustavus. *History of the Great American
Fortunes.* New York: Modern Library, 1937.

80 **nipped in the bud."** Quoted in Coleman, 48.

80 **suggesting American control."** Carosso, 484.

81 **harmony would be restored.** Brinnin, 329.

82 **"under the law."** Sinclair, 141.

82 **state of inflammation."** Morris, 339.

84 **is business efficiency.** Sinclair, 145.

84 **time of war.** It should be mentioned that Cunard remained scrupulously faithful to
both conditions for almost a century. Cunard ships have played an integral part in

every British conflict, up to and including the *Queen Elizabeth 2*'s role as troop ferry during the Falklands War. As for the first of the government's stipulations, it was not until 1999 that Cunard finally succumbed to the inevitable and became—along with Windstar, Costa, Holland-America, and Seaborne Lines—a subsidiary of Carnival Cruises, Miami.

85 **bring you to ruin."** Sinclair, 162.

85 **he ever floated."** Quoted in: Corey Lewis. *The House of Morgan.* New York: G. H. Watt, 1930, 313.

86 *Gigantic,* **and** *Titanic.* McCluskie, et al., 59.

86 **the old man."** Quoted in Brinnin, 331.

Chapter 5: "A Mad Dash of Nelsonic Impertinence"

89 **aggregate of States."** Howarth, David. *The Dreadnoughts.* Alexandria: Time Life Books, 1980.

90 **on his back to steer."** Fox, 399.

91 **the whole way."** Maddocks, 37.

94 **novelty of the invention."** Fox, 399.

94 **leviathans are done for."** Maxtone-Graham, *The Only Way to Cross,* 20.

94 **Fisher later remembered.** Maddocks, 36.

94 **fastest in the world."** Fox, 400.

95 **the two Poles."** Maxtone-Graham, *The Only Way to Cross,* 20.

96 **Cunard Line in 1903.** Brinnin, 331.

96 **under foreign control."** Warren, Mark. *Lusitania.* Wellingborough: Patrick Stephens, 1986. Reprint of *Engineering,* 1907, 14.

98 **Parsons was told.** Fox, 400.

Chapter 6: Song of the Machines

102 **armed merchant cruiser.** Ramsay, David. *Lusitania: Saga and Myth.* New York: W.W. Norton, 2001.

102 **boggled the Edwardian imagination.** Such statistics may, in retrospect, seem paltry. Cunard's glistening new flagship *Queen Mary 2* weighs in at 151,400 gross tons, with a length of 1,132 feet. To put it another way, it roughly equals five *Mauretania*s. But the significance of her predecessors' size does not rest exclusively in numbers. A photograph of the *Lusitania* at Liverpool shows her surrounded by a Lilliputian army of horses and jitneys. Towering above them, the massive steel walls and sleek, modern lines of the *Lusitania* present such a jarring contrast to this nineteenth-century quaintness as to make her seem almost like a fantastic time machine dropped in from a much later century.

103 **direction of size."** Maddocks, 48.

103 **and the Admiralty."** *Engineering,* 17.

104 **and easily remembered."** Coleman, 52.

105 were also present." Hughes, 109.

112 dyed leatherette," Brinnin, 339.

112 a lilac hue. . . ." Maxtone-Graham, *The Only Way to Cross*, 33.

112 a delightful feast.' " Brinnin, 343.

114 shaken off my bridge." Hughes, 124.

114 might be desired." Fox, 405.

115 herself as such." Brinnin, 343–344.

116 city goes to sea. Maxtone-Graham, *The Only Way to Cross*, 10.

117 record-breaking *Deutschland*," An error. The Atlantic record for speed was in fact held by the *Kaiser Wilhelm II* of North German Lloyd, which had beaten the *Deutschland* in 1906.

117 machinery in later life." Hughes, 121.

118 the ocean highway." Fox, 405.

119 held it at all." Hughes, 123.

120 Mary to do it!" Maxtone-Graham, *The Only Way to Cross*, 39.

120 follow them below." Hughes, 128.

123 filled with icebergs." Brinnin, 346.

123 almost been reached." Fox, 413.

125 will be the result." Marcus, Geoffrey. *The Maiden Voyage*. New York: Viking Press, 1969.

Chapter 7: Titans

127 Cherbourg," said the man. This is only one portent among many. In the aftermath of the disaster, scores of stories would be told of dark omens, near misses, and strange coincidences. Books have been written on the subject. Yet among the whole lot there is only one genuine oddity: the publication of a novel in 1898 by an obscure British author named Morgan Robertson. Titled *Futility*, it told the story of the 45,000-ton superliner *Titan*, declared unsinkable by her owners, which collides with an iceberg on a cold April night and sinks with terrible loss of life. Aside from the book's moralizing gloss—it was, after all, a product of the Victorian era—the similarities between its events and those of April 14, 1912, are profound and inexplicable. Robertson remains a sort of macabre Jules Verne.

129 rival in England. Old Thomas Ismay's canniness for enticing the upper class aboard his ships often came with a personal touch. When the James Roosevelt family—members of a prominent New York clan—boarded the *Adriatic* in 1889, their youngest son was feeling ill. Somewhere between New York and Queenstown the child was diagnosed with deadly typhoid fever. At once, the captain gave the boy his own cabin, arranged for a doctor (his cousin) to meet the ship on arrival, and radioed ahead to the Company office. There, Thomas outdid himself. His private launch met the ship at Queenstown and carried the boy ashore; fresh flowers bearing his card brightened the sickroom every day until the Roosevelts' son recovered. It was well he did: the boy's name was Franklin Delano Roosevelt.

Black, Conrad. *Franklin Delano Roosevelt*. New York: Public Affairs, 2003, 18.

130 **listen about the heat.** Lynch, Donald. *Titanic: An Illustrated History*. New York: Hyperion, 1992.

130 **in Atlantic history.** As the loss of the *Titanic* thwarted this ambition for weekly service, so too would it elude Hamburg-Amerika, whose own trio *Imperator*, *Vaterland*, and *Bismarck* was truncated by the outbreak of war. Only Cunard succeeded in maintaining the weekly schedule, with the *Mauretania*, *Lusitania*, *Aquitania*, and, following the loss of the *Lusitania*, the *Berengaria*.

135 *Olympic* **is a marvel!"** Brinnin, 364.

139 **take high honors.** Brinnin, 365.

139 *score is two to nil."* Marcus, 32.

Chapter 8: A World's Fair Afloat

145 **sweat and suffer.** Marcus, 94.

147 **privilege of class upheld."** Brinnin, 350.

150 **luxury hotel on top."** Brinnin, 474.

151 **floating Babylon,"** Marcus, 55.

152 **where it was. . . ."** Brinnin, 380.

153 **much happier here."** Marcus, 196.

154 **can tell them?"** Marcus, 196.

Chapter 9: Talons of the Eagle

160 **short of disaster.** Maxtone-Graham, *The Only Way to Cross*, 94.

161 **trench after another."** Fox, 372.

162 **a comical effect."** Maddocks, 57.

162 **"the genial Jew,"** Cecil, 28.

168 **Hamburg-Amerika Line,"** Cecil, 106.

176 **hot and cold water."** Brinnin, 387.

178 **counteract the instability.** Maxtone-Graham, *The Only Way to Cross*, 97.

178 **pretensions to beauty."** Brinnin, 388.

178 **to New York alone.** Maddocks, 59.

Chapter 10: "The Struggle for the Sea"

181 **"FLEET ASTOUNDED!"** Howarth, 59.

182 **a German battleship!"** Cecil, 156.

184 **after appointing him."** Massie, *Dreadnought*, 707.

185 **Admiral Müller grimly.** Cecil, 196.

185 **[comment] in the Press."** Manchester, William. *The Last Lion: Winston Spencer Churchill*. Boston: Little Brown, 1983, 449.

188 **28,000 liters of beer.** Maddocks, 60.

189 **hung in each room.** Brinnin, 397.

190 **and charmingly placid."** Brinnin, 397.

190 **so damned proud."** Maddocks, 60.

190 **intelligent observer."** Maxtone-Graham, *The Only Way to Cross*, 111.

190 **This Harbor Today."** Maddocks, 61.

191 **guarantee beforehand.' "** Cecil, 208.

Chapter 11: Descent

195 **hats on board ship."** Cowles, Virginia. *The Kaiser*. London: Collins, 1963, 87.

197 **said Kaiser Wilhelm II.** Howarth, 63.

197 **out all over Europe."** Massie, 907.

199 **and strode out.** Brinnin, 401.

205 **equipped with a sword.** Maxtone-Graham, *The Only Way to Cross*, 237.

208 **say no more."** Neitzychowski, Count Alfred von. *The Cruise of the Kronprinz Wilhelm*. New York: Doubleday, 1929, 33.

215 **tribute to the enemy."** Brinnin, 409.

216 **here on the Atlantic."** Neitzychowski, 47.

217 **ship's pool.** John Maxtone-Graham relates the story of one Euphegine Ochs, daughter of *New York Times* publisher Ralph Ochs, who witnessed this spectacle on a German ship just two years before the outbreak of war. It had evidently been common practice since the mid-nineteenth century. (*The Only Way to Cross*, 237.)

Chapter 12: Armageddon

224 **Coney Island."** Ballard, Robert. *Exploring the Lusitania*. New York: Madison, 1995.

226 **in St. Helena."** Brinnin, 414.

226 **his book sales.** Hubbard was even more prescient than he knew. Three years before he had composed a rather fruity eulogy for the *Titanic's* lost First Class passengers. He wrote in conclusion: "And so all you I knew, and all that thousand and half a thousand more I did not know, passed out of this Earth-Life into the Unknown upon the restless, unforgetting tide. You were sacrificed to the greedy Goddess of Luxury and her consort the Demon of Speed. Was it worthwhile? Who shall say? . . . Hail and Farewell, until we meet again." They met again on May 7, 1915. Brinnin, 380–381.

227 **"She runs too fast."** Bailey, Thomas, and Paul Ryan. *The Lusitania Disaster*. New York: Free Press, 1975.

228 **its passengers uncomfortable."** Ballard, 31.

228 **"a pitiable exhibition."** Bailey, 131.

229 **it cannot be helped."** Ramsay, 43.

230 **they stepped back.** Ballard, 92.

231 **I shoot to kill!"** Botting, Douglas. *The U-Boats*. Alexandria: Time Life Books, 1979.

231 **well-organized affair."** Ballard, 94.

231 **waiting for a train."** Brinnin, 417.

232 **I wanted some excitement."** Ballard, 94.

232 **calling from the very depths."** Botting, 31.

233 **and human heads."** Brinnin, 417.

233 **I will look after you."** Ballard, 104.

234 **"a dirty business."** Simpson, Colin. *The Lusitania*. Boston: Little Brown, 1972.

235 **folded firmly together. . . ."** Ramsay, 97.

235 **will be fully avenged."** Ballard, 115.

238 **seemed to forsake us."** Brinnin, 420.

238 **stained German arms."** Ballard, 118.

240 **trouble, better still.** Ramsay, 202.

240 **bring on trouble."** Bailey, 231.

241 **pirate ever practiced,"** Ballard, 118.

241 **Barbary pirate apologize."** Maddocks, 137.

241 **cabled President Wilson.** Ballard, 123.

241 **secondary at best.** Bailey, 229.

242 **frivolity and avarice."** Brinnin, 422.

242 **explosives and munitions."** Ramsay, 110.

242 **U-boat campaign.** Bailey, 229.

243 **policing with Germany.** Cecil, 285.

243 **zone of operations.** Bailey, 229.

243 **novelty of the weapon.** Ramsay, 109.

244 **lives in her.** Brinnin, 421.

245 **hell freezes, Fisher.** Bailey, 36.

Chapter 13: A New Mission

250 **"like a lady."** McCluskie, 413.

252 **like the devil,"** Maddocks, 69.

253 **Kaiser built for us."** Maxtone-Graham, *The Only Way to Cross*, 134.

254 **his American usurpers.** Maddocks, 70.

259 **suffocating her crew.** One of the officers sent to combat the problem, who himself nearly died as a result of it, was a young quartermaster named Humphrey Bogart.

260 **and 8,605 wounded.** Hughes, 143.

260 **374,000 tons of coal.** McCluskie, 228.

260 **greatest ship in the world."** Maddocks, 72.

261 **life's work lies in shreds."** Cecil, 214.

262 **embodiment of her loathing.** The Kaiserin's puritanical disgust extended even to her own family. When Leopold II, King of the Belgians, paid a royal visit to his cousin the Kaiser he came accompanied with a number of young girls, none older than fifteen. The King, who had recently celebrated his sixty-fifth birthday, was a notorious pedophile. After his departure, a horrified Augusta promptly had all the

rooms of Leopold's suite exorcised for demons. Hochschild, Adam. *King Leopold's Ghost*. New York: Mariner Books, 1999, 222.

Chapter 14: The Lion's Share

268 **of the *Berengaria*."** Brinnin, 447.

270 **nothing about her."** Maxtone-Graham, *Crossing and Cruising*, 281.

272 **in her blue eyes."** Brinnin, 451.

Bibliography

EARLY IN 2001, I CAME ACROSS A SMALL, DUSTY VOLUME ENTITLED
The Cruise of the Kronprinz Wilhelm, by Count Alfred von Neitzychowski.
The book quite clearly hadn't been read in years; the last library stamp was
dated August 25, 1961. With some misgivings, I began to read. Surprisingly, Count Neitzychowski's account of life aboard a requisitioned ocean
liner turned merchant raider in the early years of the Great War was both
riveting and fantastically ironic. Here was an eyewitness account of the
wrenching transition from peacetime follies to wartime hardship, from gallantry to cruelty, from civilization to barbarism. And, perhaps most ironic
of all, this transformation was played out in the tragicomic career of an old
German steamship blundering about the Atlantic with a ragtag crew of
adventurers. It occurred to me that despite the plethora of literature devoted to the great liners of the prewar period, very few had given more than a
passing mention to this pivotal transition from peacetime to wartime roles.

With this single source as my starting point, I conceived the idea of
examining this transition by tracking the feverish Anglo-German liner race
in the twenty-five years preceding the outbreak of war. I could not have
imagined how difficult, and yet exhilarating, this task would become. As I
mentioned in my introduction, my primary task was extricating a cohesive
overall narrative from the sentimentalized "lives of the liners" historiogra-
phy that predominates the field. To substantiate my central thesis, that the
liner race paralleled the naval race and had its own crucial impact on the
course of the war, I had to do more than simply string these individual ship
histories together; I had to place them within a greater overall context of
nationalism, capitalism, immigration, and empire.

My research for this book has taken me into libraries throughout the
United States and Canada. I have examined probably every known text on
ocean liner history for that period, as well as numerous biographies including those of J. P. Morgan, Kaiser Wilhelm II, Charles Parsons, Albert
Ballin, and Theodore Roosevelt; the philosophical treatises of Walter Benjamin and Theodor Adorno; social and political histories including Adam
Hochschild's superb *King Leopold's Ghost,* and even the period fiction of

E. L. Doctorow. I am, however, particularly indebted to the authors Malcolm Brinnin and John Maxtone-Graham, whose works remain seminal in the field of ocean liner history. I would also like to thank the Special Collections department of the University of Baltimore for furnishing the beautiful photos used in this text. Following is a list of all the texts cited and consulted in the making of *Seize the Trident.*

Angas, William Mack. *Rivalry on the Atlantic.* New York: Lee Furman, 1939.

Appleyard, Rollo. *Charles Parsons: His Life and Work.* London: Constable, 1933.

Bailey, Thomas, and Paul Ryan. *The Lusitania Disaster.* New York: Free Press, 1975.

Ballard, Robert. *Exploring the Lusitania.* New York: Madison, 1995.

Benjamin, Walter. *Illuminations.* New York: Schocken, 1968.

Black, Conrad. *Franklin Delano Roosevelt.* New York: Public Affairs, 2003.

Bonsor, N. R. P. *North Atlantic Seaway.* Lancashire: Stephenson & Sons, 1955.

Botting, Douglas. *The U-Boats.* Alexandria: Time Life Books, 1979.

Braynard, Frank. *The World's Greatest Ship—The Leviathan.* New York: American Merchant Marine Academy, 1983.

Brinnin, John Malcolm. *The Sway of the Grand Saloon.* New York: Delacorte Press, 1971.

Carosso, Vincent. *The Morgans.* Cambridge: Harvard Press, 1987.

Cecil, Lamar. *Ballin.* Princeton: Princeton University Press, 1967.

Coleman, Terry. *The Liners.* New York: Putnam, 1977.

Cookman, Scott. *Atlantic: The Last Great Race of Princes.* New York: John Wiley, 2002.

Coons, Lorraine, and Alexander Varias. *Tourist Third Cabin.* New York: Palgrave, 2003.

Cowles, Virginia. *The Kaiser.* London: Collins, 1963.

Doctorow, E. L. *Ragtime.* New York: Plume, 1996.

Fox, Robert. *Liners: The Golden Age.* London: Hutton Getty, 1999.

Fox, Stephen. *Transatlantic.* New York: HarperCollins, 2003.

Gibbons, Tony, ed. *The Encyclopedia of Ships.* Enderby: Silverdale Books, 2001.

Hochschild, Adam. *King Leopold's Ghost.* New York: Mariner Books, 1999.

Howarth, David. *The Dreadnoughts.* Alexandria: Time Life Books, 1980.

Hughes, Tom. *The Blue Riband of the Atlantic.* New York: Scribners, 1974.

Hyde, Francis. *Cunard and the North Atlantic: 1840–1973.* New York: Humanities Press, 1975.

Johnson, Howard. *The Cunard Story.* London: Whitlet, 1982.

London Times, 1900–1916.

Lord, Walter. *A Night to Remember.* New York: Holt, Rinehart & Winston, 1955.

———. *The Night Lives On.* New York: William Morrow, 1986.

Lynch, Donald. *Titanic: An Illustrated History.* New York: Hyperion, 1992.

MacDonogh, Giles. *The Last Kaiser.* London: Weidenfeld & Nicolson, 2000.

Maddocks, Melvin. *The Great Liners.* Alexandria: Time Life Books, 1982.

Manchester, William. *The Last Lion: Winston Spencer Churchill.* Boston: Little Brown, 1983.

Marcus, Geoffrey. *The Maiden Voyage.* New York: Viking Press, 1969.

Massie, Robert. *Dreadnought.* New York: Ballantine, 1991.

———. *Castles of Steel.* New York: Random House, 2003.

Maxtone-Graham, John. *Crossing and Cruising.* New York: Macmillan, 1991.

———. *Liners to the Sun.* New York: Sheridan House, 2000.

———. *The Only Way to Cross.* New York: Macmillan, 1972.

McCart, Neil. *Atlantic Liners of the Cunard Line from 1884 to the Present.* Northamptonshire: Patrick Stephens, 1990.

McCluskie, Tom, et al. *Titanic and Her Sisters Olympic and Britannic.* London: PRC Publishing, 1998.

Miller, William. *The First Great Liners in Photographs.* New York: Dover Publications, 1985.

———. *Ocean Liners.* New York: Mallard Press, 1990.

———. *The Fabulous Interiors of the Great Ocean Liners.* New York: Dover, 1985.

Morris, Edmund. *Theodore Rex.* New York: The Modern Library, 2001.

———. *The Rise of Theodore Roosevelt.* New York: Coward, McCann & Geoghehan, 1978.

Neitzychowski, Count Alfred von. *The Cruise of the Kronprinz Wilhelm.* New York: Doubleday, 1929.

Ramsay, David. *Lusitania: Saga and Myth.* New York: W.W. Norton, 2001.

Simpson, Colin. *The Lusitania.* Boston: Little Brown, 1972.

Sinclair, Andrew. *Corsair.* Boston: Little Brown, 1981.

Smith, Ken. *Mauretania: Pride of the Tyne.* Newcastle: Tyneside Publishing, 1997.

Tute, Warren. *Atlantic Conquest.* Boston: Little Brown, 1962.

U.S.S. *Leviathan* History Committee. *History of the U.S.S. Leviathan.* New York: Eagle Press, 1919.

Vard, Kenneth. *Liners in Art.* Southampton: Kingfisher, 1990.

Wall, Robert. *Ocean Liners.* New York: E. P. Dutton, 1977.

Warren, Mark. *Lusitania.* Wellingsborough: Patrick Stephens, 1986.

Williams, Rosalind. *Dream Worlds: Mass Consumption in Late 19th Century France.* Berkeley: University of California Press, 1982.

Index